# Hammer of the
## Anglo-Saxon Paganism in Modern Times

### Second Edition

## by Swain Wódening

I wish to thank Jordsvin for the initial proofreading that lead to this improved edition (any mistakes made after that are all my fault). Finally, I owe a debt of gratitude to the members of the Englatheod for helping revitalize Þéodisc Geléafa.

Published in the United States of America by
Wednesbury Shire, Huntsville, MO

# Table of Contents

# Foreword

One thousand years ago a religion that had survived countless hardships was on its last legs. Iceland had just made Christianity its state religion, and the Great Temple at Uppsala would only stand 200 years longer. Prayers to Odin, Thor, and Frey would cease. But the religion never died out. Tales of its followers and their rituals were preserved in the Icelandic sagas, and esoteric information was saved in the rune poems and the Anglo-Saxon charms. Even the tales of the Gods were saved in the *Elder* and *Prose Eddas* as well as the works of Saxo Grammaticus. This religion or collection of tribal religions can be referred to as Heathenry in the plural sense, Heathen in the singular. The word Heathen comes from Old English *hæðen*, a word whose origin has been stated by scholars as a native word related to Greek *ethnos*, or a gloss for Latin *pagan* "rural dweller" meaning "dweller on the heath." Regardless of its origin, it is the preferred term when speaking of the ancient pagan religion of the Germanic culture. It can also be called the Troth, or Ásatrú, but in ancient times was simply known by various words that meant "law," or "custom." The subject of this book is a specific form of Heathenry known today variously as the Anglo-Saxon Troth, Anglo-Saxon Heathenry, or Þéodish Geléafa; the religion of the Saxons, Jutes, Angles, Frisians, Varni, and other Germanic invaders of what is now England. The preferred term is Anglo-Saxon Heathenry. However, the tribes known to us as the Anglo-Saxons, never knew such unity until well after their conversion to Christianity. Within this book you may see the term *Angelseax* used, it is a reconstruction of the modern term Anglo-Saxon. Anglo-Saxon and *Angelseax* refer not to a race of people, but to a culture that provided the basis for the modern English nation. The ancient tribes that were the ancestors of the modern English never thought of themselves as "Anglo-Saxons," but as Jutes, Angles, Frisians, Saxons, Varni, and later as Northumbrians, Mercians, and West Saxons. What we now think of as Anglo-Saxon culture was actually a collection of very closely related cultures, all speaking very similar dialects, and following variations of the same basic religion. Anglo-Saxon culture had a long history by the time the tribes invaded what is now England. The tribes' origins rest in the Stone Age when speakers of an Indo-European dialect migrated into what is now Denmark and Northern Germany. There, their culture fused with one now referred to as the Northern Megalithic. From this fusion evolved the Germanic tribes, of which the Anglo-Saxons, as well, as the modern Norse, Dutch, and Germans were once members. Their religion was practically annihilated after the coming of missionaries to some of the Anglo-Saxon kingdoms in the early 7$^{th}$ century, much as the Norse version of Heathenry was a few hundred years later. However, the Latin script brought north with the new religion, in an ironic twist, was the salvation of the old one.

Preserved in texts were many of the folk ways. The Icelanders preserved the *Elder* and *Prose Eddas*, collections of myths of the Gods, as well as much information on rituals and other customs in the Icelandic sagas. The Danes preserved some of the myths in the works of Saxo Grammaticus. Finally, the Anglo-Saxons preserved information in a rune poem, pagan charms, and the classic work *Beowulf*. These texts along with folklore and information recorded by outsiders such as the Romans and missionaries would help form the basis of a new yet old religious movement, the reestablishment of the worship of the Heathen Gods. This has been called the Reawakening, a time when the ancient Troth would be reborn in America and in Europe. Now almost 30 years after the initial steps of the Reawakening, the adherents of Heathenry, Ásatrú, and Anglo-Saxon Heathenry meet to *blót* the Gods and hail their ancestors in *symbel*.

The Anglo-Saxon troth, is, as reconstructionist religions go, a very difficult one to reconstruct. Not much lore survived that is Anglo-Saxon. We have the God names, a few charms, one ritual that survived more or less intact, and the outline of the rite of *symbel*. Therefore modern Anglo-

Saxon pagans have to borrow heavily from the Icelandic lore, esp. when it comes to the myths, and secondary rites such as the naming ceremony. Modern Anglo-Saxon tribal religion will therefore never be what the ancient form was. Not enough evidence survived to understand what the religions of the ancient Jutes, Saxons, and Angles were like. Nevertheless, through comparative studies of festivals that survived into Christian times, folk traditions, and folklore, it has been possible to reconstruct a religion that is unique in its perspective, and perhaps close to what the ancient Anglo-Saxons practiced. It is hoped this book can add to that perspective.

Finally, a word on the research of this book, this book was not, and is not intended to be an academic work. While it is based in the lore of the ancient Germanic religion, as that religion is a living one, much is taken from my own personal experiences as well as the lore. Where possible, I draw on the ancient works, and list those in the texts.

Swain Wódening, Yule 1999

# Foreword to the Second Edition

When this book was first published five years ago, there were sections I was not pleased with. In addition, there were numerous typos, as well as many grammatical errors. And I felt there was more I could add to the book to make it more user friendly. So while many of the typos disappeared with a second type setting, much of the bad grammar remained. And I still felt more needed to be done. You will find with this second edition, all the magical practices have been removed and can be found in my book *Germanic Magic*. I felt there was more than enough material for the second book, and indeed there was. Meanwhile, I also felt that I could flesh out some of the chapters of *Hammer of the Gods*, and add more material. Therefore you will find that the sections on blót, on symbel, on the Gods and Goddesses, and on social structure have been expanded. In addition, there is now a pronunciation guide as well as sample rites and appendixes on Old English day and month names, and the divisions of the day. There remains one last thing to say

3

regarding this second edition; the primary language for religious terms is in Old English (Anglo-Saxon). Where Old Norse terms are used, these will be designated as such. Finally, I wish to thank everyone that bought the first edition. May you enjoy this one even more.

Swain Wódening, Yule, 2008

# Chapter I History

## *Ancient History*

Anglo-Saxon Heathenry's ancestry rests in the tribal religions of the Germanic peoples on the North and Baltic Sea shores of Europe, especially those of the Angles, Saxons, and Jutes. The Angles, Jutes, and Saxons were all members of an ethnic group called the Germanic tribes. The Germanic peoples came from peoples who settled in extreme Northern Europe, and spoke a language that was a fusion of an Indo-European tongue, and the language of the Northern Megalithic culture (a culture related perhaps to the builders of Stonehenge). These two cultures, the Indo-European, and Northern Megalithic met and fused in Northern Europe sometime around 1200 BCE. The tribes that resulted from this fusion remained in a core area that is modern Denmark, Southern Norway, Southern Sweden, and Northern Germany until about 500 BCE when they started expanding into areas formerly held by the Celts, Balts, and Illyrians. Rock carvings in the core area dating from 4000 BCE to 500 BCE portray many symbols later connected to the Germanic tribal religions. Ships, sun wheels, wains and other pictures all show some continuality of religious belief. Archaeological finds dating from 1700 BCE to 500 BCE such as the Sun Chariot from Trundholm also confirm this.

The first mention of a Germanic tribe in history is circa 230 BCE when the Basternae migrated to the Black Sea, and came to the attention of Greek chroniclers. From 230 BCE onwards, the Germanic tribes would come in increasing conflict with the Celts, Illyrians, and Romans, eventually swallowing up most of the Celtic and Illyrian territories in Central Europe. This was the beginnings of the Migration Era which lasted from about 375 BCE to 550 CE (although the Viking expeditions should perhaps be counted as a part of this as well), an era when nearly every Germanic tribe was actively on the move. Overpopulation and a need for new farm lands sent the Germanic tribes in search of new homes.

By 113 BCE, the Romans were defending their borders from such tribes as the Cimbri and Teutons, tribes often thought to be Germanic, though, in reality may have been Celtic. In 71 BCE, a German chieftain, Ariovistus crossed the Rhine to aid in a struggle between Celtic tribes. His tribe settled in the area of Alsace only to be wiped out in 58 BCE by Julius Caesar. Julius Caesar then drove the Suevi and Marcomanni from what is now Belgium. This was the extant of Roman successes however. In 9 CE, Arminius also called Herman, chieftain of the Cherusci defeated several Roman legions under Quintilius Varus in Teutobarger Wald. This ended Roman power north of the Rhine. The Cherusci's power waned however and by the end of the century they were defeated by the Chatti, and the lands they occupied finally fell in the hands of the Saxons. Nevertheless, the Germanic tribes continued to spread south, and this lead to the eventual fall of the Western half of the Roman Empire. The Goths migrated south and split into two groups. The Ostrogoths settled near the Black Sea and eventually swept into what was then Dacia (in the region of modern Albania). Between 488–93 CE they conquered Italy, effectively ending the Roman Empire. The Visigoths raided Greece and Italy and established a kingdom in southern France. After being displaced by the Franks, they established a kingdom in Spain, which lasted until the Moors conquered it in 711 CE. The Franks, a confederation of tribes thought to have originally lived near Pomerania on the Baltic Sea settled near the Rhine around 300 CE. In time they would invade Gaul and conquer it.

At the same time, the Franks put pressure on the Saxons and other neighbouring tribes such as the Frisians who inhabited Friesland and the Frisian Islands. The Saxons and Frisians were also closely related to the Angles who lived in what is now Schleswig-Holstein, as well as the Jutes who may have lived either in Jutland or on the Rhine (scholars are unsure of the exact location). All of these tribes invaded what is now England in search of new land. In 409 CE, the Romans withdrew the last of their legions in Britain in an effort to save the empire. Left with little defence against barbarians, the Britons quickly became the target of raids from the Picts to the north, in what is now Scotland, as well as the sea roving Germanic tribes like the Angles and Saxons.

The invasion of Great Britain by the Angles, Jutes, Saxons, Frisians, and other Germanic tribes were amongst the last of the Great Migration Age. The Angles invaded Britain from the area of Schleswig-Holstein, and are mentioned by Tacitus in his writing, *Germania*. The Jutes appear to have come from Jutland and the area near the mouth of the river Rhine. The Saxons, by this time had covered a wide area, but invaded Britain from what is now primarily Northern Germany. The Saxons were not just one tribe, but a confederation of smaller ones, and are not even mentioned by the Roman chroniclers until the second century when Ptolemy placed them in the area of the Elbe River (an area once held by the Cimbri). What tribes composed the confederation is truly not known, though the Cimbri that remained in the North may have been among them as well as the Cherusci (other tribes that have been suggested as forming the confederation are the Avioni, Nuithoni, Reudigni, Suarini, and some of the Suebi). The Frisians came from what is now the Netherlands, and the Frisian coast of Germany. Other tribes such as the Varni, neighbours of the Angles, and the Geats of Sweden may have invaded Britain in smaller numbers. The Jutes were the first to invade in 450 when they established a kingdom in what is now Kent. The Anglo-Saxon Chronicle preserved how this came to pass.

> In their days Hengest and Horsa, invited by Wurtgern, king of the Britons, landed in Britain in a place that is called Ipwines fleet; first of all to support the Britons, but they afterwards fought against them. The king directed them to fight against the Picts; and they did so; and obtained the victory wheresoever they came. They then sent to the Angles, and desired them to send more assistance. They described the worthlessness of the Britons, and the richness of the land. They then sent them greater support. Then came the men from three powers of Germany; the Old

Saxons, the Angles, and the Jutes. (James Ingram, translator, Everyman Press, London, 1912)

Bede gives a slightly different account:

They consulted what was to be done, and where they should seek assistance to prevent or repel the cruel and frequent incursions of the northern nations; and they all agreed with their King Vortigern to call over to their aid, from the parts beyond the sea, the Saxon nation; which, as the event still more evidently showed, appears to have been done by the appointment of our Lord Himself, that evil might fall upon them for their wicked deeds.

Bede goes onto say:

IN the year of our Lord 449, Martian being made emperor with Valentinian, and the forty-sixth from Augustus, ruled the empire seven years. Then the nation of the Angles, or Saxons, being invited by the aforesaid king, arrived in Britain with three longships, and had a place assigned them to reside in by the same king, in the eastern part of the island, that they might thus appear to be fighting for their country, whilst their real intentions were to enslave it. Accordingly they engaged with the enemy, who were come from the north to give battle, and obtained the victory; which, being known at home in their own country, as also the fertility of the country, and the cowardice of the Britons, a more considerable fleet was quickly sent over, bringing a still greater number of men, which, being added to the former, made up an invincible army. The newcomers received of the Britons a place to inhabit, upon condition that they should wage war against their enemies for the peace and security of the country, whilst the Britons agreed to furnish them with pay. Those who came over were of the three most powerful nations of Germany Saxons, Angles, and Jutes. From the Jutes are descended the people of Kent, and of the Isle of Wight, and those also in the province of the West Saxons who are to this day called Jutes, seated opposite to the Isle of Wight. From the Saxons, that is, the country which is now called Old Saxony, came the East Saxons, the South Saxons, and the West Saxons. From the Angles, that is, the country which is called Anglia, and which is said, from that time, to remain desert to this day, between the provinces of the Jutes and the Saxons, are descended the East Angles, the Midland Angles, Mercians, all the race of the Northumbrians, that is, of those nations that dwell on the north side of the river Humber, and the other nations of the English. (translator unknown, E.P. Dutton, New York, 1910)

The religions of these tribes were related to the tribal religion of the Goths, and that of the Norse (whose myths are recorded in the two *Eddas*). Their Gods and Goddesses were Wóden, Ing, Þunor, Fríge, Eostre, Seaxnéat and others whose names have been forever lost. Their common place of worship was in a grove (Old English *hearg*) or a temple (Old English *ealh*). They held sacred feasts, and paid homage to their ancestors. Tacitus, writing in the first century, when the tribes were still on the continent of Europe, covered in some detail the worship of a goddess called Nerthus by the Angles and other tribes near them, and makes brief mention of other practices. Collectively we can refer to the religions of these tribes, once in what is now England, as Anglo-Saxon Heathenry, though in truth, there must have been some minor tribal variation in worship, customs, and beliefs.

The remains of Anglo-Saxon Heathenry are few. Wóden is mentioned in the "Nine Worts Galdor" of the *Lacnunga*, an Anglo-Saxon healer's manual surviving from the 8th century. Þunor is recorded in the Anglo-Saxon Chronicle entry of 640 CE as killing the brother of the Christian Ermenred, king of Kent and his two sons. Ing is recorded in the Anglo-Saxon Rune Poem, and there is the semi-heathen ritual the "Æcer-Bót" or "Field Remedy" recorded in the *Lacnunga* as well. Such small mentions in the Anglo-Saxon literature as these, place names, and archaeological evidence are all that remains of ancient Anglo-Saxon Heathenry.

The Anglo-Saxon invasion began about 449 CE when Hengest and Horsa landed in what is now Kent. Hired as mercenaries by the Celtic leader Vortigan, they came to take land promised them in return for defending the Celts from the Picts. Thus, began the invasion of Great Britain by the Angles, Saxons, and Jutes. The Jutes came first with Hengest and Horsa, then the Saxons followed, and finally the Angles. Other tribes such as the Frisians would also invade in smaller numbers. By 519 the Saxons had established Wessex, Kent was established not long after the arrival of Hengest and Horse by the Jutes. Other kingdoms would be established later. For almost 50 years, the Germanic tribes in what is now England went unmolested by Christianity. They kept to the religion of their ancestors, and practice rites as they had for eons. Then in 593 CE, Pope Gregory dispatched Augustine as a missionary to the Germanic tribes in England. He arrived in 597 CE on the Isle of Thanet, and started preaching to the Heathens. By 601 CE he convinced Ethelbert, whose wife was a Christian Frank, to destroy the Heathen temples and repress Heathen worship. Missionaries were sent to the West Saxons. Kings would convert their kingdoms to Christianity, then their successors convert the kingdoms back to Heathenry, and folks would lapse back to the old religion when the Church was not looking. But this was the beginning of the end for Anglo-Saxon Heathenry. For the next two hundred years the two religions would struggle for the upper hand. But by 633 CE, the last great stand of Anglo-Saxon Heathenry was to begin. King Penda, Heathen king of Mercia sought to conquer the other Anglo-Saxon kingdoms that had converted. Over the next 22 years, Penda, the last great Heathen king in England killed the Christian kings Edwin, Oswald, Oswin, Ecgric, and Sigebert before he himself died at the battle of Winwæd in 655 CE. In 685 CE, Cadwalla took the throne of Wessex to become the last Heathen king. In 686, the Isle of Wight, the last truly Heathen stronghold was converted to Christianity, and King Cadwalla of Wessex converted to Christianity in 688 CE, baptized by the Pope in Rome. This was the end of ancient Anglo-Saxon Heathenry in England amongst its kings, and spelt the doom of the religion as a whole.

While the kings and ealdormen of the Anglo-Saxons were converted to Christianity, it was not quite the same Christianity as was practised in Rome however. Christ was portrayed as a Germanic hero. Heathen charms were converted to Christian uses. Heathen rites were converted to Christianity. Symbel, or ritualized drinking rounds continued to be practised, with the toasts being Christianized, and the sacred feasts continued almost unchanged. Temples were converted to churches.

> "When Almighty God shall bring you to the most reverend Bishop Augustine, our brother, tell him what I have, after mature deliberation on the affairs of the English, determined upon, namely, that the temples of the idols in that nation ought not to be destroyed, but let the idols that are in them be destroyed; let holy water be made and sprinkled in the said temples - let altars be erected, and relics placed. For if those temples are well built, it is requisite that the be converted from the worship of devils to the service of the true God; that the nation, seeing that their temples are not destroyed, may remove error from their hearts and, knowing and adoring the true God, may the more familiarly resort to the places to which they have been accustomed.......

> And because they have been used to slaughter many oxen in the sacrifices to devils, some solemnity must be substituted for them on this account, as, for instance, that on the day of the dedication, or of the nativities of the holy martyrs whose relics are there deposited, they may build themselves huts of the boughs of trees about those churches which have been turned to that use from temples, and celebrate the solemnity with religious feasting, no more offering beasts to the devil, but killing cattle to the praise of God in their eating, and returning thanks to the Giver of all things for their sustenance; to the end that, whilst some outward gratifications are

11

permitted them, they may the more easily consent to thee inward consolations of the grace of God." (translation of The Letter to Mellitusof 601 taken from J. H. Robinson, Readings in European History, Boston, 1905)

For the common folk merely the names of the Gods changed. They continued to practice Heathenry in their homes, and throughout their lives. A long period of mixed faith continued long after the conversion of the Anglo-Saxons. Perhaps until as late as the time of Cromwell, Heathen tradition, although not worship survived in many areas. Plows which had been blessed in the fields in Heathen times were brought into the Churches to be blessed in the spring. Christian festivals were celebrated with Heathen customs such as Maypole dancing, and the dead honoured in funeral feasts as they had prior to the conversion. Even the Heathen Gods were still being invoked in charms for healing as late as the 10th century. As late as the reign of King Canute in the 11th century, laws had to be enacted against Heathen practices.

Heathenry lived on in Frisia and the Saxon homelands as well as Scandinavia. Radbod of Frisia in 714, after the country had nominally been converted, threw out the missionaries and burned all the Christian churches. He then reinstated the Heathen rites, and the country remained Heathen until after his death. In his life he managed to reconquer much of the Frisian territories taken by Pepin of the Franks. In the 8th century, Charlemagne began what would be a 33 year struggle against the still Heathen Saxons. The war ended in 804 CE with the defeat of the Saxons and their forced conversion. During this time countless atrocities had been committed by the Christians. In 782 CE, 4500 Saxons, unwilling to convert to Christianity, were massacred. The Irminsul, a pole thought sacred to Tiw (Tyr) was cut down in what is now Marsberg. The pagan shrines there were desecrated. And in Hesse, Boniface, cut down an oak sacred to Þunor (Thor). Despite this, the Heathenry survived. Iceland did not convert until 1000 CE, and then only from coercion from Norway who held important Icelanders hostage. Even then private practice of the old religion was accepted. The Great Hof (temple) at Uppsala, Sweden stood until 1200 CE. Its fall is generally counted as the end of ancient Heathenry.

In the meantime, the religion was preserved in many ways. Some folk practices were adapted to the new religion, while others continued to be practised by the peasants despite the Church. Writers contemporary with Heathenry from the time of Tacitus onward recorded bits and pieces of information, often preserving information on rites and even myths. Tacitus recorded what the culture was like and gave details on daily life. Later, Arab trader Ahmad ibn Fadlan would record his interactions with Heathen Rus Vikings, and record a funeral performed by them. Other writers would contribute to this information, giving us a wealth of lore from the outsiders' point of view.

In the early Middle Ages we would see legitimate Heathen information recorded in the form of the Elder Edda, the Anglo-Saxon charms, and the rune poems. Many of the skaldic poems were composed by Heathens as well. Records of the Christians at the time such as the Anglo-Saxon Chronicle also recorded Heathen beliefs. The Prose Edda by Snorri and Saxo's History of the Danish Nation would preserve myths alongside the Heathen accounts in the Elder Edda. Finally, the Icelandic sagas preserved many Heathen beliefs and rites including the description of temples, an outline for blót, and beliefs regarding the runes and seer craft.

Modern archaeology has enriched this information through the examination of homesteads, artefacts, rune stones, and burials. Linguistics has delved into the meanings behind words used in the old tongues and revealed more beliefs of the ancient Heathen peoples. Finally, folklore and festival survivals have helped fill out the knowledge of Heathen beliefs. All of this information comprises what modern Heathens call the Lore. The lore is the information that using scholarly analysis modern Heathens have based their beliefs and practices upon.

## Modern History

Anglo-Saxon Heathenry is intimately tied to Ásatrú (here used in the sense of only the Norse version of Heathenry), the two being the same religion with only tribal variations the difference between the two. It is therefore safe to trace the origins of modern Anglo-Saxon Heathenry to the early 70s when Norse paganism was revived both in Iceland and America. In 1973, Sveinbjörn Beinteinsson brought Ásatrú back to Iceland and Stephen McNallen founded the Ásatrú Free Assembly (AFA), then known as the Viking Brotherhood. The AFA closed its doors in 1987, and in 1988 the Ásatrú Alliance was founded. The Ring of Troth, another Heathen organisation was founded only a little before then in 1987. Since then, these two organisations have been the main promoters of the Elder Troth in the United States, although in recent years many other organisations have arisen.

The modern Anglo-Saxon troth owes its origins to the experiences of Garman Lord, a former Gardnerian Wiccan in 1976. On July 4, 1976, Garman Lord prayed to Wóden and received an answer. Shortly, thereafter, the Witan Theod was founded, and the modern Anglo-Saxon troth was born. The Anglo-Saxon troth of that day and age was not quite what it is now. Many steps were taken in the reconstruction of the ancient religion, and it was not until 1988 after many false starts that Theodish Belief found a form even close to what folks know today. In 1992 after many disappointments, Theodish Belief exiled one of its groups, Moody Hill Theod. There had been several problems between the two Theods, with Moody Hill not ascribing to what was thought to be general Theodish practice. Moody Hill has not generally been accepted as a part of Anglo-Saxon Heathenry since. Only Gering Theod remained with Garman Lord and Gert McQueen as any form of Anglo-Saxon organisation.

They were far from being alone in practising Anglo-Saxon Heathenry however. Two Ring of Troth members Swain and Eric Wódening also had been practising it since 1989 (having practiced Norse Heathenry prior to that). Contact between the Wódenings and Gering Theod was made in 1993. Since that time, the Anglo-Saxon troth has grown to be the second largest form of Germanic Heathenry in the world. In 1996, a group calling its self Esacynn was founded, and in the same year, Swain Wódening, disenchanted with Theodish Belief, and in the process of being exiled, founded with Winifred Hodge the Angelseaxisce Ealdriht. Esacynn and the Ealdriht merged in 1999, only to separate again with Esacynn becoming a separate organisation again.

Anglo-Saxon Heathenry, as stated before is a part of Germanic Heathenry. Modern Germanic Heathenry has many different forms, the two major ones being Ásatrú, and Anglo-Saxon Heathenry. Ásatrú or the Norse (sometimes called Icelandic) version is the far more diverse of the two major varieties, being made of many different groups with many different views. These can basically be classed in three groups: 1) Folkish, a term slowly falling out of use, but once used to describe any individual that felt one must be of Northern European descent to be Ásatrú. Folkish can be broken down into two subgroups. The first is the racialist, those that feel only those of Germanic descent can be Ásatrú. The second group have never been defined by any term, but feel Germanic descent is needed due to certain spiritual qualities passed down family blood lines. These spiritual qualities however can be transferred to a non-Northern European through adoption or blood brotherhood allowing them to become Ásatrú. 2) non-Folkish, sometimes called Universialist (another term falling out of use) feel anyone can be Ásatrú regardless of race. 3) Tribalists are those that follow a version of Ásatrú more closely styled on the structure of the Anglo-Saxon troth, but using Norse customs. Tribalists can again fall under the heading of Folkish or non-Folkish as well, but generally fall into the realm of the second variety of Folkish individuals.

The Anglo-Saxon troth, *þeodisc Geléafa*, Theodish Belief, or Hæðengyld (as it is sometimes called) differs from Icelandic Heathenry in that it has been more innately "tribal" or *þeodisc* in nature. Traditional tribal societies share several features 1) A chieftain, usually elected for life. 2) A tribal assembly consisting of free adults of the tribe. 3) A way of determining status in the tribe. 4) Customs and traditions

15

particular to the tribe. Both the Ealdriht and the Winland Rice of Theodish Belief operated using tribal assemblies and ways to determine status within their organisations. And both drew their thews from the ancient Anglo-Saxon law codes and other ancient materials. Many tribal organisations feel that one must be accepted into the tribe to be thought Heathen.

While modern Anglo-Saxon Heathens are attempting to reconstruct the ancient religion, modern Anglo-Saxon Heathenry is not and cannot claim to be an authentic reconstruction of the ancient religion. The myths of its Gods it owes in a large part to the Norse *Eddas* and the Dane Saxo. Other beliefs have been reconstructed from comparison to the Icelandic sagas, and many of its traditions are drawn from later English folklore. Modern Anglo-Saxon Heathenry is therefore a synthesis of many Germanic traditions and beliefs that have been interpreted using the best scholarship in modern Germanic Heathenry. Despite this, it never can or will be the ancient religion. It is in truth a fusion of Icelandic rituals, medieval folk festivals, and a hodge podge of information gleaned from English and German folklore. Still, what survived of the Anglo-Saxon Heathen beliefs are being followed by many in the Americas, Australia, and Great Britain. And while it is not exactly as the ancient religion of the Jutes, Saxons, and Angles was, it captures the spirit and soul nonetheless.

# Chapter II The Nine Worlds

It is not known, precisely how the Anglo-Saxons saw their universe. In the Anglo-Saxon charm, "The Nine Worts Galdor," it is said, referring to the nine herbs, that Wóden, *sette ond sænde on VII worulde;* "set and sent to seven worlds." Many have taken this to mean that the Anglo-Saxons did not share with their Norse neighbours the idea of nine worlds. Others maintain that yes, the Anglo-Saxons believed in nine worlds, and the number seven was a substitution for nine due to Classical influences. Regardless, neither the Norse nor the Anglo-Saxons saw a simple universe with a heaven above and a hell below. Instead they saw a complex of other planes and enclosures interconnected with our own. To even get close to an idea of how Anglo-Saxon pagans saw the cosmos, we must turn to the Icelandic *Poetic* and *Prose Eddas.*

According to the *Eddas*, these planes or worlds were born when the realm of fire, Múspillheimr, in the south moved north to meet the realm of ice, Niflheimr in the south. They met in what is known as the Ginnungapap "the yawning void." From this union sprang forth two beings Ymir the primeval giant and Audhumla, the primeval cow. By licking the ice, Audhumla made a new being appear, Buri. From Buri sprang Borr who married Bestla, who gave birth to Wóden, Willi and Wéh. They slew Ymir and from him created the Nine Worlds and the World Tree that supports the worlds.

Although the Nine Worlds are linked by the World Tree, they by no means lie near each other, there are hills, valleys, mountains, and even rivers between them formed by the bark of the tree. Beyond the Nine Worlds are unknown worlds resting in the *Útgard,* an Old Norse term meaning roughly, "that outside the enclosure". Each world as well as the World Tree and the Well of Wyrd are described below with the Old Norse name followed by the Anglo-Saxon version or an Anglo-Saxon reconstruction where possible.

## Yggdrasil/ *Éormensyll

Yggdrasil, perhaps, known as the Irminsul in Old Saxon (the Anglo-Saxon reconstruction being Éormensyll) is the World Tree and holds all the known worlds and rises out of the Well of Wyrd. It is often spoken of as an ash, though it was thought to have needles like a yew and also bore fruit. More than likely, the tree cannot be compared to any mortal species of tree, but may, indeed be a combination of them all. The World Tree gives the universe its infrastructure. The Nine Worlds rest within its branches and under its roots. Due to this, the World Tree often serves as a pathway for travel between the worlds.

## Niflheimr/ *Nifolham

Niflheimr "the misty home" was thought of lying in the metaphysical north of Miðgardr below Hell. It is a world of pure cold or ice, shrouded in mist. From it flowed the rivers into Ginnungagap at the beginning of time that now flow into Hvergelmir, a part of the Well of Wyrd. It is believed that the Nibelingen (MHG) or Niflungar (ON) of the Sigurd myth may have originated there.

## Ásgarðr/*Ésageard

Ásgarðr literally means "enclosure of the *Ése* (Æsir)" or "enclosure of the gods." It is possible it was also called *Heofonríce* in Anglo-Saxon, but there is no way to prove this definitely. Ásgarðr is centred on a higher plane above Midgarðr and can be reached through several means. Chief is Bífrøst or Ásbrú, the fiery rainbow bridge that links the world of men to the realm of the gods. It can also be accessed from Hell by Gjallarbrú "the resounding bridge."One can also reach Ásgarðr through the Myrkviðr the "mirk wood" which separates Ágarðr from Múspillheimr. Finally there are the rivers which flow around Ágarðr and these Þunor (Thor) must cross as he is too heavy for the bridges.

There are many halls in Ágarðr; Valaskjálf of Wóden, Bilsskirnir of Þunor, Fensalir of Fríge, Víngolf (AS Wyngeard) of the goddesses, Glitnir of Forseta and Valhøll

(AS *Wælheall) of the fallen heroes.

## Jøttinheimr/*Eotenham

Jøttinheimr is home to the Jøtnar (AS Eotenas) or ettins, the giants. Traditionally it is seen as north of Midgarðr. In Eotenham lie the fortresses of the ettins. Within its borders also lies the Jarnviðr or the "iron wood."

## Alfheimr/ *Ælfham

Alfheimr is the home of the elves and was given as a gift to the god Fréa (Frey) for his first tooth. It was thought of as a place of great beauty, as were its inhabitants. Many believe it lies near Ásgarðr.

## Midgarðr/Middangeard

Midgarðr is the realm of Man and is thought of lying in the centre of the Nine Worlds. It is surrounded by a vast ocean and about it lies a wall built by the gods to protect it. Several variants of the name survive, amongst them Middenerd and Tolkien's Middle-Earth.

## Múspellheimr/Múspell

Múspellheimr is a region of pure fire ruled by the Surtr. Others like him inhabit the realm and are the closest thing to evil incarnate that can be found in Northern European mythology.

## Hel/Hell

Hel is the lowest of the Nine Worlds besides Niflheimr resting below the World Tree, although there are references to worlds which lie beneath it. It is not at all a bad place, parts of it are an afterlife paradise while other parts are seen as dark and gloomy. Unlike the Christian purgatory, it is not an abode of punishment, but simply a resting place for the dead. It may be reached by the road Helvergr "the Hell way" or "Highway to Hell" if you like, a river of blood called Gjøll, or a cave called Gnípahellir. Hel's gate called Helgrind or Nágrind is guarded by the ettin woman Modgud and the hound Garmr.

Below Hel and in a northern part of it lies the mansion of the goddess of death Hel. It is called Elviðnir "misery" and is surrounded by a wall called Fallanda Forad "falling peril." Still deeper is Kvøllheimr, a place of punishment for the wicked. Within it is Nástrønd/*Néostrand "corpse strand" a dwelling made of adders for which there may be an Anglo-Saxon term in *Wyrmsele* "snake hall." Here the evil dead are sent forever to have burning poison drip down upon them.

## Svartálfheimr/*Sweartælfham

Svartálfheimr is the home of the Svartálfar, the black elves. Their identity is unclear, though a few believe them the same as the Dokkálfar or "dark elves." Still others hold they are the dwarves of Norse mythology. It is thought of as a subterranean region and folk tales suggest it can be accessed through caves in Midgarðr.

## Vanaheimr/*Wanaham

Vanaheimr is the home of the Wena (Vanir) the second family of Gods of which Fréa (Frey) and Fréo (Freya) are members.It is thought to be west of Midgarðr and like Ágarðr is said to have many mansions.

## Urðarbrunnr/ *Wyrdesburne

Urðarbrunnr or the Well of Wyrd lies at the base of the World Tree. There lies the dwelling place of the Norns as well as the thing stead or assembly area of the Gods.

The various directions given in the above descriptions should not be thought of as literal directions. They come down to us from many sources and we cannot be certain of their accuracy. Certainly Earthly directions would have little bearing on what are essentially metaphysical planes bordering our own. Still, it may be that these directions may give some idea of where the planes lie in relation to each other and which may be closest to our own.

# Chapter III Wyrd and the Multiverse

Wyrd, the look and feel of the word is rather archaic today. Its modern spelling of weird has long lost its original sacred meaning. Simply defined in its older sense, Wyrd is the way the universe operates. Action in the present has results in the future that are based on similar actions in the past. The ancient Heathens defined this by using the model of the World Tree, Yggdrasil, and the Well of Wyrd, much as we use models to demonstrate concepts today.

At least three factors played a role in this model: 1) the World Tree, Yggdrasil (ON) or *Eormensyl 2) the Well of Wyrd, Urðarbrunnr (ON) or *Wyrdesburna 3) the Nornir (ON) or Wyrdas (OE), three godly figures in charge of the multiverse's destiny. Above the Well of Wyrd stands the world tree, dew forms everyday on its leaves:

Ask veit ek ausinn,--- Heitir Yggdrasil, Hárr baðmr heilagr, --- Hvíta-auri; Þaðan koma döggvar, --- Es í dala falla; Stendr æ yfir gronn --- Urðarbrunni.

> An ash I wit standing --- Called Yggdrasil, A high holy tree --- Sprinkled with white clay, Thence come the dews --- That in the dales fall; Stands it always ever green --- Over Wyrd's Well. (Gylfaginning 16, *Prose Edda*)

Here beneath the tree at the well, the Nornir or Wyrd Sisters oversee the events of the multiverse. We are told in the *Elder Edda:*

> Þaðan koma meyiar, --- margs vitandi,
> þrár, ór þeim sæ, ---er und þolli strendr;
> Urð héto eina, ---aðra Verðandi
> --scáro scíði--, --- Skuld ina þriðio;
> þær lög löumlgðo, ---þær líf kuro
> alda bornom, ---ørlög seggia

> Thence come the maidens, --- Mighty in wisdom,

Three from the place, ---Under the tree,
Wyrd is called one, ---Another Werðende
Scored they on wood, ---Scyld is the third;
There Laws they laid, ---There life chose,
To men's sons, ---And spoke primal laws (Völuspa
20-25)

Each of the actions the Wyrd sisters performed daily had a
specific purpose in the maintenance of the multiverse. The
first of these is --*scro scíði*-- "to score on wood." This is an
activity one usually found linked to the carving of runes, and
indeed, the Wyrdas may be divining what they should do, or
using the runes to ensure that which should happen will
happen. Next they *lög lögðo*, "laws lay down" or more
literally "lay layers."

The scholar Paul Bauschatz feels these are not laws
per se, but physical strata or layers (in the spiritual sense) :

> "The phrase lög leggja is the usual term in Old
> Norse for the act of making laws, but the literal
> meaning of the phrase suggests something else.
> Leggja is "to lay," "to place," "to do." Lög (the
> plural of lag) is literally 'strada' or 'that which
> has been deposited or laid down.' Lög leggja is,
> then, to lay down that which is laid down, or to
> lay down or implant strata. They also líf kuro
> "choose life" and ørlög seggia "say ørlög.""
> (Paul Bauschatz *The Well and the Tree*, pages
> 6-7, University of Massachusetts Press, Boston,
> 1982)

Bauschatz feels the phrase to "choose life" is too vague to
make any decision on as to its context. But it is parallelled in
the lore by another phrase which is valkyrja "chooser of the
slain." The valkyriur are Wóden (Odin)'s and Fréo (Freya)'s
hand maidens and it was their duty to choose who fell in
battle. Just as the valkyriur choose whom dies in battle, the
Wyrdas could easily guide the lives of men. A close look at
*Beowulf,* shows Wyrd being mentioned at crucial moments
such as in the passage above, or when Beowulf boasts in

symbel. Beowulf boasted he would slay the monster that had been killing warriors in the hall, and ended his speech with *Gað á wyrd swá hío scel*, "Goeth ever Wyrd as she shall." This is typical of references to Wyrd in relation to crucial events. Wyrd determines the outcome of any such crucial event based on the past actions of those involved. In this sense, Wyrd is choosing life or life's paths.

The final activity of the Wyrdas is to speak *ørlög* (*orlæg* A-S), the "speaking of the primal layer." The prefix *or-* was used in Old Norse and the other Germanic tongues to mean something that was "primal", "fist", "ancient," or "primeval." Thus, the *orlæg* is the earliest, most significant layer. All of these activities are in relation to the well and the tree. Our word "to do" derives from an Indo-European root related to Sanskrit *dadhti* meaning "to put or lay." Other words related to action or law also refer to this idea of "layers." Thus, a deed is a layer in Wyrd's Well

By scoring on wood, choosing life, and speaking *ørlög*, the Wyrdas created the layers or laws within the Well. These layers represent the past, deeds that have been done by beings living in the World Tree. In addition however, the Wyrdas also water the World Tree from the Well each day:

> Enn er aat sagt, at nornir aær, er byggva við Urðarbrunn, taka hvern dag vatn i brunninum ok með aurinn aann, er liggr um brunninn, ok ausa upp yfir askinn, til aes at eigi skulu limar hans treena eða fœna, en aat vatn er sv heilagt, at allir hlutir, aeir er aar koma í brunninn, verða sv hvítir sem hinna sœ, er skjall heitir, er innan liggr við eggskurn.

> And it is said that, these Norns there, that dwell at Wyrd's Well, take every day water from the well and with that clay, that lies in the well, then sprinkle it upon the ash, to the end that the tree's limbs shall not wither or rot, for this water is so holy, that all lots, that come there into the well, become as white as the white within an egg shell. (Gylfaginning 16)

By watering the tree and speaking the *orlæg* of all things, the Wyrdas ensure that the present is built upon the past. The Well of Wyrd with its layers of past deed symbolizes the past, the World Tree holding the Nine Worlds, represents the present. The Wyrdas would water the Tree, this water being the result of deeds, and these deeds and results would then run back into the Well, where they would again become part of the past.

These deeds and their results do not just sink into the Well to be lost forever. Within the well itself, deeds never sank to the bottom only to be pushed back up to the top by the natural action of the well, for Urðarbrunnr is not a cistern, but a spring fed well. The Old Norse word, brunnr referred specially to wells of a special variety, those fed by springs which force the water up from the bottom, through natural pressure.

The deeds therefore bubble back up to the top, to be brought back to the present again. In the process of watering the tree the Wyrdæ choose the lives of men, and spoke the primal law, this ensured that the cycle of past influencing the present was an ordered, rational one. It remains, however, an ever changing, ever growing pattern with each layer or strata representing a deed or related event being brought from the past to present and back again.

All of these actions can be summarized as thus: The results of deeds in the present as symbolized by the tree Yggdrasil, which holds the nine abodes, flow into the Well of Wyrd, representative of the past. There they sink, to surge back up to the top again through the natural action of the well. The Norns then bring these results to the present to serve as the basis for the results of new deeds when they water the tree. These deeds may also be drawn up by the roots of the tree, or by evaporation from the well condensing on the tree as the dew. The results of deeds in the present are drawn from outcomes of similar deeds in the past.

This is true of events not only for the entire multiverse, but also for each individual in the multiverse. The results of deeds in the present for any individual, are based upon his or her deeds done in the past. This is one's personal *orlæg*. Each and every thing in the Nine Worlds has its own *orlæg*. And the *orlæg* of each and everything is linked and affected by the *orlæg* of those things around it. The closer a person or thing is to something else, the more the *orlægas* affect each other. Thus deeds that a family member does, will affect members of that family immensely at times, but not that of someone unrelated half the world away. The ancients demonstrated this through the Web or "woven cloth" of Wyrd.

Unlike the Well and the Tree model, we have no ancient descriptions of the Wyrdas using a loom to create the Web (unless one counts the Hegi lays where Helgi's life is woven by the Wyrd sisters). We only have hints in the form of kennings referring to the threads of life. At least one is a very clever reference in the Anglo-Saxon riddles in the Exeter Book. The word Wyrd its self derives from words that once meant "to turn or to spin." The Anglo-Saxons seem to have preferred the loom and web model to that of the Well and the Tree, which seems to go unnoticed in the surviving Anglo-Saxon literature.

The model of the web follows the operation of a loom while weaving. Horizontal threads called the woof cross vertical threads called the warp. Every warp thread runs parallel to the other warp threads on the loom. The woof thread is passed back and between the warp thread interweaving them by means of the shuttle. A comb then forces each warp thread against the next warp thread creating the woven cloth. This cloth or web is then taken up in a roll on the cloth beam of the loom. As weaving continues, more warp threads are rolled up from the back of the loom where they rest on the warp beam. Thus, the Web and Loom model may be reconstructed something like what follows:

In the process of the weaving, the woof threads, or the threads of the lives of men, pass across the warp threads, which can be seen as the events in men's lives. As the Wyrdas weave they speak the *orlæg* of all things. This is to ensure that the weaving is ordered and controlled. The Web its self, the woven cloth is the past, those threads ever being woven into the weave are the present. Eventually the cloth is ripped up and spun into new thread. Modern Anglo-Saxon troth often holds that it is the goddess Fríge (Frigga) that spins the threads of life on her distaff. Once spun the thread again goes to the Wyrdas, and is woven by the Wyrdas back into the Web. Thus as with the Well and the Tree, it is an ever repeating, ever changing, ever growing cycle.

This model unlike the Well and the Tree model emphasizes the link amongst all things. No thread stands alone isolated, but touches many others. And through the process of weaving, may come contact with many other threads. Those closest, are those that have the most impact upon it, those farthest away, the least.

The belief in Wyrd has many implications for believers in the Anglo-Saxon troth. One's own deeds determine their fate, so free will is ever present. Yet at times, when similar deeds have been repeated often enough, one's destiny may seem unchangeable. It is the repetition of deeds that impact the "primal layer" the most, and these deeds once in the past lend their results to similar deeds in the present. Ethically, this has strong meaning for Anglo-Saxon Heathens, to do wrong once may be admissible, maybe even twice, but eventually the full weight of such deeds will come again to the present.

## Wyrd and the Basis of Law

Ancient Germanic law codes operated on the idea of how Wyrd and *orlæg* operated. Even today the basis for English Common Law is the concept that the past determines what shall be done in the present. The ideas that past precedents in court rulings determine what should be done in the present go all the way back to when the ancient Heathens believed in Wyrd.

To the ancient follower of the troth, Wyrd and law were inseparable. Old English *dóm*, our word "doom" is defined as "judgment, ordeal, sentence, law, and custom." It derives from the word *dón* "to do," and thus like the word law, carries with it the idea of the layers in the Well of Wyrd.

27

In essence, it referred to the *orlæg* of the tribe, the results of their combined actions at times that were most significant. Other ancient legal terms also reckoned back to a strong belief in Wyrd. Old English *ordál*, our word "ordeal," originally had a meaning much closer to that of ørlög, an *ordál* being an "ancient portion." When one underwent a trial by ordeal, they were essentially showing themselves to be a virtuous person innocent of the crime, by calling upon the witness of their own past.

In essence, the ancient Heathens saw *orlæg* as no different from law. Each individual, family, community, tribe, even Middangeard had its own *orlæg*. Some deeds affect the entire realm of men, while others affect only tribes or their communities. Other deeds may only impact families or individuals.

## Wyrd and Sin

Wyrd affects everything, and there is hardly a theological construct in the Troth that it does not play a role in. Just as the way the ancient Heathens viewed law as tied to Wyrd, so was the way they viewed "sin." The very name of the third Norn was Skuld "debt," a concept which plays an important role in Heathen ideas about "sin." Three basic principles play a role in Heathen conceptions of sin. The first is Wyrd, the second is mægen "spiritual strength or might," and the third is Skuld, or in Anglo-Saxon *Scyld*, "debt."

Every individual has its own personal *orlæg* (OE) or *ørlög* (ON). *Orlæg* dictates how actions taken by a being or thing resolve themselves in accordance with wyrd. It is the *fylgja* (ON) or *fæcce* (OE), the fetch that regulates how this is done. The fetch is one's guardian spirit, and passed down family lines. The fetch is often confused with the hamingja (ON) another word for *mægen* (OE) or *megin* (ON) "the 'luck' or spiritual strength" of an individual. *Orlæg* too was thought to be passed down family lines. When inherited, so were the duties and obligations of the dead ancestor, that ancestor's *orlæg*. This could mean the physical duties of the dead ancestor, but that is likely not the case. It is unlikely that an individual would be responsible for the physical debts of a long dead ancestor. Instead the inheritance of *orlæg* means the individual inherited the spiritual abilities and obligations of that long dead ancestor, his or her "karma" or "metaphysical baggage." Evidence of personal *orlæg* is usually found in the Old Norse texts, the other Germanic tribes using instead the term Wyrd, which has implications of universal law more so than personal *orlæg*. However, Old English *dóm* "law" which is found in several poetic passages and usually translated "renown, reputation," has earlier meanings more keeping with the term Old Norse *ørlög*. In such passages, either renown or personal karma could be meant. In the passages below, I substitute *ørlög* for *dóm* in the translations in an attempt to see if it is *ørlög* that is truly being referred to.

se þé fore duguþe wile --- dóm áraran, eorlscipe æfnan ---oþþæt eal sceaceð, léoht ond líf somod --- lof se Gewyrceð, hafað under heofonum --- héahfæstne dóm.

He that before his war band will --- Orlæg establish, Manliness must fulfil --- Or all shakes, Light and life together --- Fame he works, That has under heaven --- Highfast orlæg. (Widsith, lines 140-144)

[...]--- Nu) is se dæg cumen, þæt þ- scealt aninga --- oððe twéga, líf forléosan --- oððe lange dóm ágán mid eldum --- Ælfheres sunu. ... --- Now is the day come,

That you shall among any men --- Of two things do Life forfeit --- Or long orlæg earn, Go with the others --- Ælfhere's son! (Waldere I, lines 8-11)

As can be seen in both passages, the substitution makes sense. This is true of most passages containing the word *dóm*. It only seems to mean "fame" or "renown" when used in the contexts of passages above, when it could just as easily refer to *ørlög* or orlay. At all other times it takes the meanings of "law," "decree," "fate," sentence," or "power, might." We see *ørlög* used in similar senses to this in Old Norse, and there it is clear that only one's "personal karma" can be meant. Within the Anglo-Saxon passages, it is implied (as it is sometimes in Old Norse texts containing the word *orlæg*) that *dóm* must be earned or somehow won. This would be true if the word meant" renown," but if it means "personal law, wyrd" this would hardly be possible. Renown is something others bestow upon you, wyrd is something one can only bring about or influence for you or your self. There are at least two possibilities here. First, *dóm* also meant "power, might" and therefore might be equitable with mægen. Second, the ancient Anglo-Saxons might have confused *dóm* with mægen, just as the ancient Norse confused *hamingja* with the fetch. All of these terms are related, and therefore may have become confused. The fetch was said to keep track of one's *ørlög* and to regulate one's *hamingja*; therefore that the various terms become confused and interchangeable late in the Heathen Era might be expected.

Mægen (OE) is the spiritual energy contained in every living thing in the multiverse. It could be lent to others or given away. This exchange could be done between the living and the dead. There were several terms for it besides *hamingja* such as *gipta* (ON) and *gæfa* (ON), both words meant "luck, fortune," but are related to our word "gift." Mægen seemed to have been passed down family lines along with the fetch and *orlæg*. How far these acts of transference go is anyone's guess, but based on the passages above and other passages, one might assume that mægen was acquired as the results of one's deeds. In Waldere I, it is said, *Weorð ðe selfne, gódum dædum,* "Worth gain for yourself, thru good deeds." Throughout the lore we are faced with the improvement of one's *orlæg* or the gaining of strength thru deeds of renown. It is one of the central themes of Beowulf and plays a major role in the other epics. If mægen can be earned thru good deeds, then can it not be lost thru bad ones (deeds that harm the tribe)? We are told in the Eddas that the fetch flees the wicked, since the fetch is the carrier of mægen, it might be assumed that the wicked loose mægen every time they commit an evil act.

On the physical plane, fines were the primary form of

punishment for any given crime. In a sense, (OE) laws reduce every offence to 'theft,' for which a monetary equivalent can be found. " In fact the term for crime was *scyld* (OE) "debt." The Old English word *gylt*, our modern word "guilt" packed similar connotations. Other terms, such as *dolh* (OE) "injury," are related to words meaning "debt" such as Gothic *dulgs*. When the Christians first needed a word for "sin" they chose the word *scyld*. This seems to be true of most Germanic languages. One can only assume that this was because the term *scyld* packed not only the threat of physical retribution or the need to pay compensation, but also a spiritual penalty. Finally, the third Norn's name is Skuld, which means that the concept of "debt, obligation" must have played some role in Wyrd. The only other mention of Skuld outside of Völuspa 20 and the Gylfaginning is in Völuspa 30, where she is mentioned in a list of valkyriur, the valkyriur as choosers of the slain, were often the collectors of debts owed to Wóden for a promised victory in battle.

If as it appears the ancient Heathens used the term *scyld* as a word for "sin," then what was the currency of exchange? The only logical answer would be mægen. If as the lore seems to indicate, one gained mægen by doing good deeds, then by inference they would lose mægen by doing evil deeds. One can further assume that if tribal laws could be changed by "setting a new precedent" so too could be one's personal *orlæg*. This would most likely be done thru an expenditure of mægen. Any deed one does will have a result influenced by his or her *orlæg* straight from the Well of Wyrd. The results of deeds or actions depend on two things; 1) the past actions of the thing or being doing the deed, and their personal *orlæg*, 2) the amount of mægen the thing or being has and is willing to expend to change the influence of *orlay* on an action currently being done. In order to set a new precedent, the thing or being must expend mægen to bring about change. A new precedent forever changes the results of all actions similar to the one being taken, at least until another new precedent is made. This is the way English Common Law works, so it is only reasonable to assume the spiritual parallels the physical.

The amount of *mægen* any sentient being has is determined by their deeds. Deeds helpful to the tribe, earns one more mægen. Deeds harmful to one's community, a crime or sin, result in a loss of mægen, unless those harmed are recompensed for the harm done. Any harmful deed is a *scyld*, a "debt" or "obligation." The one committing the crime by harming another or stealing their property is in debt to the harmed or obligated to correct the problem. Failure to do so, will result in a loss of mægen by the one who committed the deed. Another form of sin was that expressed by *synn* (OE), our word "sin." *Synn* originally meant "inaction or stasis." A *synn* may have been a failure to take appropriate action or simply action that did not gain one mægen. This type of sin may have been represented by such Old English words as *undæd* and *misdæd*. Non-action may have interfered with the operation of the Well and the Tree making non-action a sin, *synn*. Regardless, this form of sin seemed secondary to that of *scyld* "debt for causing harm." One must be careful not to start thinking that *scyld* is an entirely negative term. The world *scyld* merely meant "debt" or "obligation" and often that debt or obligation resulted in a reward. Béowulf for example created a *scyld* to slay Grendel when he made his boast. Upon paying that *scyld* he received rewards in the form of gifts from the king of Héorot, as this was a deed beneficial to the tribe.

In summary, every deed one does has a consequence based upon some *orlæg*. If the deed is a good one, a Heathen will gain mægen or spiritual strength, if it is a bad one he or she will incur a *scyld* or "debt," and lose *mægen* until he or she can pay that debt with another deed.

# Chapter IV The Sacred and the Holy

## *Sacredness and Holiness in the Heathen Mind*

The Elder Heathens had more than one concept of what was holy and sacred; in truth, they had two separate concepts. The readily familiar is *hálig* (OE) (OFris. *hélich*; OS *hélag*; OHG *heilag*; (ON) *heilagR*; Gothic *hailags*), our word holy. The other concept after nearly twelve hundred years of Christianity has been largely lost to us, but when looked at from a Heathen context is easily understood. It is one of separateness, otherworldliness, and is represented by Old English *wíh* ((ON) *vé*, OHG *wíh*) "religious site." Both *hálig* and *wíh* can be represented by the Latin words *sanctus* (Greek *agios*) and *sacer* (Greek *hieros*) respectively.

The concept of something that must remain whole or healthy must be a very old concept. Etymologically, Latin *sanctus* is related to Old English Gesund (High German gesund) as in "healthy, in good condition," just as our word "holy" is related to other Indo-European words for health. The concept of "health and wholeness" was widely used in the Germanic tongues, and even then seemed to be the more important of the two concepts of the holy and the sacred. *Hálig* and the words immediately related to it were used in a variety of ways, amongst which were Old English *hálsian* (ON *heilla*) "to invoke spirits," not to mention our words, health, hale, whole, and hail. All of these words revolve around the concept of health and wholeness, and the ability of healing. It was therefore a quite attractive term to the ancient Heathens, and was thus widely applied to the realm of Man.

Unlike *hálig*, *wíh* and its proto-Germanic ancestor *wíh* were applied more to the realm of the Gods. Proto-Germanic *wíh* comes from IE *vík*-"to separate," and has a cognate in Latin *vic*-as in *victima* "sacrifice." As an adjectival prefix it survives today in German Weihnacten "the sacred nights" used of the Yule season. Formerly, however, *wíh*-

and the words derived from it, saw a variety of uses all revolving around that which is separate from the everyday. Such terms as Old English *wíh* (ON *vé*; OHG *wíh*) "sacred site;" *wéoh* "idol;" and *wíhian* (ON *vigja*) "to consecrate" saw fairly extensive use at one time. It was largely applied to things that were seen as "otherworldly;" and, even more so than the enclosures of Mankind; must remain separate from the "wilds" around them. The term was applied to words for cultic centres, temple sites, idols, and grave mounds, the very symbols of godly order as opposed to the "wilds" outside. This can especially be seen in Old Norse *Véar*, a general term for the gods. Anything that was *\*wíh*-was something that was, at least partially, in the realm of the gods, separate from all else. An *ealh* (OE) or "temple" was therefore *\*wíh*-, as was a *friðgeard* (OE) "cultic site, vé," thus proto-Germanic *\*wíh*- came to mean such sacred sites. With *wíh*-, we are seeing the ultimate opposition of *innangarðs* versus *úttangarðs*, which is the enclosure of the gods versus the "wilds," all that lies beyond the enclosure of Mankind. Whereas hallowing something makes it whole, *\*wíh*-ing something makes it separate from the ordinary (places it in the realm of the gods), and therefore gives it something of the Gods' power (protection from the "wilds").

A term that may be a combination of the concepts of *hálig* and *wíh* appears on the Gothic ring of Pietroassa, at the end of a runic inscription; *wíhailag* would appear to be synonymous with the Latin term sacrosanct, "that which is whole and separate from the ordinary." A similar phrase appears in Old Norse *vé heilakt* "sacrosanct," as well as in Old English *sundorhálga* "saint." While *sundorhálga* may have been a creation of the Christian missionaries, it could just as well been a term used to replace a more familiar, though Heathen term. The fact that Old English *sundor*- appears in the place of *wíh*-indicates it may have been a substitution of a more acceptable Christian term for one with strong Heathen connotations.

What can be drawn from these concepts of the holy and the sacred are that while the concept of "health/wholeness," was represented by the term *hálig* for both Man and Gods, *wíh*-represented yet another concept, that of "separateness, otherworldliness." This "separateness" or "otherworldliness" would be the divine forces themselves, the gods, and the powers of their realm. Anything that was *wíh*-was endowed with the qualities of the gods and their realm, it contained their mægen. This concept can be difficult to understand at times, but perhaps it is best not to try to understand it, but realize that if something is *wíh*-it has qualities of the gods' realms, and carries with it powers that leave Man in awe. It can be seen in what Tacitus had to say about the drowning of the slaves who washed the goddess Nerthus' cart.

> There is a fear of the arcane attached to this custom for there is a reverence sprung from ignorance about that which is seen only by men who die for having done so. (Tacitus, *Germania*)

The slaves may have had to die because they had touched something of the godly realm, and therefore may have ceased to be of this realm. The kindest thing to do then, would have been to send them to the realm of the gods. This type of action is reflected in the Latin term *victima* "sacrifice," a term which shares etymological origins with the Heathen term *wih*-. This type of religious awe can be seen elsewhere, as in Tacitus' tale of the grove in which the Semnones worshipped a god they believed ruled all. To enter the grove a Semnone had to be bound with rope, and if he fell, he could not stand up, but had to roll out of the grove.

The concept of *wíh*-forms part of a greater Heathen perception of reality, one which is best defined by Kirsten Hastrup in *Culture and Society in Medieval Iceland*.

> When we turn to the layout of immediate space, it appears that the most significant distinction pertaining to the spatial arrangement of the farmstead was inni:úti ("inside:outside"). The borderline between the farmstead as centre and the world outside as periphery was drawn along the fence that

35

surrounded the farm. The opposition between innangarðs and úttangarðs ("inside" and "outside fence" respectively) had important socio-legal implications. (Kirsten Hastrup, Culture and History in Medieval Iceland)

These implications were applied to more than the simple farmsteads of the Icelandic farmer, and can help us better understand the concept of *wíh-. But before we can fully understand the concept of *wíh-, that which is a part of the gods' realms, we must first look at how the ancient Heathens viewed their own socio-cultural order, and how that understanding of themselves extended to their understanding of the other nine realms.

## *The Sanctity of the Human Enclosure*

The concept of *wíh-, "that which is a part of the gods' realms" was related to other concepts revolving around how the ancient Heathens viewed society and the law. Hastrup in her book addresses this concept of "separateness" between that of a husbandman's farm and the wild lands outside it and expands this explanation to Heathen society itself.

The important point is that in our period a structural and semantic opposition was operative between "inside" and "outside" the society-as-law, allowing for a merging of different kinds of beings in the conceptual "wild." This anti-social space was inhabited by a whole range of spirits...landsvættir "spirits of the land," huldufolk "hidden people," jötnar "giants," trölls "trolls," and álfar "elves"...all of them belonged to the "wild" and it was partly against them that one had to defend ones-self... In this way the secure, well-known and personal innangarðs was symbolically separated from the dangerous unknown and nonhuman wild space outside the fence, úttangarðs. (ibid)

As Heathen familiar with our own cosmology, we know this paradigm not to be entirely correct. In truth, what the ancient Heathens truly saw, was a series of enclosures comprising even larger enclosures. Thus individuals comprised the enclosure of a farmstead, and several

36

farmsteads comprised a godord, and all the godhords, the Icelandic state. In most ancient times, individuals made up families, families made up clans or kindreds, clans or kindreds made up tribes, the tribes made up Middangeard. Middangeard and the other eight abodes made up the multiverse and were held in the world tree Yggdrasil. Hastrup points out later in her book:

> Horizontally the cosmos was divided into Míðgarð andÚtgardR. Míðgarð was the central space..inhabited by men (and gods), while ÚtgardR was found outside the fence . (ibid )

This view of the universe as a series of enclosures governed nearly every socio-political factor of an ancient tribesman's life and extended beyond a socio-political philosophy into the very theology of ancient Heathenry. At the base of all of these enclosures was the individual. An individual was part of a *mægd* "a family" and as an individual held certain responsibilities towards that family. He or she was expected to contribute to *wergild* should another family member commit a crime, avenge any fellow family members wronged, defend the family's enclosures from encroachment, and generally contribute to the common good of the family. As an individual he or she possessed mægen, his or her own spiritual energy, and a fetch inherited from some ancestor. Individuals determined their own Wyrd through their own actions, each action resulting in an appropriate outcome according to a personal law that individual had laid down throughout his or her life time. All of an individual's actions had to be in keeping with that which is good. That which is good was determined by the tribe as a whole, and generally came down to "that which did not harm the tribe or one of its individuals," but actively contributed to the tribe as a whole. The word good, which has cognates in every Germanic tongue, derives from Old English *gód* which in turn derived from proto-Germanic *\*gad*-"to unite, bring together." It is related to the word gather and referred to the collectiveness of the family and tribe. Individuals are rarely treated as solely responsible for their deeds in the ancient law codes. According to Bill Griffiths, "Compensation itself would be collectable and payable to a kin-group rather than an individual, suggesting communal responsibility." In time, an individual's lord or guild would be held responsible (notably after the Conversion when Heathen custom was dying), but in the earliest times it was the family or kindred that were responsible for the individual's actions. The *mægd* was the institution that enforced the law for its members. Should a *mægd* fail in preventing a member from committing a crime, it was then held responsible for making compensation to the victim's family. If the *mægd* held that their family member was innocent, they could then take the matter to thing, or fight the ensuing blood feud. Even should the culprit of the crime flee, the family was still responsible for half the victim's wergild under some Anglo-Saxon law codes.

A notable absence in the ancient law codes, are laws dealing with crimes within a kindred. These crimes were dealt with by the *mægd* itself without outside interference. This was because the *mægd* formed a legal unit in and of its self. A glance at the Icelandic sagas will quickly reveal the strength of the family in this respect. The strength of the family as a legal unit, also extended into the spiritual realm. Just as the individual possesses a fetch, the family possesses a kin-fetch called in Old Icelandic the *kinfylgja*, and as an individual possesses mægen, so too does a *mægd*. Similarly the collective actions of a family comprised that family's wyrd. Families were the most important enclosure within a tribe. While within Anglo-Saxon England there were hundred courts, and Iceland, the godords, that came between the families and the tribal assembly itself, it was the family that wielded the most power.

While families were the principal enforcers of the law, they were not its creators. In a metaphysical sense, every individual lays down law as personal wyrd, as does every family. But the laws that governed individuals' behaviour were generally decided upon by the tribe as a whole in various mæþels and things. The *þéod* or tribe was the enclosure, the innangarðs. The law created by the *þéod* was customary in nature. The tribal assemblies did not "make laws" so much as rule on how existing customs or traditions would apply to a given situation (for example the dispute between two families over a boundary). The customs or traditions of a *þéod* were considered its wyrd, its doom, the actions that as a collective whole the *þéod* had laid down in the Well of Wyrd. Kirsten Hastrup maintains that "In Iceland 'the social' was coterminous with 'the law'...it was eloquently expressed in the notion of *var lög* ('our law'). By logical inference 'the wild'...was coterminous with 'non-law.'" (Hastrup, Culture and History in Medieval Iceland) This philosophy was expressed when the Heathens and Christians in Iceland declared themselves *ýr lögum* "out of law" with each other at the Icelandic Althing of 1000 CE.18 Ancient Germanic law was not connected to political boundaries as modern law is now, it was by tribal membership, by blood. That is, an ancient Jute would only be tried under Jutish law, not by the law of the þéod he had committed his or her crime in. The tribe was the law, was that which was good, was the innangard, and all outside the tribe was úttangarðs for all practical purposes. The tribe as an innangard served as "contained space" for deeds to be done. It is the sort of contained space Bauschatz is talking about in his book the The Well and the Tree:

> For the Germanic peoples, space as it is encountered and perceived in the created worlds of men and other beings, exists, to any significant degree only as a location or container for the occurrence of action...The container is action, whether of individual men, of men acting in consort or in opposition, of men and monsters, or whatever. In all cases, immediate actions are discontinuous and separable deriving power and structure from the past. (Bauschatz, page 109)

These deeds done within the innangard of the tribe by its tribesmen are its law, its orlay. A *þéod* is no different from a *mægd* or an individual in that it too lays down its own wyrd in the Well of Wyrd. This wyrd or doom is the law of the tribe. Just as there are spiritual correspondences between the individual and the family, so too are there between the tribe and the family. The tribal leader was seen as possessing the mægen of the tribe, and for the tribe to remain successful, it had to obey its laws. Failure to do so would result in a loss of mægen. Anglo-Saxon Heathens generally believe that our law, orlay, wyrd, and mægen operate on the very same principles; the same principles that the ancient Heathens may have believed in.

Here we are brought back to the discussion of *wíh-*. The tribe in ancient times was the largest social enclosure of Mankind. In a sense, that which was *wíh-*, was also outside its realm, outside the *innangarðs* of Mankind, though not a part of the "wilds," the Útgard. Not all outside the realm of Man was thought threatening. In sooth, much of what lies outside Man's realm is helpful, esp. the Gods. Perhaps then we have struck upon the primary reason for worship, to build a bridge between the enclosures of the gods and the enclosures of Man.

## Good and Evil

The ancient Heathens however did not see all outside the guarded enclosures of their home as dangerous, not to be trusted. They were fearless adventurers, routing the Roman navy on the open seas, colonizing Russia, and even sailing to the coasts of America. It could be argued that the physical unknown did not faze the ancient Heathen, but that the spiritual unknown was quite a different matter. To a great extant, this may be true. In the ancient lore when we are met with otherworldliness, it is often of the dangerous variety. Grendel is a prime example as are the countless tales of ettins and thurses. Yet, we are faced with the concept of *wíh-*, that which was part of the realm of the gods, and therefore seemed to be desirable to achieve. To the ancient Heathen, there were but two types of beings outside Mankind, those that would help Man, and those that would harm Man. There were countless shades of gray between, but most beings fell into these two categories. The ancient Heathens worked charms to rid themselves of arrows shot at them by ill wishing elves and sang prayers to invoke the gods. All of this constituted an interaction between enclosures. It also constituted the ancient Heathens' concepts of good and evil.

Good was, of course, that which helped the entirety of one's tribe. Included in this would be the members of the tribe, their dead ancestors, the tribal gods, land wihts, and other beings that had proven themselves worthy in a time of need. Evil was that which sought to destroy the tribe. The contrast between the two can be seen in the early words for evil. The majority of words fall into two groups. The first group is in stark contrast to the concept of the "holy" for these words deal with evil as illness. Old English *bealu*, our word bale "evil," derives from an Indo-European root meaning "illness" and is related to Old Slavic *bolu* "sick person." Similar is Old English *traga* "evil" a variation of *trega* "grief, pain," and Old English *niþ* with its secondary meaning of "affliction." A term that came down to us as meaning "sick" originally meant "evil" in Old Norse; *Illr* should be readily recognizable as our word "ill."

This concept of evil as an illness can be seen in the Anglo-Saxon charms where wights from outside the enclosures of Mankind are blamed for causing illnesses. Illnesses, growths, and sharp pains are seen as *ésascéot* "arrows or spears" from elves, witches, and other wights or *fléogende áttres* "flying poisons."

Evil was not only seen as illness, but also as the wights outside of the *innangarðs* of Man that might cause illness. Thus Old English *wearg* meant not only "outlaw" but "evil" as well. Similarly, Old Norse fiandR "outsider" was cognate to Old English *féond* "demon," our word "fiend." Just as *illr* is in opposition to holy, so was *wearg* to good, and such words as Old English *sibb* which meant not only "relative or kinsman" but "peace."

How the ancient Heathens handled these "out dwellers" can only be seen in the Old English charms and in

41

the interaction with outlaws in the Icelandic sagas. Throughout the Old English charms, "outdwellers" are threatened with sheer magical strength. In the charm "Wiþ Færstice," the spellcaster after stating he has shielded himself from the "mighty women" causing the sudden pain in the victim goes on to say:

> Stód under linde --- under léohtum scielde
> þær ða mihtigan wíf --- hyra mægen
> beradden and hie giellende --- gáras sendan
> ic him oðerne --- eft wille sendan
> fléogende fláne --- forane tógeanes.

> I stood under linden --- Under light shield
> There the mighty women --- Are deprived of their strength
> And their yelling --- Spears sent
> Another I will --- Send back at them
> Flying arrows --- Forward in reply!

Here it is clear that the spellcaster has taken an active and somewhat combative role in chasing off the wights causing the sudden stitches in the victim. Other charms are not quite so dramatic, but clearly reflect the ancient Anglo-Saxons belief that illnesses were caused by "outdwellers," and that these "outdwellers" must be dealt with in, an aggressive way. Outlaws fared not much better in the Icelandic sagas. They were open game for anyone that came upon them (it was not illegal to kill an outlaw as they were no longer a member of the tribe and therefore, not protected by its law), and could not expect the aid of anyone. They were stripped of any lands they might own, and more often than not wound up dead at the hands of some citizen. Outlaws were men without tribe, and men without tribe were without law. Not even hospitality, one of the greatest of Heathen virtues, need be extended to an outlaw.

Of course, not all "outdwellers" were considered a threat to the enclosures of Mankind, and many such as the Gods were considered necessary, so that while *illr* and *wearg* came to be used of wights intent on harming Man, holy and *wíh-* came to be used of those that were helpful to Man. Here we come to one of the primary reasons for engaging in Heathen worship: to provide a way in which modern Heathen can interact with those beings that help Mankind. This may mean more than just performing rites and prayers however, for to receive the aid of any wight, much less the Gods, one must first prove to be trustworthy, brave, and worthy of the other qualities our forbears found desirable.

# Chapter V The Thews or Virtues of Heathenry

## *Introduction*

Over the years, there have been several attempts to consolidate in one list, the thews or virtues the ancient Germanic Heathens followed. This probably is not possible. The old religion never relied on such things as lists of thews. Instead these thews were implicit in their laws, maxims, and gnomic verses. Many of them can be seen in the "Hávamál" of the *Elder* Edda, and others in the sagas and tales such as the Sigurd lays. Still, others can be seen in the law codes of the time. Yet for the modern Heathen, such lists do come in handy.

## *The Various Lists of Thews*

The most popular of the various lists of thews or thew related material is the Nine Noble Virtues. The Nine Noble Virtues have been around for at least 15 years, and few are certain as to who came up with the list. It is as follows:

Courage - Bravery or boldness, the ability to stand and fight in the face of any threat.

Truth - Honesty and the ability to standby what is true.

Honour - Reputation, renown. Your personal worth as well as that of your family's.

Fidelity - Troth or loyalty to those around you be that family, friends, or fellowship.

Discipline - Self control, the ability to be in command of one's own *orlæg*.

Hospitality - The ability to make a guest feel welcome.

Industriousness - The ability to work hard in maintaining one's self and family.

Self Reliance - The ability to rely on one's self without the aid of others.

Perseverance - Steadfastness, or the refusal to give up even when things are rough.

Many of the Nine Noble Virtues involve oneself. Few of thethews, listed in the Nine Noble Virtues, deal with community. Ásatrú at the time of the list's formulation was the only widespread Heathen religion, and at the time very much into the self reliant, independent Viking warrior image. With the rise of more tribal forms of Heathenry, and a less romantic view of the ancient past, a need became apparent for a more community oriented list. The Nine Noble Virtues were and are a fine guide for how a Heathen should conduct themselves in everyday life, but seems to fall short when a true Heathen community is involved. Therefore, other lists evolved. One such list is The Twelve Æþeling Þews. These twelve thews were formulated about five years ago and first appeared in the work *Beyond Good and Evil: Wyrd and Germanic Heathen Ethics*. They are:

Boldness- Bravery, courage in the face of adversity.

Steadfastness- Tenacity, the refusal to give up.

Troth- Fealty, faith, fidelity. Loyalty to one's tribe, friends, and family.

Givefullness- Generosity, the ability to give to others at the appropriate times Gestening,

Guestliness- Hospitality, or the ability to be kind with guests.

Sooth- Truth, the avoidance of lies.

Wrake- Justice, or the drive to always see the wrongs done one's tribe corrected.

Evenhead- Equality. The recognition that those of the opposite sex are equal.

Friendship- The ability to treat those that one calls friend as family.

Freedom- Self reliance and perseverance as well as responsibility
for one's actions
Wisdom- Adherence to the ancient wisdom of our religion and the use of it in life.
Busyship/Workhardiness- Industriousness or the ability to work hard.

The Twelve Æþeling Þews came about at a time when Heathenry was becoming more family and community oriented. It can be noted that the additional thews all relate to family or community, or the individual's obligations to both. A slightly older list of thews is one created by Garman Cyning of Theodish Belief. It is known as The Three Wynns. They are:

Wisdom - Adherence to the ancient wisdoms of our religion. Worthmind - The maintenance of a personal sense of honour. Wealthdeal - Generosity with one's family and friends.

Like the Twelve Æþeling Þews, The Three Wynns show there is a clear obligation to something other than oneself, and perhaps one of the most balanced (although the shortest) of the thew lists. The most recent list of thews appears in Eric Wódening's book *We Are Our Deeds: The Elder Heathenry Its Ethic and Thew*. This list is even more community oriented than The Twelve Æþeling Þews, and thus reflects the ever changing face of Heathenry. The thews listed are:

Bisignes - Industriousness
Efnes - Equality, equal justice for all.
Ellen - Courage
Geférscipe - Community mindness, putting the good of the commu
nity above one's self.
Giefu - Generosity
Giestlíðness - Hospitality

Metgung - Moderation or self control.
Selfdóm - The ability to be an individual, true to one's self.
Sóð - Truth, Honesty.
Stedefæstnes - Steadfastness
Tréowð - Troth or loyalty.
Wísdóm - Wisdom

There are points of overlap among all of the lists. This does not mean the thews, the lists hold in common, are the most important. It merely means they are the most often thought of. There are less obvious thews that appear not at all that are just as important. Frith rarely appears on any such list due to its complex nature, and is usually handled alone in articles, yet no one would doubt its importance.

## *A Brief Look at the Thews Mentioned*

As stated all of the lists have certain thews in common, and all fail to mention other thews such as frith. Therefore, frith will be covered first here, followed by a brief description of other important Heathen thews.

### Frith

While now a very important part of Heathenry, frith was barely ever mentioned prior to 1994. Then two articles, one by Eric Wódening and the other by Winifred Hodge detailed the ideas behind frith. Since then, it has become a very important part of Heathen life. Frith, roughly defined is "the maintenance of the peace, security, and refuge of the community; the peace and security enjoyed by that community." Frith is a far cry from meaning simply "peace, "the word most would use to define it. One can live under a despot with no freedom and have peace, yet one could not have frith. Similarly, one's tribe could be at war (not at peace), yet the local village be enjoying frith. Frith unlike peace is not the "lack of strife." War and feuds maybe used to enforce the frith or restore it when a threat comes from outside the frithstead, i.e. village, tribe, or family. When within a frithstead, other more peaceful means would be used, such as mediation and reconciliation. If those methods failed, then Thing could be resorted to.

The word frith derives from Indo-European *priyas,* "one's own." Many other words derive from this root word such as Old English *fréogan* "to love," *fréodom* "freedom," and the name of the god Fréa. According to most Old English dictionaries, the word frith meant "peace, tranquillity, security, or refuge."  It also referred to the special protection offered by the tribe and the penalty for breaching that protection. A verb form, *frithian* meant "to make peace with, cherish, guard, defend, or keep."  Eric Wódening in his article "The Meaning of Frith" (*Ásatrú Today*, Dec., 1994) put forth that frith's original meaning was most likely "the peace enjoyed while among one's own (that is one's family or tribe)."

Compound words made with frith reveal a wide array of meanings. *Friðsumian* "to reconcile," *friðhus* "sanctuary," *friða* "protector," *friðlic* "mild, lenient," *friðscon* "asylum, sanctuary," *friðowaru* "protection." Frith clearly did not translate literally into our modern word peace, but a concept far deeper. Its secondary meanings taken from compounds would seem to indicate elements meaning "to protect, defend, give asylum to, to reconcile." A brief look at the definitions of the compound words, as well as that of the word frith its self, reveals words such as peace, refuge, mild, lenient, cherish, protect, defend, asylum, sanctuary, and reconcile. All of these words have in common the idea of maintaining the peace, security, and refuge of the community.  This maintenance would include ways to seek asylum, as well as chances for reconciliation.

This definition would also include maintenance of the law. The ancient Heathens saw the law as the tribe itself, and frith was the ideal state of the tribe, its welfare so to speak. When the law was broken so was frith. Indeed, one could not enjoy the frith of the tribe unless one was a part of it. And one could not be kept out of the tribe once made a part of it unless they had broken the law. While peace is a very sedate idea, frith is an active one.

# Ár/Honour

*Ár* is the native Anglo-Saxon word for honour as is *weorthmynd* "worth mind." Both involve a sense of dignity, reverence, self and family worth...in essence, good self esteem and respect for others. Honour in short is respect for oneself, one's family, and one's tribe. To be dishonourable is to fail to respect others, be it one's family, or other members of the tribe. Dishonour can even result from failure to respect oneself. Heathen honour goes beyond adhering to some later day code of chivalry. For the individual it means respecting the wishes of others, not insulting their person or position. It involves a certain amount of compassion for the under privileged, and respect for those that have earned their status thru good deeds. Other words from the old tongues that mean honour refer to respect, glory, and achievement. One who does not do good deeds does not have much honour, and only those that attempts truly great deeds can be called truly honourable. These deeds will always be exceptional in commitment to the other thews.

George Fenwick Jones in his work, *Honor in Germanic Literature*, concludes that honour was not an inner thing, but more akin to fame or reputation. Honour was something given to someone. It was more akin to fame or renown than any inner sense of virtue. This can be seen in some of my findings as well. Old English ár can be defined as "glory, rank, respect given one." It also relates well to the concepts of *weorð* and especially *dóm* whose primary meaning is most often when not being used of law, "fame, renown." The problem with this is we have a whole host of definitions that point in a different direction. For ár can also be defined as "reverence, dignity" and these are largely inner qualities. The key I think is in the word respect.

Jones in his thesis, discusses early Germanic concepts of honour in relation to Germanic shame culture, as opposed to the guilt culture of Christianity. The difference being that shame is an external thing applied by those outside one's self. Guilt on the other hand is a regret for doing something that one has done. Thus when an ancient Germanic tribesman thought about doing something wrong it was fear that the community would shame him for it, expose him to

49

ridicule or worse, that kept him from doing it. In contrast, a 15th century Christian Englishman's fear was that he would feel guilt over what he had done. This represents two different approaches to a solution to the problem of wrong doing that significantly affects how we think and act. Just as shame was an external thing for the ancient Germanic Heathen so too was honor. Honor was given to one by his or her community. It was not something one developed on one's own. So that while virtue for the Christian was more an inner sense of living a clean life, for the ancient Germanic tribesman, honor was more akin to renown. Yet, this still meant one had to behave according to certain expectations. And herein lies the problem, for without certain inner qualities, one could never hope to achieve honor in ancient Heathenry.

Honor or ár therefore is as much about how one behaves as it is about how one is perceived. There are many ancient Germanic figures that achieve fame through victories in battle. The hero Starkaðr, while very well known, and spoken of in the ancient literature, did not know honor in his life. Indeed, he was often subject to shame. He definitely was well known, and had success in battle, but as he was often the antithesis of Germanic ideals on what a hero should be, he did not know honor. Starkaðr lacked certain qualities that the ancient Germanic Heathens deemed needed to fulfil the Germanic heroic ideal. In essence, he did not do the good deeds needed to win public approval, and did do deeds that won him the scorn of many. It is safe to say therefore, that ár cannot be simply translated as fame or renown. Starkaðr, after all was very well known, but not necessarily liked. A better translation would be "well known for a good name." This concept is seen repeatedly in maxims in *Béowulf* and the *Hávamál*. One's good name was thought to be everything to the ancient Germanic Heathen.

Then as today, a good name had to be earned. This was done by keeping to certain thews or virtues. Jones makes as a prerequisite for these, wealth. His argument is that lack of wealth was evidence of "cowardice, weakness, or shiftlessness; and poverty" (Jones, *Honor in German Literature* page 4). Today's world is quite different from that of ancient Northern Europe as we do not win wealth in battle, nor in the mead hall as gifts for deeds done. Instead, the lack of wealth may reflect more poor planning, a lack of hard work, or medical problems. Indeed, today when nearly everyone enjoys luxuries in the USA, it is difficult to define what wealth means in comparison to a time when most probably lived in mere hovels. Were we to dump the average Middle Class American with an equivalent amount of gold to his or her net worth in ancient Mercia we may well find they would be counted wealthy. Therefore, one might say, that for the modern Heathen wealth is not so much the indicator of honor as much as the appearance of poverty is an indicator of dishonor. Poverty being of course the inability to afford the basic necessities of food, shelter, and basic medical care. This definition does not necessarily fit well, but as our concepts of how to earn wealth have changed so vastly, it is difficult to use it as a prerequisite in a day and age when most everyone basically has wealth. Therefore, we might want to look at whether one owns their own house, do they manage to provide for themselves, are they capable of supporting themselves or their family? If the answers to these are yes, then they have probably met the minimum requirements for what Jones considers needed for honor. Wealth beyond that of course would gain one more renown, but still be reliant on the appearance of other worthy deeds. One that is a miser, and therefore not generous would not in ancient Heathen Germania have honor.

Generosity is perhaps one of the highest Heathen thews or virtues. Kings were called beaggiefas in "ring givers" in *Béowulf.*, and those that failed to give of their wealth were shunned, or brought down. Jones points out the tale of King Rörik told in Saxo's *Gesta Danorum*:

> "In one of them a hero named Hjalte tells of an avaricious king named Rorik, who has accumulated wealth instead of friends and then tries, unsuccessfully, to bribe his enemies to spare him. Because he has been unwilling to give arm rings to his friends, his enemies

finally take all his treasure and his life too"
(Jones, *Honor in German Literature*, page 4)

This wealth ensured that an ancient Germanic war band leader stayed in power, as he or she had to be able to gift his or her men, and to a degree support them. It was a part of the war band system's economics. Today, we might translate this for a Theodish lord as the ability to gift their folk. It might be also seen in the ability to organize and afford to host gatherings of the folk, publications for the furthering of Heathenry, amongst other things. Again, no longer living in a purely Heathen culture whose economics are based on war, it is hard to translate what even generosity may mean to the modern Heathen.

Wealth also meant success for the sibb or extended family. But this was a relationship that was reciprocal in ancient Germania. A powerful sibb meant that one had a better chance at honor or ár. Under ancient Germanic law codes, wrongs were not just that of the individual, but of the family. It was the family that paid wergild, not the individual. Thus, to truly win fame and power, and thus honor, one had to have a family of some means. This is difficult for modern Heathens when many have Christian relatives, and few have fellow Heathen kinsmen. There is a reason that Theodism fell back on the war band culture to formulate its structure, few Theodsmen early in the movement's history had fellow kinsmen that were Heathen. Therefore, with modern Heathen, having well known and respected Heathen kinsmen is merely a bonus, but not a prerequisite. Yet, having Heathen kinsmen may reflect one's luck or power in that it shows the Gods have favored more of the clan than just one individual. To be without kinsmen for the ancient Germanic Heathen was a disgrace, a sign of having no luck. The family, the kindred, was for them everything. Perhaps is powerful more than wealth was a reflection of honor. It is in many ways like the Old South, where it was often said, and still is on occasion, "he comes from a good family." Still, this creates difficulties for the modern Heathen that may not be resolved for a generation or two. We cannot deem every Heathen lacking Heathen family members a disgrace as it would mean most modern Heathens are living in disgrace. It does perhaps though point to the importance of starting families, and raising our children Heathen.

With wealth and a good family as prerequisites we can now move on to the thews or virtues. Jones' list is different from those of most modern Heathens. He names prowess in battle, courage, ambition, fealty, largess, vengefulness, and pride. Prowess in battle is difficult to have in a day and age when battle means using a ranged weapon to pick off a sometime unknowing target. Rare is hand to hand combat as it was amongst the ancient Germanic Heathens. Prowess for today's Heathen might be better translated into those skills needed to obtain wealth today such as having a sharp mind. Staying physically fit however could still be counted as a Heathen thew for this purpose. Courage however, virtually remains unchanged. We still face situations where we must be brave, for whatever reason must face either the consequences of our actions or the circumstance in which we are in. These can mean not fleeing from a mugger, but fighting them off, or simply being brave enough to tell a creditor you have not the money to pay them. Courage comes in many forms as it did then. Ambition for the modern Heathen may seem difficult. Christianity has taught us to be modest, to be humble, and not seek to attain greatness. Yet, for the ancient Heathen ambition was needed to obtain a good name, to get renown. One could not attain fame without it. Still, ambition is seldom seen amongst modern Heathens, and when it is, is often ridiculed. There is no reason though that a modern Heathen should not seek to be more than they are. Even if they are without the means, it at least indicates that they have goals in mind. It certainly beats being content to be humble. I blame this, again on Christianity. We are taught from a very young age that humility is a virtue, that to seek glory is wrong and self serving. This, I think has skewed our thinking as Heathens. Every Heathen, I think should seek to make their name in some way. For me, it is through writing. For my former wife Tee Wodening, it was through being the ideal Heathen lady, for others it may mean being an expert craftsman, songsmith, or a leader of a theod. But one should have the ambition to do what it takes to make a name for themselves. Jones state fealty or troth, loyalty was important to ancient Heathens and it remains at least in my mind unchanged. It means not betraying or turning on those you are blood kin to, or those you have sworn oath to, or count as friends. Troth was counted as one of the highest virtues of ancient Heathenry, and is still highly admired today. To turn on one's friends or those one loves is seen as the greatest of disgraces, as it should be. Largess or generosity, being liberal with gifts also still remains a thew which can be practiced now as in ancient times. Gifts can take many forms, although arm rings and weapons were the common gift in ancient times. Today, it can mean virtually anything. Gift giving brings in a whole other dynamic as gifts exchanged creates a bond between two people. That is why kings so often gave gifts to their thanes. It was a way of strengthening bonds within the war band. Today, it can be used to strengthen the bonds of any Heathen fellowship. Vengefulness again is a difficult thew to see in the modern world. For the ancient Heathen it did not mean being petty, and taking insult to every minor trespass. What it meant was the ability to protect one's family, to take revenge if one of them was killed or wrong. Rarely, do we see revenge taken for one's self, it is always for a kinsman. The problem today of course is that we have laws against being a vigilante, it is thought wrong to take the law into one's own hands. Even in ancient times, vengefulness may have meant accepting wergild and not taking revenge. For today's Heathen, then it may mean seeing that every legal thing that can be done to bring down a wrong doer is done. Finally, Jones list pride as one of the virtues. This like ambition is perhaps hard for the modern Heathen. Those with pride are seen as arrogant, uncaring, sometimes even boisterous. Christianity with sayings like, "pride cometh before a fall," has given us a bad taste in the mouth for those that are proud of the things they have done. The only time it seems okay to speak well of one's accomplishments is in symbel. It should not be this way. Heathens should be able to brag on themselves, to take pride in what they have done. A notable thew missing from his list is hospitality, which is well attested to in the *Hávamál,* and appears on nearly every modern Heathen list. In ancient times, when there were no motels or hotels, hospitality was needed to ensure folks could travel with ease. We see in the ancient tales, folk entertaining travelers. For today's Heathen it should be no different, not to mention, we should try to host gatherings often as well.

There are other exceptions to Jones' list that modern Heathens may see as thews. Both the NNV and my own Twelve Æþeling Thews have thews he does not list. But his list is sufficient to show that these are things one had to do to win renown. For Jones, the aim of keeping these thews or virtues was to obtain renown or glory. Doubtless, this was the aim of many an ancient Germanic Heathen warrior, and is well represented in the lore. However, perhaps the greater aim was to obtain a good name, or to earn the respect of the community (however community could be defined for the ancient Germanic Heathen). The difference in meaning here is subtle. Renown or fame can be had without these thews as can be shown by the example of Starkaðr who while he showed courage and prowess lacked many of the thews, yet had enough fame to have his name remembered. Having a good name means having one without shame, not giving the community any reason to shun one's self. For the ancient Heathen, as for the modern this is the true meaning of ár or honour. Regardless, of what list of thews one uses, to exemplify them, and thereby avoid shame is perhaps the greatest form of honour. It is not enough to give the appearance of being thewful, as sooner or later one's wrongs will be discovered, one must be thewful to acheive true honour.

## Freedom

The recognition and defence of one's own rights are a part of keeping one's honour. Those that allow themselves to be ridiculed by others were not likely to survive long in the Migration Era. Therefore, every Heathen had certain rights. No one could take the horse or sword of a free man, and one could always count on being able to take a dispute to Thing and see due process obeyed. These rights evolved into the "human rights" Americans and the English now enjoy.

Beyond defending one's own rights though, to be honourable meant also to defend the honour of others as well.

## Sooth

Dedication to sooth or the truth is a good part of honourable behaviour. Lies, rumours, hearsay can quickly destroy a tribe. Often simply remaining silent is only a way to allow lies and hearsay to perpetuate themselves. Therefore, part of being honourable is to speak the truth when it is known, especially in the face of lies and hearsay, even if that means one is alone in trying to reveal what is sooth.

## Troth

Another part of honour is troth, or loyalty to one's friends and family. To be in troth with one's family, friends, or lord/lady is not to betray them in even the slightest way. It goes beyond the normal aspects of honour, for troth makes their honour your own as well. Troth breached can always be restored, and it is never a one way street, but one must always remain true to one's own folk. Its sentiment can be seen in this passage from Hrólf Kraki's saga:

In foul winds as in fair--- Keep faith with your lord, He who withheld no hoard for himself, But gave freely of gold and silver

## Wrake

Justice or vengeance for the wrong done one's family was also thought a part of honour. Ancient Heathenry relied on the family for law enforcement. It was the family that defended its own, and often chastised its own.

## Boldness

Ellen, courage, bravery... all of these words are something all of us know, but yet find hard to define. Bravery is the ability to face potentially life threatening situations without regard for one's own personal safety, while accomplishing something for the good of another individual or individuals. Bravery is not the lack of fear. Any veteran praised for his bravery in the face of insurmountable odds in battle will tell you, fear was always present. Bravery is the ability not to allow that fear to take control, and to accomplish what needs to be done regardless. Many passages in the lore demonstrate the Heathen belief in boldness such as Hávamál (passage 15)

> Silent and attentive-- and battle bold should a chieftain's son be. A man should be glad and happy,--- until defeated by death. Such sentiment is further expressed in Fáfnismál

> (passage 29): Ever the fearless--- but never the fearful fares the better in a fight; 'tis better to be glad than in gloomy mood whether all is fair or foul.

## Busyship

Industriousness or the ability to work hard when there is need was not a thew or virtue to the ancients. It was a necessity of survival. In the harsh north with no modern technology one had to work when the weather was good to make sure the community survived the winter. Fields had to be tended, herds protected and maintained, wood cut for fuel, spinning and weaving had to be done for clothing. The lazy were likely to find themselves freezing or starving come winter. Today, it is no less important that we work hard to maintain our families and ourselves.

## Evenhead

Equality of the sexes, equality in the eyes of Heathen thew or law is something that our spiritual forbears passed down to modern America. Regardless of whether one was a lord or a churl, the same laws applied. Punishments may have been different based on the status of the victim, and laws differed on who need oath helpers in trial, but was a lord to kill another lord, his punishment was the same as if a churl were the murderer. Women were highly respected in the ancient era, and one would often find them taking care of farmsteads or advising kings and jarls. They were not treated as chattel or near slaves as in the Southern cultures.

## Friendship

Friendship is the ability to treat one's friends as family. This thew is actually a combination of a couple of others. Troth or loyalty plays a role, as does hospitality and guestliness. The Hávamál has perhaps more verses on friendship than any other subject.

## Givefullness

Looking at the ancient sagas we can tell kings and warband leaders were known for how generous they were. Ring giver was a common kenning for "king." The Hávamál contains several verses on the importance of generosity, but particularly on the importance of sharing with friends.

## Guestliness

Hospitality was almost a necessity of survival for the ancient traveller. Weather could turn bad, there were no inns in that day, and a warm place to sleep was a welcome sight. Hospitality ensured that the tribe's individuals would survive. One knew, that by putting up for the night, that someday the favour would be returned. Today with Heathens often far apart, and travel distances far, hospitality is just as important. The Hávamál (passage 135) has this to say about guestliness:

I give you rede Loddfafnir--- heed it well! You will use it if you learn it, it will get you good if you understand it. Do not abuse a guest--- or drive him out the door. Instead do well for the wretched.

## Moderation

Heathens do not believe in sins of the flesh, yet the ancient Heathens clearly understood even too much of a good thing could be bad. The Hávamál warns against talking too much, drinking too much, eating too much, and even thinking you know more than you do. The point of all these verses is that one should try to do everything in moderation. Included in moderation is self control, the ability to, for example, stop drinking before one is made a fool, or worse yet becomes ill. Overindulgence in anything is not a good thing.

## Neighbourliness

Community mindedness or the desire to be a part of a community was important to the early Heathens. The antisocial did not contribute to the survival of the tribe and therefore account for little in the greater scheme of things. This goes for groups as well as individuals. Groups and individuals that try to isolate themselves and do little for the rest of Heathenry are likely to find themselves snubbed when they try to take advantage of the things the greater community provides such as teaching materials and gatherings. After all, if they have not contributed to the survival of the greater community, why should they enjoy its benefits? Any community takes the mutual cooperation of all involved. For the ancients this mutual cooperation meant mutual survival, the tribe could not afford to defend a village that refused to help others in a time of need. It is not different today. We are a small religion, few in number, and prone to attacks from anything from Fundamentalists to Wiccans. National organisations may mean little to the local kindred, but the national organisations provide teaching materials, ordained priests, and organize the major gatherings...benefits most local kindreds enjoy. According to Neighbourliness, it is the duty of the local kindreds to return in some form, some of the help they have been given, even if indirectly.

## Steadfastness

Modern life can be as difficult as life was for the ancient Heathens. We have traded the daily hardships of physical survival for other hardships that cause stress, heart disease and other problems. At the sometime, we have lost many of the simple pleasures such as living near friends and family that could make modern life more pleasurable. While the ancient Heathen had to worry about keeping enough food and wood on hand to keep the family fed and warm during the winter, we have a different set of problems relating to the same concerns. Commuting to work, problems with coworkers, illnesses, financial problems, all cause the same amount of stress for us as it did for the ancient Heathen. None the less, we as they must persevere, refuse to give up, and be steadfast in our work.

## Wisdom

Knowledge of every kind was valued in the ancient era. To know the meaning of words, or a way to do something was highly prized. Wisdom consists of many things: folk wisdom and common sense, reasoning, and the willingness to learn. The lore shows over and over the quest for wisdom. Woden's self-sacrifice on the Irminsul was to gain knowledge, not power (but then, wisdom and knowledge lead to power). The drink from Mimer's Well was to gain wisdom, the ability to use knowledge, foresight and common sense. Modern Heathens have many ways to seek wisdom. One can read scholarly works on the religion, discuss it with others, and seek out knowledgeable teachers.

## *Conclusion*

There are as we are always told, even more thews than those covered here. However, ancient Heathenry was an organic tribal religion. Such wisdom as the thews was not passed on in lists such as these but in tales like Beowulf, imparted in gnomic verses such as those of the "Hávamál" and "The Anglo-Saxon Maxims." It is only through the study of these early sources of the lore that one can truly learn what it means to be a thewful Heathen. Yet for one new to Heathenry, these lists let them know what is expected of them and when.

# Chapter VI The Soul

Modern Christian thought has the soul being a single entity somewhat divorced from the human body. The ancient Heathens did not see the soul this way, for them the soul was composed of many parts, each with a different function, and intimately tied to the mortal body during life. In the "Völuspa," from the *Elder Edda*, we are told Wóden and his brothers gave man *ønd* or divine breath, *oðr* or moods/emotions, *lá* or appearance, and likr or health. These gifts are parallelled in the *Anglo-Saxon Dialogue Between Saturn and Solomon* where God is said to have given man *þang* or thought, *æðungem* or divine breath, and *modes unstadalfæstenss* or unsteadfast moods. Finally, a twelfth century poem in Middle High German states God gave man *muot* or mood and *aethem* or divine breath.

Research of the various ancient Northern European tongues reveals that the soul can be broken down roughly into: 1) The Lich or body 2) The Hyge or high, the intellect 3) The Mynd or memory 4) The Willa or will 5) The Æþem or the breath of life, the "silver cord" 6) The Hama or the skin of the soul 7) Orlæg or one's personal wyrd 8) Mægen or one's personal energy 9) The Fetch or one's personal guardian spirit 10) The Mód or the emotions. 11) The Wód.

## *The Lich*

The lich or in Old English *lic* is the human body, and it, like other parts of the soul requires special treatment. One should get plenty of exercise and eat the right foods. Humans are naturally omnivorous that is they eat both meat and plants. It is for this reason we have incisors or canine teeth which are designed to tear meat as well as molars to gnash hard grains. One should keep in mind though that most meat on the market today is loaded full of fat that ancient man did not see in his diet. It is best for that reason to choose carefully what meats one eats. As for plants one should eat a variety of plant foods and not eat too much of one thing. One should be certain to eat a variety of green vegetables, nuts, and berries. For those that prefer a vegetarian diet, foods

that are high in protein such as nuts and some types of beans
should be eaten regularly. As for physical appearance, one
should try to keep their hair long as the ancient Heathens
held that one's power resided in the hair, thus kings and
nobles always wore long hair. Nails on the other hand should
be kept trimmed as the ship of the evil dead used to assail the
gods' realms at the twilight of the gods is made of the
untrimmed finger nails of corpses.

## The Hyge

The high or in Anglo-Saxon *hyge* is the intellect, that
part of the soul which rules rational thought. Its dominion is
that of the "real world." While the *hyge* seems to rule the
rational part of Man the ancients may have also felt it ruled
some emotions. The word *hyge* itself is related to words
meaning "to love" or "to care for." The idea of the *hyge* being
connected to the thought of "caring" isn't quite far fetched.
Caring is after all, an active emotion, that is it is one that
requires deeds be done. "To care for" one's sick mother
requires some activity after all, and it may be the ancients
thought "caring" required some form of rational thought.
The memory in the ancient soul structure is also linked to
words for love, although this is in a more romantic sense.
The difference could be between love that is of one's own free
will that of the *hyge,* and one that is innate, that of the
*mynd.*

## The Mynd

The *mynd* is the memory and all functions surrounding it.
This includes all that has been learned, memories of one's
life, and one's ancestral memory or instinct. Like the *hyge,*
the word *mynd* is related to words meaning "to love," though
of a far more romantic variety. Many of the words dealing
with the human mind and loving or caring seem to have
evolved with the sense of "keeping one in mind." That is the
memory or mynd is linked to words meaning "to love"
because one's loved ones will be ever present in the memory.
Similarly the *hyge* is related to words meaning to care for, as
one will actively think of one's loved ones often. These  ideas

of remembering or thinking about those we love or care for or even have been kind to us is deeply ingrained in the Germanic culture. The phrase "thank you" evolved from a sense of "I will think of you" meaning the kind act would be remembered. Heathen scholars have yet to explore these possibilities, the link between active rational thought and emotions such as caring or loving.

## The Willa

The will is the source of voluntary self assertion or determination. It is the ability to "wish" something into being by sheer desire, and be in control of oneself and one's wyrd. It is related to words meaning "to wish or desire " and deals primarily with what one wants instead of necessarily what one needs. However, unlike the *hyge* or the *mynd*, it is not linked to any words meaning "to love" or "to care for," strange for that part of the soul which rules self initiative and desire.

## The Æðem

The æðem is the breath of life, it is the animating principle of the body and is what links the body to the rest of the soul. It is roughly the equivalent of "the silver chord" of some philosophies. Without the *æðem* the soul would separate from the body and leave. At death, the *æðem* dissolves setting the soul free to fare to the afterlife. Another term for the *æðem* is the *ealdor*, which also refers to the life span of a man as well as eternity. Yet another term is *blad* which means "breath or spirit," and like *æðem* refers to ancient beliefs involving the idea of the breath of life as the soul of a man.

## The Hama

The *hama* is an energy/matter form surrounding the soul that protects it outside the body. It is roughly analogous to the skin of the body. The *hama* looks like the body it belongs to although very powerful creatures can shape shift theirs. The *hama* is the "ethereal image" of any ghosts one might see. It is the hama that keeps the soul's energies from

63

being dispersed when the body fares forth. After death the *hama* may be referred to as the *scinn* or *scinnhíw*.

## The Orlæg

The *orlæg* is one's personal wyrd. It is an individual's "law." The *Orlæg* contains all the events of one's life and their consequences. These events and their results further determine the results of one's future actions. It is tied to one's fetch and regulates the amount of one's mægen.

## The Mægen

*Mægen* is the spiritual energy possessed by every living creature and thing in the universe. *Mægen* like wyrd exists on many levels. There is the mægen of the individual that shared by the family, and that shared by entire nations. *Mægen* is expended in everyday life with the deeds we do. How much *mægen* one has is regulated by Wyrd and based largely on our deeds. When one commits an evil act, they incur a debt known in Anglo-Saxon as a scyld "debt, or obligation." Failure to pay this debt results in a loss of mægen equal to the amount of *mægen* lost from the evil act. Thus, theft of a piece of jewellery would result in a loss of *mægen* from the thief equal to the amount of mægen contained in that piece of jewellery. *Mægen* can be earned through the doing of good deeds that is the doing of deeds that benefit others or the community.

## The Fetch or Fæcce

The fetch, or in Anglo-Saxon *fæcce*, is one's guardian spirit and is said to appear as an animal resembling one's disposition or as a member of the opposite sex (which if corresponded to Jung's theories on the *animus* and *animi*a would resemble one's true love). If the fetch is seen as an animal, it will always be seen in that form unless the spell caster wills it to shape change. In ancient times fetchs were generally seen as wolves, bears, cats, hawks, eagles, sea faring birds, and livestock (horses, pigs, cattle, etc.). Its form can sometimes be seen by those with second sight. It is the fetch that usually controls the allocation of one's mægen in accordance with one's wyrd. The fetch also records one's actions in one's wyrd. Fetchs are said to flee the wicked in the *Eddas*.

## *The Mód*

The *mód* is the self. In many ways it is the "totality of being," the cognizance of an individual or state of being. It is a concept that is very difficult to understand because of the vast array of uses of the word in the ancient Northern European languages. The reason for this complexity probably lies in how the early Northern Europeans viewed the world.

In modern thought there are two ways of viewing things. The objective view is one that always views things for what can be scientifically proven about them. It tends to be rational and materialistic in the way it views things. Most of the Western world uses objective viewing. Alongside objective viewing, the West also practices activism or the tendency to submerge oneself in the physical or material world. In the West, thus materialism exists as the main drive in life. A second way of viewing things belongs to the great Eastern culture of India. Subjective viewing sees objects for the emotions they can evoke. Usually cultures that practice subjective viewing also practice quietism or rather they tend to submerge themselves in their own thoughts and not the physical world. These differences in Western and Eastern thought have resulted in the East as seeing only psychic reality or "the reality of the mind" while the West sees only "the material world."

Neither set of views seem to have been held by the ancient Northern Europeans. They seem to have believed in a metaphysical reality or "psychic reality" as much as they did a physical reality or material reality. As such, they probably viewed everything both objectively and subjectively while practising activism in both forms of reality. This would account for such a large part of the soul as the *mód* with its multitude of uses for both the intellect and the emotions. The *mód* is most likely a reflection of the integrated self, one that can both view things subjectively and objectively.

# The Wód

The *wód* is the seat of the "passions" or those emotions that bring about inspiration. The *wód* is the providence of Wóden, and many believe its power comes directly from him. The *wód* is responsible for a higher state of being edging on the divine and can only be defined by such words as enthusiasm, agony, and ecstasy. It is responsible for poetic inspiration, "madness," and the berserk rage. It most closely resembles the modern principle of the *daimonic* as described by psychologist Rollo May. Failure to integrate it into the rest of the soul can result in a myriad mental illnesses, if one uses May's theories as an example. Successful integration on the other hand can result in artistic genius or simply a well balanced sense of being. Strangely enough, the *wód,* was gave to Man by Willa, the god of the will, and therefore self control.

Collectively the soul minus the fetch is known as the *feorh, gæst,* or *sawo*l in Anglo-Saxon There are many other terms in the Elder Tongues for each of the soul parts as well. The lich can also be called the *hræw*; the *æðem*, the *ealdor*. The other terms have related words as well, but these are often more obscure. There is much we still do not know about ancient Heathen soul lore, and the above information is by no means complete. We have little idea what such terms as *sefa, angiet*, and *orðanc* refer to. Whether they are synonyms for the other terms, or other parts of the soul we do not know. However, what knowledge we do have on ancient soul lore will lead us to learning more about how our souls are constructed, and why we do the things we do. The soul is intimately tied to Wyrd, and no study of the soul would be complete without one of Wyrd and concepts concerning good and evil also.

# Chapter VII Afterlife

Not much information remains about what the pagan Anglo-Saxons believed about the afterlife. Some scholars wrongly believe, despite the grave good evidence to the contrary, that the Anglo-Saxons had no belief in the afterlife. They base this on several phrases in Old English poetry and Norse texts such as the "Hávamal" stating the best a warrior can hope for is everlasting fame. This logic of course would be the same as saying Catholics have no belief in Heaven because they do not use grave goods. Nevertheless, they cite phrases found like the following from Beowulf:

Grieve not, wise warrior. It is better to avenge one's friend than mourn too much. Each of us must one day reach the end of worldly life, let him who can win glory before he dies: that lives on after him, when he lifeless lies. (lines 1384-1391)

As well as phrases such as the following from the "Hávamal":

Cattle die, and kinsmen die, thyself eke soon wilt die; but fair fame will fade never: I ween, for him who wins it. (Hollander translation, verse 76)

What the scholars are seeing, however, is only half the formula. The purpose of a heroic life was, indeed, to gain everlasting fame. But the purpose of that fame was not an end unto its self, its purpose was to better one's position in the afterlife, and that of one's descendants. Only those that had done things for their folk could hope to make it into one of the abodes of the Gods. And the proof of these heroic deeds were the boasts made in symbel by descendants, the songs sung by the scop in hall, and the general retelling of one's life. In essence, one's fame served as a witness to one's deeds that showed they were worthy of such a hall as say Valhalla. In addition, if one did not go to one of the abodes of the Gods, but instead was reborn, it improved the Wyrd one was reborn with. Everlasting fame was not immortality its self, but a step unto becoming immortal. That the ancient Anglo-Saxon Heathens believed in an afterlife can be demonstrated by the use of grave goods. Regardless, of whether the bodies were cremated (as is most common in Anglian areas) or buried (as is most common in Saxon areas) grave goods can be found. These grave goods abruptly stop after the Conversion, and can confidently be identified with pagan beliefs. Whether the ancient pagan beliefs of the Anglo-Saxons included a *Wælheall, or "Valhalla" where all warriors went or a *Néostrand comparable to the Norse Naströndr, where the dead were punished is unknown. That information, barring the discovery of some long lost manuscripts is forever lost, if indeed it ever existed.

It is probable that the ancient Anglo-Saxon Heathens felt when they died they joined their ancestors. A substantial number of Frisians invaded along with the Jutes, Angles, and Saxons. And it is recorded that Radbod (leader of the Frisians around 696 CE), when about to be baptised asked the missionary Wolfram if when he died he would join his ancestors. The answer was, of course, "no," and Radbod changed his mind, kicked out the missionaries, and destroyed their churches. It is also likely that at some point the Anglo-Saxons believed in reincarnation or rebirth much like the Norse, but more on that later.

The ancient Anglo-Saxon Heathens had several terms that were cognate to Old Norse words associated with the afterlife. Old Norse *Hel*, *Folkvangr*, and *valkyrie* appear in Old English as *Hell, Folcwang*, and *wælcyrge*. Further there are terms for the afterlife in Old English that do not appear in Old Norse such as *neorxnawang*. Since this term along with others are used in a Christian context however, it is not known if they were used of the Heathen afterlife. It is therefore not a question of whether the ancient pagan Anglo-Saxons believed in an afterlife, but a question of what sort of afterlife they believed in. For answers, we are almost entirely dependant on borrowing from Norse and Danish materials which are very diverse in their views.

Interestingly though Anglo-Saxon beliefs regarding the afterlife may have survived into modern England and America. The present day belief that when people die, they go straight to Heaven or Hell, is not an orthodox teaching of the Christian Church. Orthodox Christian belief teaches that people die to be resurrected on Judgement Day, (there being no activity of the soul between the time of death, and Judgement Day and during that time, you either rest in limbo, go to purgatory, or are just dead). It is therefore entirely possible that this belief was passed down amongst the folk and is a relic of ancient pagan belief in an afterlife.

## The Soul After Death

While the soul or essence of a person would go onto an afterlife domain such as *Heofon, Hel*, or Valhalla, other parts of the soul went onto another form of existence.

### Heofon

Heaven is not commonly used of the Heathen paradise in the afterlife today. The primary reason is because it does not appear in the Old Norse version of the myths as an abode of the dead, and Germanic Heathenry in general today is based on the Norse material. However, there are several indications that the ancient Anglo-Saxon Heathens may have used the term *Heofon* "heaven" to mean the afterlife paradise. Even in the earliest Christian poetry, the term *heofon*, or more commonly, a compound of it such as *heofonríce* "heaven kingdom" appears as either the abode of God, or as the home of the dead. This usage is not unheard of in the Old Norse texts either. The home of Hama (Heimdall) in the Eddas is said to be Himinbjörg "heaven mountain" or "heaven cliff." Himinvanga "heaven plains" appears in Helgakviða Hundingsbana I used of an earthly place when speaking of valkyries riding to Helgi. However, it is entirely possible that this usage harkens back to an older usage of the term as referring to heaven (the valkyries appearing out of the heavens to ride to Middangeard). In the Old Saxon poem Heliand, a cognate of the Old Norse Himinvangr (the singular form of Himinvanga), *hebanwang* is used of the

Christian heaven. It may be then, that at one time, the word Heaven was the common Germanic Heathen term for the afterlife abode.

The word heaven is thought to derive from Indo-European '*ke-men-, a compound word originally thought to have had the meaning of "stone." *Ke-is believed to have derived from PIE *ak "edge," while *-men meant "to think," and dealt with states of mind and thought. Heaven is related both to the word hammer and the word mind, and its earliest meaning *The American Heritage Dictionary of the English Language* takes to mean "the stony vault of heaven." Former Ealdriht priest, Brian Smith in his article, "Heaven" states it as meaning "that which has a quality like stone," and points out the family of Þórólfr Mosturskeggi, in the *Landnámabók,* believed their family would go to reside in a mountain after death (covered below). Others feel that the ancients thought the sky was made of stone, and thus the meaning of the word heaven. It would seem apparent though that both ideas could relate to the concept of Heaven. The most common usage of *heofon* in Old English was for sky. This was also true of its Old Norse cognate *himinn.* Other theories on the word's origins relate it to Old English *hama* "covering, skin," and this would make sense if the word has always meant sky (the sky "covers" the Earth). It could be that mountains, because of their sheer height, were associated with the sky and the Gods. This is so in other pantheons. The Greek Gods resided on Mount Olympus, and many other peoples associated holy mountains with their Gods. Similar to the belief of Þórólfr's family that they "died into the mountain," is one concerning Holda and the Brocken. With Holda we are offered a belief, though late, and potentially influenced with Classical myth, of a Goddess associated with a mountain and people residing in it with her. In 1630, during a witch trial in Hesse, Diel Breull, confessed to have travelled in spirit form to the Venusberg (Blocksberg or the Brocken). There he was shown by Frau Holt the sufferings of the dead reflected in a pool of water, inside the mountain (Marion Ingham, The Goddess Freya and Other Female Figures, p.251). This source is very late however, and therefore very suspect. However, perhaps it does retain a part of Heathen belief in associating Germanic deities with mountains as an abode of the dead. What is clear however is that *Heofon* was seen as above *Middangeard* while Hell was seen as below. It could be then that the ancient Anglo-Saxons saw a world of opposites; *Heofon* as the bright and shining sky, and Hell as the dark and dreary underworld. It can perhaps be considered the same as *Ésageard*.

## Hell

Hell has already been covered with the other nine worlds, however, it requires further mention here as an abode in the afterlife. The term Hell carried over into Christian usage originally as purgatory, not an abode of eternal punishment, but one of a temporary stay, a limbo of sorts. We do not know if the pagan Anglo-Saxons held this view of Hell as a limbo where good and bad both go. And we are given few clues as to whether the pagan Anglo-Saxons viewed Hell as a place of punishment. Nor are we given clues of the happy home of Balder after his death seen in the *Eddas* (indeed that is nearly the only place in Old Norse Hel is not shown as dreary). All we do know is Hell is an abode of the dead, unlike that of the Christian version, but an abode of the dead nonetheless.

In Old English literature, we do see evidence of native beliefs regarding Hell, ones that are not borrowed from the Christian concept of a fiery abode. Either the Goddess Hel, or her domain appears as taking those that die. When Grendel dies in Beowulf, it is said in *fenfreoðo feorh alegde, hæþene/ sawle; þær him hel onfeng,* "in his fen abode, his soul he laid down, his heathen soul Hel took." It is not clear though if this is the Goddess or the place. Hell, as a place, is mentioned again in the Old English Christian poem, "Soul and Body I" where it is used of the grave and not some abode of punishment by fire. Interestingly though, when describing the body being eaten by worms, it uses Old English *wyrmas* "serpents." *Wyrm* had not yet quite acquired its modern meaning of worm, and therefore it could be possible, the poem, while Christian, contains a memory of what the Norse called Nástrønd. Other Old English poems such as "Judgement Day II" contain this torment by *wyrmas.* In the Old English poem, "Christ and Satan" it is very clear serpents, and not worms, are meant when describing Hell (although fiery) as *Hær is nedran swæg, wyrmas gewunade,* "Here is the adder's noise, here serpents dwell." Interestingly, while mentioning the Christian Hellfire, the poet also keeps referring to Hell with such phrases as *dimme and deorce,* "dim and dark," and *ðissum dimman ham,* "this dim home." It could be the Christian poets fell back on native belief of a cold, dark, viper ridden Hell in order to fill out descriptions of the Christian abode of punishment.

In the Norse Eddas, Hel is a very complex place composed of several different places. There is Hel, which can be used of the entire realm, a place where the dead, both the good and the bad go. Then there is Nifolhel, where those that have committed evil go. And finally, for the most evil, there is the Norse abode of punishment, Nástrønd, a place where poisonous snakes drip venom on the evil dead. Old English preserves a word that may have described this place in *Wyrmsele,* used of Hell in the Christian poem Judith. Taken literally, *Wyrmsele* would mean "serpent hall." This word, coupled with evidence from the other Christian poems mentioned above shows the pagan Anglo-Saxons may have known a place not unlike Old Norse Nástrønd as a part of their version of Hell.

Finally, the word Hell derives from an Indo-European root, *\*kel-,* which meant "to conceal or cover." *\*Kel-*also gave us the words hole, hollow, and hall from Old English, as well as cellar from Latin. Hell, just going by the origin of the word then would be some place hidden, covered, or enclosed in some way. This corresponds with the underworld abode seen in the Old Norse *Eddas.* Some scholars have suggested that like Hebrew *sheol,* it just meant the grave. However, if that were the case, we would expect other words derived from the same IE root to have similar meanings. Yet the words hall, hollow, and cellar all derive from the same root, and little about them would imply a relation to a grave. It would seem then, that Hell would be a bit larger than a grave, dark and enclosed like a Hall perhaps, but not small and narrow like a grave. If Hell did indeed mean "grave" at some point, it would likely refer to the burial mounds or perhaps the ancient megalithic graves of Denmark which the Germanic tribes would be very familiar with. Too, it seems unlikely that a people who provided the dead with expensive grave goods to have believed that those goods would never be used. Regardless, this etymology suggests an enclosed place whether a grave, a hall, or walled realm of some kind. Along with the poetic evidence we can surmise the pagan Anglo-Saxon Hell was a dark and dreary place, probably a nether world, perhaps where souls stayed until reborn (or just stayed), with a special place where the truly evil were punished with serpents (not unlike the Norse version).

## Mounds

In the Icelandic sagas the dead are often pictured as living in their burial mounds. Similar burial mounds have been found in England, good examples of which are the Sutton Hoo mounds, and the mound at Taplow. It could be then, that the Anglo-Saxons, or some segment of them shared this belief. The best example of life after death within the burial mound can be seen in *Brennu-Njál's Saga*.

> "There was a bright moon with clouds driving over it from time to time. It seemed to them that the howe was open, and that Gunnarr had turned himself in the howe and looked up at the moon. They thought they saw four lights burning in the howe, but no shadow anywhere. They saw Gunnarr was merry, with a joyful face..." (translation taken from H.R. Ellis Road to Hel)

This idea appears in several other sagas, and therefore seemed a common Heathen belief. In the "Helgakviða," Sigrun enters the mound of her husband to embrace him as in life, he then must ride to Valhalla. Burial mounds were also connected with the Elves, and there is some indication because of this that the Elves may have been nothing more than souls of the Dead. In *Kormak's Saga*, a sacrifice is made to Elves that live in a burial mound so that Thorvard

73

Eysteinsson would be healed of a wound. King Olaf, Olaf the Unholy's ancestor Olaf was buried in a mound at Geierstað, and was known as Olaf Geierstaðaálf "Olaf the Elf from Geierstað."

## Mountains

The *Eyrbygga Saga*, preserves an account of an Icelandic family that felt when they died they would go to live in the mountain Helgafell.

> ".....he saw the whole north side of the mountain open up, with great fires burning inside it and the noise of feasting and clamour over the ale horns. As he strained to catch particular words, he was able to make out that Thorstein Cod-Biter and his crew were being invited to sit in the place of honour opposite his father"(Palsson and Paul Edwards translation)

This belief is also mentioned in the *Landnámabók*, in reference to the same family. *Brennu-Njál's Saga* gives an account of fisherman claiming that Svanr the wizard was received into the mountain Kaldbak after he had drowned on a fishing trip. Several other sagas make mention of the belief or infer it, though it is not mentioned in detail. The concept of people "dying into a mountain" however, may be parallelled in more southern beliefs concerning the Venusberg. The 1630 confession of Diel Breull cited above could be dismissed as a borrowing from Italy, or as sheer fantasy, were it not for these Icelandic accounts. However, Holda is portrayed in German folklore as a leader of the Wild Hunt, and is connected with a cult of witches once fabled to have met on the Brocken. Bruell's confession then may have had a thread of truth about it, and the idea of dying into mountains may be a legitimate Heathen belief.

## Realms of the Gods

The most famous of the God realms where the dead go is of course, Valhalla, which would have occurred in Old English as *Wælheall*. No mention or even a hint of it can be found in the Anglo-Saxon poetry, not in that of the Old

Saxon literature either. However, that does not mean the ancient Anglo-Saxon Heathens did not believe in it in some form. *Wælheall* is mentioned in the *Prose Edda* as being roofed with golden shields, and having more than six hundred and forty doors, its warriors are served mead by valkyries, half the battle slain every day go to it. In addition, the dead warriors there feast on the boar, Sæhrímnir, who comes back to life every evening only to be slaughtered again, while mead flows from the utter of the goat Heiðrún into a cauldron to provide drink. This view taken from the *Prose Edda*, is no doubt highly romanticised. However, the core beliefs are there, warriors and others can die and go to *Wælheall*, there they fight every day to train for the war with the legions of the underworld. This belief could easily have been held by the ancient Anglo-Saxons as well, although we have no evidence of it.

Other realms of the Gods besides *Wælheall* are said in the *Eddas* to receive the dead. Vingólf (which can be reconstructed in Old English as *Wingéolf*) is mentioned in the *Prose Edda* as receiving some of the Einherjar (though Snorri states in another place the righteous), as is a place called Gimlé (which Snorri holds to be one and the same). Vingólf is also said to be the hall of the Goddesses by Snorri. Other of the battle slain or Einherjar are said to go to Freo's hall Sessrumnir "many seated" in Folcwang. The Norse Goddesss Ran and Gefion (Geofon) are said in the Icelandic texts to take in the dead. Ran in particular takes in the souls of those have downed in the ocean.

## Rebirth

There is some evidence that the ancient Norse believed in reincarnation of a sorts. There is no evidence that the Anglo-Saxon tribes shared this belief, however, the lack of evidence does not mean they did not. Indeed, it would be odd if they did not share this belief with the Norse. The ancient Norse appeared to have believed in two forms of reincarnation. The first was thought to occur with everyone, and involved the inheritance parts of an ancestor's soul. The *hamingja* was thought to be passed from an ancestor to a child named after them. This can be seen in the *Finnboga Saga* when a man begs his son to name a son after him so that his *hamingja* would follow, and Glumr in *Viga Glum Saga* claims to have the *hamingja* of his grandfather. This belief also appears in Svarfdæla saga, where Þórólfr says he will give all his *hamingja* to a child that bears his name. The *ørlög* of an ancestor was also thought to be passed to a descendant. This is most clearly seen in the Helgi lays, even though the three Helgis were not all related to each other. The soul then was reborn in part, but only those aspects that did not clearly define one as an individual. That is the *ørlög*, *hamingja*, and perhaps even the fetch may have been passed on, but not the mind, and mood of the individual. The *hugr* (Old English *hyge*) and *munr* (Old English *mynd*) would exist on in the afterlife with the soul that had possessed them in life.

There is evidence though for another form of reincarnation, and this may be what is referred to in the Helgi lays and certainly inregard to Óláfr Geirstaðaálfr and his descendant King Óláf (sometimes called Saint Olaf) as told in the *Flateyjarbók*. Throughout the tale there are indications Óláfr Geirstaðaálfr is King Óláf reborn. When King Óláf's mother is giving birth, she had great difficulty until the belt from the earlier Óláf 's mound is brought to her. As a grown man Odin (Woden) comes to King Óláf , and tells him that he is Óláfr Geirstaðaálfr, and not long after one of the king's followers inquires as to whether the king had been buried in Óláfr Geirstaðaálfr's mound. This could be reincarnation of the soul as a whole, and not just rebirth of parts of the soul.

## Conclusion

The archaeological evidence of Anglo-Saxon graveyards along with the Norse texts show that the ancient Anglo-Saxons probably had a very rich belief in an afterlife. Many modern Heathens believe that when they die, provided they have committed no hideous crimes, they will be given a choice of where they wish to go. Regardless, the afterlife, like birth, and death seems all a part of one continuous life cycle.

# Chapter VIII The Gods and Goddesses

Detailed information on the Gods of the pantheons of the Jutes, Saxons, and Angles is forever lost. We know from mentions in Anglo-Saxon literature that Wóden, Þunor, Ing, Eostre, Hreðe, Eorðe, and Seaxneat perhaps were worshipped. We know further from place names that Tiw, Fríge, and Fréo were also worshipped. Finally, we can infer from continental sources in the homelands of the Anglo-Saxons and their neighbours that such Gods as Irmin, Holda, Fosite, Nehalennia, and Nerthus may have also made up the pantheon. For the most part we are indebted to the Norse and Danish sources as well as German folklore, not to mention our own ongoing experiences with the Gods and Goddess for information.

## *Finding the Anglo-Saxon Pantheon*

One of the problems with the reconstruction of the ancient Anglo-Saxon pagan religion (better known as Anglo-Saxon Heathenry) has been finding out exactly what Gods were worshiped. History was not kind to the literature produced by the Anglo-Saxons. Most of the poems are contained in four volumes, and most of the prose is about the lives of saints, Christian sermons, or if it is historical in nature, it neglects to tell us anything about the Heathen faith. Time, Viking raids, and Henry VIII's closure of the monasteries probably cost us any information recorded on the Anglo-Saxon Gods.

We can find information on them however. The first place to look is in the Roman accounts, a time when the Germanic tribes were still on the continent. We know, for example the Angles, along with other tribes are mentioned in Tacitus' *Germania* in passing as worshiping the Goddess Nerthus. There are other clues mentioned in *Germania*. In discussing the origin myth of the Germanic tribes, Tacitus mentions that the Germanic tribes were descended from the three sons of Mannus (son himself of Tusito). The three groupings of tribes that were descended from these sons were the Ingaevones, Herminones, and Istaevones. From this we can derive that the ancient Angles may have also worshiped deities named Ing, Hermin (or Irmin), and Istæ as well as Mannus and Tuisto. Collaborated evidence can be had for Ing and Irmin. Ing is mentioned in the Old English Rune Poem while Irmin is seen amongst the Old Saxons in the compound Irminsul, a sacred pillar first mentioned by that name by Einhard, Charlemagne's chronicler, and in the Heiland in the compund Irmingott, a title of the Christian God. The Old Norse version of this name is a byname of Oþinn, Jormun. For Istæ and Tuisto we have no further evidence, and for Mannus we have to turn to other Indo-Europeans such as that of the Aryans of India. Their deity Manu (cognate to Mannus, both meaning simply "man") was seen as the progenitor of humankind and the first king. Sadly though, most Roman sources are silent on specifically the Angles, Saxons, and Jutes, and the Gods they worshiped. We can glean though from Tacitus' generalization that all Germanic tribes worshiped Mercury as most high, that the Angles, Saxons, and Jutes knew his worship as well. Most scholars today feel that when Roman writers spoke of a Germanic deity Mercury they were indeed referring to Woden. Jonas Bobiensis in *The Life of Columbanus*, in the seventh century, equates Mercury with Vodan when telling a tale of Columbanus interrupting a libation to the deity.

For more information, we must turn to the Anglo-Saxon's own literature. While the information is scant, we can find some mention of Germanic deities. The easiest is Woden, mentioned in the "Nine Worts Galdor" (also called the "Nine Herbs Charm"), "Maxims I " and as progenitor of Anglo-Saxon kings in the various kings lists. Seaxneat, a deity known from an Old Saxon renunciation formula recorded in Vatican Codex pal. 577 listing a Saxnot along with Woden and Thunor as deities to be renounced appears in the kings list of the kingdom of Essex. As mentioned earlier Ing is mentioned in the "Old English Rune Poem" verse for the rune named for him. A rite is preserved in the form of the Æcer Bót (also known as "A Field Remedy" and a "Charm For Unfruitful Land ") to a Goddess presumably Eorðe, although a name Erce is also invoked which may indicate a separate Goddess who is mother of Eorðe. Bede mentions two Goddesses as having been worshiped in association with months named for them, Eostre and Hreðe. For other deities we have to make a bit of a stretch. Heimdall may be behind the Hama mentioned in Beowulf as bringing the Brosingamene to his fortress. The Old Norse poem "Husdrapa" mentions a battle between Loki and Heimdall over the necklace Brisingamen. Hel may be mentioned in Beowulf as well. In verse 852, it says of Grendel, þær him hel onfeng "Hel took him." It is unclear whether a place or person is meant. The most obvious literary evidence comes in the form of day names. We know from the days of the week that the Anglo-Saxons worshiped Tiw, Woden, Thunor, and Frige. Beyond this, for information close to the Heathen period of England we must look to place names. According to various scholars Frige, Thunor, Tiw, and Woden all seem to have had places named for them. There may be more deities for whom places were named, but as we have no other reference for them, we will never know.

Later evidence from the period of Middle English merely confirms what we already know. Geoffrey of Monmouth, for example, has Hengest saying that they worship Woden. There is one exception to this however. Heliŏ is mentioned by William of Coventry, Benedict of Rochester in his tale of Augustine's life. Supposedly, Augustine destroyed an Anglo-Saxon idol of a deity named Heilth.

Unfortunately, we cannot draw much on archaeological evidence. The Angles, Saxons, and Jutes did not leave inscriptions as many of the Germanic peoples did on altars such as those at Hadrian's Wall.

This is pretty much the extant of the evidence for an Anglo-Saxon pantheon. To fill it out, we must assume that the Angles, Saxons, and Jutes may have worshiped the tribal deities of neighboring tribes such as the Frisians. Here we are treading on dangerous ground as we do not even know if the Angles for example even worshiped the Saxon deity Seaxneat, or for that matter if the Saxons worshiped Eostre (Bede being a Northumbrian was writing from the perspective of an Angle). However, if we do assume they did, at least worship the major deities that their neighbors shared with the Norse we can add Fosite, whose name is cognate to that of the Norse God Forseti. Fosite is mentioned in Alcuin's The Life of Willibrord as having one of the Frisian islands sacred to him, and some equate him with the giver of the Frisian law in the tale "Van da tweer Koningen Karl ende Radbod (Of the Two Kings Karl and Radbod)." Altars to a Goddess Nehellenia have been found in Zeeland, perhaps indicating Frisian worship of her. We can also draw on such information as Saxo's *Gesta Danorum*, much of the information in it dealing with the Angles. For the most part this only gives us deities we already know about, but it also adds ancestral heros such as Offa and Scyld (who are mentioned in the Old English literature only briefly). Archaeological evidence can also be of an aide as seen already with Nehellenia. We know from altars erected along Hadrian's Wall and elsewhere that Germanic mercenaries followed the cult of the matrones. This cult strongly resembles the Norse mentions of the Dísir. These altars or votive stones are found all the way from Hadrian's Wall to what is now Bonn, Germany. The names of these deities generally referred to giving or protecting. Drawing once on Bede, and his treatment of the Anglo-Saxon Heathen calendar, we know the first night of the year was called modra nect. This indicates that perhaps the "cult of mothers" was known to the Anglo-Saxons as well. Going father afield we must look to the Norse. It is probably unwise to equate every Norse deity with a potential Anglo-Saxon one as I have done in the past. However, one deity in particular deserves mention. Gefion is mentioned in Snorri's *Heimskringla* as having ploughed out the island of Zealand. She is said in the Prose Edda to have married Scyld, mythical first king of Denmark. It is possible then that the Angles, Saxons, and Jutes knew of her.

This is as perhaps as full a reconstruction of an Anglo-Saxon pantheon one can attempt. Even then all we really have are names. The closest thing to a myth in Anglo-Saxon is the "Nine Worts Galdor" where we are told Woden gave the nine herbs to seven worlds (much like he gave the runes). We can assume based on the kings lists that Woden was considered God of kings, and on other clues as the giver of runes. Otherwise, we are bereft of information on Anglo-Saxon mythology.

## The Æsir (Ése)

### Wóden/ Óðinn

Wóden is perhaps the most documented of the Heathen gods, both in the ancient lore and modern writings. His name derives from words such as Old Norse *örðr* and Anglo-Saxon *wód*, both meaning "madness, fury, inspiration." This "fury" can be seen when he acts as leader of the Wild Hunt, a group of spectres riding the winds of winter storms with their hounds preying upon those unwise enough to go out into the night air alone. Stories of the Wild Hunt are scattered all over Europe, and in most Germanic areas one of the leaders of the Hunt is none other than Wóden himself. It can also be seen when one examines tales of the berserkers, warriors dedicated to Wóden that would go into a battle frenzy, killing all that got into their path. This image of Wóden as a god of the fury can be seen throughout the lore. He bears such names as Yggr "the terrible" in the *Eddas*. The tales of berserkers come from the Scandinavian countries and Iceland, while the tales of the Wild Hunt come primarily from Germany, and our earliest records such as Tacitus show he is a battle god.

Wóden as god of fury is also Wóden, god of violent death. To reach his hall Valhalla (Anglo-Saxon *Wælheall; Old Norse Valhøll), one must die a battle death (although many scholars such as H.R. Ellis Davidson have shown any violent death will do). He is also god of the hanged, his primary human sacrifices in ancient times being hung and stabbed with a spear such as King Vikar of *Gautreks Saga*. Other followers of his met such varied deaths as drowning and being thrown in snake pits.

Yet, Wóden, god of fury and violent death was also the god of poetry and speech. The Eddas speak of how Wóden won Óðroerir... "the mead of inspiration" which allows poets to compose great poetry; how he won the runes, and gave

81

man the gift of "divine breath." The *Anglo-Saxon Rune Poem* credits Wóden with being the origin of all language.

> Ós biþ ordfruma --- ælcre spæce, Wísdomes wráþu --- ondwítena frófor Ond eorla gehwám --- éadnes ondtóhiht
> One of the Æsir is the primal source of all speech Wisdom's support and wisemen's help, And every earl's riches and happiness.

As god of poetry, Wóden was also god of galdor(OE), "magical incantation." In the "Hávamál," Wóden is shown to have won the runes for the gods and men. He is also mentioned by name in the "Nine Worts Galdor," an Anglo-Saxon charm for healing some ailments, as having given nine healing herbs to Mankind. Wóden is again mentioned in the "Second Merseberg Charm" as a healer, which shows him healing a horse with a broken leg. Here we see a kinder, gentler Wóden, the same Wóden whose horse German peasants once left a sheaf of corn for. These two seemingly opposed views of Wóden as battle god and Wóden as god of healing are difficult to reconcile. Yet, both views seem to revolve around the concept the ancient Heathens refer to as wód, a word that had meanings ranging from "fury to inspiration." According to Eric Wódening in his article "Wode and the Daimonic," wód can be equated with a psychological construct known as the daimonic.

Psychologist Rollo May defines the *daimonic* as "any natural function which has the power to take over the whole person." He also sees it as the centre of all self assertion, not to mention the link between that which is mortal and that which is divine. Most of all, May sees the *daimonic* as being the drive behind all self assertion, be it rage, love, or the need to create poetry. Eric Wódening therefore views the *daimonic* as being equivalent to *wód*; "wode is the faculty by which all human beings can enter into a higher state of self-awareness, thus entering the realm of the divine. In other words, wode is the source of all *daimonic* urges." This somewhat reconciles Wóden as god of war and god of healing. All these seemingly extreme aspects of the deity stem from that creative force known as *wód*, and are merely variations of the same divine nature. Fire after all can be used to burn an enemy's house down, or warm one's own. Similarly, *wód* can inspire one to compose poetry, go into a berserk rage, or perform healing magic.

This view of *wód* as Rollo May's *daimonic* is somewhat confirmed by Woden's byname of Oski (ON) which means "wish." The word *oski* and its Anglo-Saxon cognate *wúsc* are related to words dealing with desire and the will. May maintained that the will must be used to control the *daimonic* for one to achieve mental health. In Wóden we find the *daimonic* and the will combined. It is somewhat fitting that the god of "shamanic ecstasy" not to mention wisdom would rule such qualities as required for an "integrated self." This would also somewhat explain how Wóden can be both healer and god of the fury for both stem from how the god uses *wód* or "inspiration." In war, when ruthlessness is called for, the *wód* would be used to call up the berserk rage, while in times of illness it may be used to heal. Much like a knife, *wód* can be used to kill or heal, it all depends on how one chooses to use it.

Finally, Wóden was also seen as the King of the gods and the god of kings. In this, he was often called "oath breaker," as many of the kings dedicated to him eventually lost their lives in battle. A careful look at the lore however will reveal that it is not Wóden that was the "oath breaker," but the kings. In *Gautek's Saga*, King Vikar promised Wóden a sacrifice when his ship was caught in stormy seas in return for good weather. Lots were drawn and King Vikar's lot was drawn. Yet, instead of offering himself as a sacrifice, Vikar planned a fake one, calf gut would be put around his throat instead of rope, a twig would serve as the tree, and he would be poked with a small stick instead of stabbed with a spear. He would thus cheat Wóden of his sacrifice, and preserve his life. Wóden transformed all these items into the real thing none the less, and received his sacrifice anyway.

Ancient Germanic kings were credited with the gift of ræd, or the ability to "intuit" divine wisdom. This ability was also seen amongst the skalds and in such "shamanic" deeds as "mound sitting" (sitting out on a grave to get inspiration from the dead), and "going under the hide" (sitting out with a cloak or hide drawn over one's head in meditation). This is perhaps Woden's greatest aspect, that of god of wisdom. In his own quest for wisdom, Wóden hung on the world tree to win the runes with a similar account about him winning healing herbs, gave up an eye to drink from Mimer's well, and send out his ravens daily. Woden's quest for wisdom is perhaps endless, even near Ragnarok in the *Elder Edda*, Wóden is seen consulting an ancient seeress for knowledge.

Wóden is a very complex god governing a great deal of human and divine life. He is a god of kings, and a god of healing, and he is a god of war and of poetry. To better understand him, is to first gain his gifts, wisdom, the ability to control one's *wód*, and the runes or "mysteries." If one does not understand these things and is unable to work the ancient forms of magic known as seiðr and galdor it is doubtful one will ever understand the god Wóden.

## Fríge/Frigga

Wóden's wife and the most powerful of the goddesses, Fríge's primary domain was the household. This domain of hers is not that of the household we think of today however, for Northern European women were fully their husbands' equals and often made the most vital decisions in household affairs. Like Wóden she is a figure of immense wisdom. She is said to be all knowing and to know the *ørlög* of all men and things. However, she never speaks these things. Fríge in myth gave Wóden advice on at least two occasions, actually tricking him to achieve the just ends in the situations. In the legend of the naming of the tribe of the Lombards the Vandals called on Wóden for victory in battle. Wóden states that whomever he saw first in the morning, he would award victory to. The Lombards, at that time called the Winni appealed to Fríge for aid. Fríge told them to have their women comb their hair over their faces and stand before the sunrise. Fríge then moved Wóden's bed so it faced the east. When Wóden awoke that morning and saw the Winni, he exclaimed "Who are these long beards?' Fríge responded

"Now you have given them a name, you must also grant them victory."

Fríge plays the role of Asgardr's noble queen and as such bears the responsibility of any noble's wife. This role meant advising her husband and making many decisions herself. It was usually women who played the role of *frípwebba* or "peace weaver" the one who makes and maintains peace. This role was one very necessary in ancient Northern Europe, making Fríge a very important goddess in the elimination of strife.

Fríge was associated with spinning and weaving as a constellation in the sky was called Frigga's Distaff. It could be she spins the threads of men's lives that is then woven into the web of Wyrd. This would explain how she knows the *ørlög* of all men. The German goddess Holda may be yet another guise of Fríge. Like Fríge she is named as Wóden's wife, and is even said to lead the Wild Hunt on occasion. Holda was a maternal goddess, concerned with motherhood and spinning. She abhorred laziness and punished those who could not finish their spinning and weaving in ample time, yet being a kind goddess, she rewarded the hard working. The scholar Jacob Grimm believed Holda to be one ad the same as Fríge, and many scholars agree on this assessment giving us plenty of information to supplement the scarce Norse material. Fríge is the goddess of household affairs, married love, child birth and child rearing, wisdom, peace, and spinning.

## Þunor/Thor

Þunor may have been the most widely worshipped god of the ancient Northern Europeans, more places bear his name than any other god save possibly Wóden. Þunor is the god of the thunderstorm and the rain, things necessary for the growth of crops. But Þunor is no simple storm god for it is he that defends both man and god from the giants. This made him ideal for the act of hallowing and many passages in Old Norse refer to men invoking Þunor to hallow ground or items for a sacred purpose. One of his nick names in fact meant "hallower" or "he that makes sacred." Þunor is seen as a god of raw strength and even mægen. This is tied to his position as hallower for it is the strength of one's mægen that truly defends against evil.

Þunor was also seen as god of the thing or the assembly and as responsible for the support of society. In Iceland, this association was especially strong as assemblies met on Thursday "Thor's day." He was also one of the three gods oaths had to be sworn by, the other two being Wóden (Odin) and Fréa (Freyr).

The symbol of Þunor's hammer was seen as a talisman of great power being a representation of that god. Hammers were worn to ward off evil and the shape of the hammer itself was thought to have the effect of hallowing things. Hammers were laid in the laps of brides at the wedding feast in order to hallow them. This may have been an extension of Þunor as fertility god as well.

Þunor was the most popular god of the common folk and this is largely due to his position as bringer of the rain for crops, defenders of man, as well as his associations with justice. Þunor like Wóden (Odin) can be seen as a god of many things, but foremost is his position as protector of the common man.

## Tiw/Tyr

Tiw is one of the greater gods about which little is really known. He survived in some of the tales of the Eddas, some references are made to him elsewhere, but by the time of the Viking Age, his worship had either dwindled, or simply was not recorded. Evidence in England however, and on the continent show that his worship was once widespread. The Romans refer to the Germans sacrificing to Mercury and Mars, and Mars is often assumed to have been Tiw. While in England there are more places named for Tiw than for Ingui Frey. Many modern Heathens feel he is Seaxnéat, tribal god of the Saxons, and indeed the frequency of place names on the continent and England would point to this. Widukind in *Deeds of the Saxons* states the Saxons celebrated a victory in Mars' name, and as Seaxnéat is their tribal god this would again be evidence they are one and the same.

What literary evidence we have of his worship reveals Tiw to be a war god. In the "Sidrifumal," Sigdrifa counsels Sigurdr to carve runes on the edge of the hilt of his sword then call three times on Tiw. He was also a god of troth or loyalty, a god of oaths, and of the nobles who lead the folk. The "Old English Rune Poem" verse for Tir or Tiw states:

> Tiw is a token --- who holds troth well with princes --- he is ever on course over night's mists --- he never betrays.

The rune poem verse reveals Tiw as a god of troth and loyalty amongst princes of the folk. If he is indeed Seaxnéat, he can be counted as a god of kings, and the use of the word athelings in the rune poem point to this. The Anglo-Saxon Essex traced their lineage to Seaxnéat and not Wóden. This would place him in the realm of Wóden, a god of nobles and kings, and not the lower classes. In the Old Icelandic Rune Poem he is called "Ruler of the Temple," another indication he was a god of the ruling aristocracy.

However, Tiw is also god of thing, the public assembly, a position he shares with Þunor. Germanic mercenaries erected an altar on Hadrian's Wall to Mars Things, "Mars of the Thing." The Old High German name for Tuesday "Tiw's Day" is Dienstag "Assembly Day." This link to thing does not make Tiw a peacemaker however, and indeed is only an extension of his being a god of war. Loki states in the *Lokasenna* that Tiw has never been able to bring justice between two men. It could be Tiw was the god of ordeals in which only one man could win, thus his connection to war and trials in thing.

Mention is made of Tiw's wife in the *"Lokasenna"*, although she is not named. Continental sources have a goddess named Zisa, the feminine of Zio, Old High Germanic for Tiw. *The Excerpts of Gallic History* mention her under a variant name Cizae. A city was named in her honour Cizerim. During a siege by Romans lead by Titus Annius, a festival was held in her honour. When the Romans attacked, they were defeated. This would seem to indicate she like her husband governs victory.

## *Forseta/Forseti

The *Eddas* have Forseti as the son of Balder and Nanna. However this is most likely a post Conversion development as Forseta appears to be the much older God. It is very unlikely a deified hero could have produced one of the greater Ése (Æsir). Snorri states of Forseti's home in Ésageard (Asgard) that, ""Glitnir (Glittering) is the tenth (hall), it is supported with gold, and silver thatches it as well; and there Forseti dwells most of the day and settles all cases." In Snorri's "Skaldskaparmal," he is listed amongthe Ése's 12 judges. He appears as a law giver amongst the Frisians who knew him as Fosite.

In the legend, "Van da tweer Koningen Karl ende Radbod," Charlemagne demands that the Frisians produce a law code. The 12 Elders of the Frisians managed to put him off twice, but finally were punished by Charlemagne. He sent them out in a rudderless boat. The boat was overtaken by a storm, when a man appeared, and with a golden axe steered them to an island. Here he threw his axe to the shore and a spring appeared. He then ordered them to disembark the boat. Upon getting out of the boat each drank from the spring, it was then the man begin to speak, and gave them their laws. They thereafter called the island Fosite's Island or Helgoland "Holy Island." A sacred spring was there and no one could drink from it save in silence. We are told in various sources as well as The Life of Willibrord by Alcuin that the Christian missionary Wilibrord defiled the spring by baptizing three men in it. Some of his men killed a few of the sacred cattle. For this desecration, Wilibrord was nearly sacrificed but had the luck of the draw when they drew lots. As it was one of his men was killed, and he had to flee for his life.

There seems to have been some confusion between Balder and Forseta in some areas. Saxo credits Balder with the creation of springs in his Danish Histories. No doubt when the Northman deified Balder they may have usurped some of the older Gods attributes and gave them to him.

Forseta's name means "one that sets before," i.e. one that sets laws. A fitting name, for a God that appears to be the God of judges and Things.

## Fulla

Fríge's sister and handmaiden, Fulla is rarely mentioned in the lore and never in detail. She is listed by Snorri as one of the twelve most divine goddesses, "The Lay of Gimnir" as one of Fríge's handmaidens, and mentioned in the "Second Merseberg Charm" as Fríge's sister.. The *Gila saga Surssonar* preserves a brief prayer said to her shortly before the hero's death:

> My Fulla, fair faced, the goddess of stones Who gladdens me much, shall hear of her friend Standing straight, unafraid in the rain of the spears.

Her name would seem to indicate she is some sort of goddess of plenty, although as the *Gisla saga* would seem to indicate she may also have been a goddess of stones. Grimm felt her to be a moon goddess due to her name and relation in the Merseberg Charm to Sunna.

## Geofon/Gefjun

Gefjun is a Danish goddess whose name appears in Old English as Geofon, a word for "ocean." There are Danish place names for her such as Gentofte and Genvnö. Her name derives from the verb "to give" and is related to words seen amongst the Cult of Mothers practised by Roman mercenaries in Britain and on the continent. They usually had names like Garmangibi "Giving."

In the *Prose Edda,* Snorri relates the following tale of the creation of the island of Zealand:

> It is told of him that he gave a ploughland in his kingdom, the size four oxen could plough in a day and a night, to a beggar-woman as a reward for the way

she had entertained him. This woman, however, was of the family of the Æsir; her name was Gefjon. From the north of Giantland she took four oxen and yoked them to a plough, but those were her sons by a giant. The plough went in so hard and deep that it loosened the land and the oxen dragged it westwards into the sea, stopping in a certain sound. There Gefjon set the land for good and gave it a name, calling it Zealand. But the place where the land had been torn up was afterwards a lake. It is now known in Sweden as 'The Lake'.[Malar]. Young translation)

In the "Ynglinga Saga," Snorri also tells the tale, and adds that Geofon married Skjold, first king of Denmark and son of Wóden. Skjold, founder of the Skjoldung royal dynasty is the same as Scyld Sceafing mentioned in Beowulf, and ancestor of Hrothgar. Looking at this myth it becomes apparent that Geofon was associated with the tilling of soil, as having some connections with the sea (she created the lake), and the marking off perhaps of boundaries. Snorri also attributes her in the Prose Edda with receiving all women that die unmarried into her hall (this despite the fact she is married). In the "Lokasenna," Loki accuses Geofon of having sold herself to a youth for a ring or a jewel.

Geofon seems to be the only literary evidence of a group of Goddesses that were known to be giving and open handed.  As stated above names associated with giving appear frequently on the Roman-Germanic altars in England and on the mainland, and H. R. Davidson maintains that the Old English Charm "A Field Remedy" or Æcer-Bót which is considered to contain a prayer to a pagan Earth Goddess, may well be to such a Goddess. We do see the same elements in Geofon in the lines of the Æcer-Bót, the plow, the asking of the one praying for the gift of a good harvest. In some areas of Germany there were plow processions instead of those using wagons (as Freda's) or ships (as in the Germanic Isis mentioned by Grimm), and plow blessings in the spring were nearly universal in Northern Europe.

## Hama/Heimdall

Hama the watchman of the rainbow bridge (Bifrost) is one of the most often mentioned Gods in the *Eddas*. He is also one of the few Gods listed with several names, a trait scholars believe reflected the importance of a God or Goddess. In the *Eddas*, he is called Hallinskísði, Gullintani "gold toothed," and seems to be the mysterious Rígr of the Rígsþula. He is also called in some of the texts, Heimdali which means "ram" and may be a cleaver play on words. Finally, he is referred to in the "Þrymskviða" as the "whitest of the Ése" due to his purity, and Snorri in the Prose Edda too calls him the "White God.". His hall in *Ésageard (Asgard) is called *Heofonberg (in Norse, Himinbjorg) which means "Heaven Mountain." And he bears the *Giellerhyrn (Gjallarhorn) a horn with which to alert the Gods to attack on Ésageard.

His Norse name Heimdall corrensponds to one of Fréo's (Freya's) other names Mardoll. The heim in Heimdall means "home" or "earth" while "mar" means "mare" or "sea." This is only one link between the Goddess Fréo and the God Hama. In the "Þrymskviða" it is Hama that advises Þunor to disguise himself as Fréo. He is also said to have done battle with Loki, both as seals, for the Goddesses' necklace Brísingamen. His connection with the necklace also appears in Beowulf.

> Nænigne ic under swegle --- selran hyrde
> hordmaðum hæleþa --- syþðan Hama ætwæg
> to þærc byrhtan byrig --- Brosinga mene,
> sigle ond sincfæt,--- searoniðas fleah
> Eormenrices, geceas ecne ræd.
> Ne'er heard I so mighty, --- 'neath heaven's dome,
> a hoard-gem of heroes, --- since Hama bore
> to his bright-built burg the Brisings' necklace,
> jewel and gem casket. --- Jealousy fled he,
> Eormenric's hate --- chose help eternal.

This connection is strong enough to make one wonder if the mysterious Oðr who is said to be Fréo's husband is not

91

one and the same as Hama, who as Rígr roamed Middangeard.

Snorri references the lost "Heimdallargaldr" which says Hama was born of nine mothers. They are named in the Hyndluljóð, "Gjálp bore him, Greip bore him, Eistla and Eyrgjafa bore him, Úlfrún and Angeyja bore him, Imðr and Atla and Járnsaxa. He was made greater with the main of the earth, the spray-cold sea and holy boar's blood". Some connect these with the nine daughters of Ægir and Ran despite the difference in names. Snorri also states that he "needs less sleep than a bird, and can see a hundred leagues in front of him as well by night as by day. He can hear the grass growing on the earth and the wool on sheep, and everything that makes more noise." These abilities are needed of course for his duties as watchman for the Gods. We are told in the "Völuspa" his hearing his hidden beneath the World Tree.

There is one extant lay about Hama, and it is the "Rígsþula" of the *Poetic Edda*. In it he roams the earth as Rígr and stays with three couples. First he stays with a couple known as "Great-Grandfather" and "Great-Grandmother" and begats on "Great-Grandmother" the child known as thrall. Next he stays with "Grandfather" and "Grandmother" and begats with "Grandmother" the child known as Karl. Finally he stays with "Father" and "Mother" and begats Jarl. Thus according to the lay the three classes of men were born. He later returns to teach Kon, son of Jarl runelore and how to rule.

## Wær/Vor/Var

Wær is the Old English cognate of the Goddess name Vor. Var and Vor are probably the same goddess, their names are merely variations of each other. Var is said by Snorri in the *Prose Edda* to be "who is so wise and searching that nothing can be concealed from her. It is a saying that a woman becomes vor (ware) of what she becomes wise." Vor is mentioned in the *Elder Edda* as the goddess of oaths, contracts, and also marriage. Wær, vor, and German wehr all mean truth as well as "pledge, compact, oath." It is therefore fairly easy to discern what she is Goddess of. Ideally, she should be invoked at the taking of any oath, but esp. at marriage along with Lofn whom is said to bring men and women together according to Snorri, and of course Fríge (Frigga) and Fréo (Freya).

## The Vanir/Wen

### Ingui Fréa/Yngvi Freyr

After Þunor (Thor) and Wóden one of the most popular of the gods was without a doubt Ingui Fréa. He is above all else the god of peace and the Northern Europeans gave him credit for times of peace and plenty. Ingui Fréa was above all else a fertility god, seen as bringing fertility to the crops, livestock, and members of the community. This is not to say Fréa is a pacifist, as some of his nick names suggest he did serve as a war god also. However, he was a god of defensive war, a sort of divine policeman. The boar was his symbol and any emblem of a boar was thought to bring protection to its wearer by the early Northern Europeans. Peace is necessary for good harvests. Unnecessary warfare pulled men out of the fields they were tending and often destroyed the very crops themselves, so Fréa's position as provider of peace went hand in hand with his role as god of fertility. It was Fréa who along with the goddess Sunne that was thought to send the sunshine necessary for crops and to send the gentle rains that were also needed. Fréa was also seen as making livestock fertile so often rites were performed to him for this purpose. And just as he governed fertility in animals he also governed human sexuality, although this was usually the realm of his sister. Adam of Bremen stated that sacrifices to Ing took place at midsummer when weddings were preformed.

In the "Flateyjarbók," Gunnarr Helming posed as the God after having wrestled with the idol. He then rode with the sacred wain through from village to village. While this may be one of the earliest Swede jokes as they mistakened a mortal for their God, it also serves as evidence that like Nerthus Ing was taken about in a wagon. Wains seem to have been important to his cult as they also appear in the Anglo-Saxon Rune Poem:

> Ing wæs ærest --- mid Eastdenum
>     gesewen secgun, --- oþ hé siððan eft
> ofer wæg gewát, --- wæn æfter ran;
>     þus heardingas --- þone hæle nemdon.
> Ing was first --- among the East Danes
>     Seen by men --- but he since went eft (back)
> Over the wet way --- his wain (wagon) ran after
>     Thus the Heardings --- named the hero

Like Wóden, Ing is said to have fathered lines of kings, Yngling royal line of Sweden traced its ancestry to him. Fréa is married to Gearde (Gerðr) whom he sent his servant Skirnir to court for him as portrayed in the "Skirnismal." Elfham (Alfheimr) was his tooth gift and he is its ruler. He is therefore connected to the Elves. Ing's ancient cult may have involved cross dressing. The Wodenic hero Starkad left the temple of Uppsala "at the time of the sacrifices, he was disgusted by the effeminate gestures and the clapping of the mimes on the stage, and by the unmanly clatter of the bells." Tacitus also mentions in *Germania* of the tribe the Naharvali "The presiding priest dresses like a woman; but the deities are said to be the counterparts of Castor and Pollux. This indicates their character, but their name is the Alci." The Alci have always assumed to be twin male Gods, but in truth they could just as easily be Ing and his sister Fréo. Finally, Tacitus mentions a group of tribes which included the Angles that he called the Ingvaeones. They felt they were descended from a man called Ing who was said to be a son of Mannus. If this Ing can be identified with Ingui Fréa, then all the English may claim descent from him.

**Fréo/Freya**
Fréo is reputed to be the most beautiful of goddesses, and is for the most part the goddess of love. She was also goddess of magic however and is said to have taught Wóden

seiðr. Seiðr was largely seen as a woman's craft and it would seem natural that such magic would fall to her. While Fríge governed married love, Fréo governed human sexuality and eroticism. She is the goddess of unbridled passions and in some of the tales of the ancient Northern Europeans she is said to have even taken mortals as her lovers. Fréo was also a war goddess however, half the dead that die in battle are said to go to her hall, the other half going to Wóden. This could be a more fierce side of the goddess rarely spoke of today and lost in the ancient tales. Like her brother Fréa she was connected to wealth and plenty, but esp. to the kind of wealth associated with gems and precious metals.

## Neorð /Njördr

Neorð is Fréa (Frey) and Fréo's (Freya's) father and was thought of as a god of the seas not to mention commerce. The name of his palace is *Nacatun (Nóatœn) which literally means "harbour" or "place of ships." It is said he was invoked by sailors and fisherman alike for good seas. Like his children, Neorð was linked to material wealth and especially fertility of the sea. He married the giantess Sceadu (Skaði). Sceadu came seeking revenge for her father's death, and the Ése offer wergild. Sceadu said that the wergild be to make her laugh. Loki manages to accomplish this. The Ése allowed her to chose a husband, but it must be on the basis of their feet. She chose Neorð as he had the most beautiful feet. The marriage did not work out though as she missed her mountains, he, his sea. Oaths were sometimes sworn before Neorð in legal assemblies so that he may also have some connection to law. Njörðr's name is cognate to that of the Goddess Nerthus mentioned by Tacitus in Germania and quoted below:.

> Nor in one of these nations does aught remarkable occur, only that they universally join in the worship of Nerthum; that is to say, the Mother Earth. Her they believe to interpose in the affairs of man, and to visit countries. In an island of the ocean stands the wood Castum: in it is a chariot dedicated to the Goddess, covered over with a curtain, and permitted to be

95

touched by none but the Priest. Whenever the Goddess enters this her holy vehicle, he perceives her; and with profound veneration attends the motion of the chariot, which is always drawn by yoked cows. Then it is that days of rejoicing always ensue, and in all places whatsoever which she descends to honour with a visit and her company, feasts and recreation abound. They go not to war; they touch no arms; fast laid up is every hostile weapon; peace and repose are then only known, then only beloved, till to the temple the same priest reconducts the Goddess when well tired with the conversation of mortal beings. Anon the chariot is washed and purified in a secret lake, as also the curtains; nay, the Deity herself too, if you choose to believe it. In this office it is slaves who minister, and they are forthwith doomed to be swallowed up in the same lake.

The ritual is similar to one in *Gunnars þáttr helmings* whereupon it is Fréa that is carted around place to place. It could be possible that Tacitus confused a Vanic male deity with a Goddess. Saxo in his account of Starkad's visit to one of Fréa's temples mentions men dressing like women and effeminate gestures. It may well be the idol of the God Njörðr was dressed like a woman and taken on the rounds, and this is what Tacitus informant witnessed. Njörðr does not appear in material before the Viking Age, and Nerthus is only mentioned the one time by Tacitus, so it is not unlikely. In the "Lokasenna," Loki states that Njörðr got Fréa and Fréo on his sister. So it could also be that Nerthus is that sister. This would be the preferred view as the deity Tacitus describes must have some connection with fertility of the land, while the Eddic Njörðr is clearly a God of sea commerce.

## *Other Gods and Goddesses*

### Éagor/Ægir

Éagor does not appear in any of the continental

96

sources or the Anglo-Saxon ones. However, the cognate of his Norse name Ægir did in the form of Éagor "flood, high tide." Apollonaris Sidonius also commented that when the Saxons would sail they would sacrifice one of every ten prisoners by drowning or hanging him the night before. Ermoldus Nigelus writing about 826 CE said the Danes, the Saxons' neighbours on the continent worshipped Neptune. While Neptune may have been Njörðr, it is likely that suchsacrifices were to Éagor or Ran as both were the closest thing the ancient Germanics seem to have had in the way of sea Gods. Snorri identifies him with Hlér "the shelterer" and Gymir "Concealer." Gymir was also the name of Gearde (Gerd)'s father, but it is not known if they are one and the same. The Vikings referred to the River Eider as "Ægir's Door." The name Eider its self meant "seamonster" in Old English. Éagor is not listed amongst the Ése (Æsir) or Wen (Vanir), however they do frequent his hall, and as such he played a major role in the Norse myths.

In the *Eddas*, Éagor is portrayed as brewer of the Gods. Thehall in the symbel portrayed in the ""Lokasenna"," is Éagor's. The drowned were seen as going to his hall, and those that had gold for Ran were treated kindly. Egil after one of his sons drowned, said in his poem "Sonatorrek," "Could I have avenged my cause with the sword, the Ale brewer would be no more." Generally though, it is Ran and not her husband that is accredited with the taking of life. Her name means "robber," and she was said to have a great net which with to drag down men. This is not much unlike the nixies of Germany folklore. Many areas believed that if the river nixies were not given a life a year, they would take one of their own. Apollonaris Sidonius said in his commentary on the Saxons that they loved storms at sea so they could take foes by surprise. This was their reason for giving one man in ten chosen by lot to the sea, to kept hem safe in the storms. Éagor and Ran were said to have nine daughters named in Norse as Himminglæva, Dufa, Blóðhadda, Hefring, Unn, Hrónn, Bylgja, Bara, and Kolga.

## Eorðe/Jörð

Eorðe is the Old English cognate of Jörð, and both words mean "earth." According to Norse lore, Eorðe was the mother of Þunor (Thor) and daughter of goddess Niht (Nott) and her husband Annarr. Throughout the *Eddas* and even in the Anglo-Saxon corpus she is seen under many different names, in Old Norse she is called Fjörgyn, Hlóðynn, Fold "earth," and Grund "ground." In Old English she is called Folde, Fira Modor "mother of Mankind," and possibly Hrúsan. There is little evidence of active worship of her as with some of the other Gods and Goddesses, however, there is much evidence of passive worship. Galdres in both Old Norse and Old English say to call on her for might and main. This connection with sheer strength is seen in her son Þunor as well. Two Old English works mention her with some detail, in the Anglo-Saxon Rune Poem the verse for Géar may be referring to her in some form of divine marriage:

> Géar biþ gumena hiht, --- þonne god læteþ,
>     hálig heofones cyning, --- hrúsan sellan
>     beorhte bléda --- beornum and þearfum.
> Géar (Year) is man's hope --- if God lets, Holy
> heaven's king, --- the Earth sell (i.e. "give") Bright
> fruits, --- to nobles and needy.

Despite the obvious Christian reinterpretation, the fact that *Hrúsan* "earth" is mentioned at all is significant. Another Anglo-Saxon work the "Æcer-Bót" also called For Unfruitful Land contains what may be a prayer to her (and evidence of active worship), and contains lines that can only be interpreted as divine marriage
.

> Hal wes þu, folde, --- fira modor!
> Beo þu growende --- on godes fæþme,
> fodre gefylled --- firum to nytte.
> Wassail Earth --- Mankind's mother;
> Be growing --- in God's embrace,
> Filled with food --- man to joyously help..

Old English *nytte* is cognate to Old Norse *nýta*. Kveldulf

Gundarsson notes in *Our Troth*, that *nýta* appears in Sigrdrífumál in the compound *fjölnýta*. Thorpe translates this in a prayer that Sigrdrífa says on awaking as "bounteous earth." Kveldulf notes however *nýta* is hard to translate and can mean "helpful, good-bringing, enjoyable." Unfortunately, Eorðe never appears in the Norse lore in person, but is only referenced to by the other Gods or mortals. Therefore, it is difficult to get a real image of her. That she is no Kubaba type Earth Mother is clear. Any Goddess the ancient Germanics would call on for might and main would not be likely to be pictured as overweight and out of shape even when pregnant. We can therefore assume she is a Goddess of some strength, with strong bearing, perhaps built much like her son Þunor. We can also see her as a mother, as she is seen as the mother of Mankind, not to mention the thunder god. Finally, there is the obvious connection with fertility. Eorðe is the ultimate fertility goddess. Without her the fields will not grow no matter how much we mortals may coax the other Gods and Goddess.

**Eostre**

Eostre is a very obscure Goddess. She is not mentioned at all in the Norse corpus and only fleetingly in the Old English by Bede in *De Temporum Rationale*. Her material is so scant that some scholars have speculated she was not a Goddess at all, but that Eostre was merely a name for the holiday. Her name is connected to words for "east" and "shining." It is therefore related to the Greek god name Eos, Goddess of the dawn in their pantheon. Finding place names indicating her worship is difficult due to this relation to the word east. Her name survived in the German name of the Christian holy tide as Ostara, therefore if she was a Goddess, she was worshipped there as well.

In order to understand anything about the Goddess Eostre (or the Goddess or Goddesses worshipped at that time) we must draw on the traditions associated with the holy tide. Grimm in his *Teutonic Mythology* maintained that "Ostara, Eástre, was goddess of the growing light of spring." The date of the holy tide would make this a reasonable conclusion. Holy water in the form of the dew or water collected from brooks was gathered at this time. Washing with it was said to restore youth. Beautiful maidens in sheer white were said to seen frolicking in the country side. Also according to Grimm, the white maiden of Osterrode, was said to appear with a large batch of keys at her belt, and stride to the brook to collect water on Easter morning. Cross buns were of course baked and eaten. While this could be a Christian addition, that cakes were often use in Heathen rites is apparent in any survey of the lore. And the cross may be symbolic of the rune Gebo or the buns may represent the sun wheel. Easter eggs seem to go fairly far back in both English and continental celebrations, and of course symbolize the beginning of new life. The hare also known for its fertility appears fairly early in Easter celebrations. Bonfires and vigils also seemed to play a role in many Easter rites.

Based on this Eostre would appear to be a Goddess of purity (the holy water), youth and beauty (the young maidens), as well as one of new life beginnings. Kveldulf Gundarsson feels she may be the same as the Norse Goddess Iðun. They would appear to have a lot in common, except apples do not seem to play a role in spring ritual celebrations in the lore, and are seen more often connected to Harvest. The likelihood they are the same Goddess would therefore seem to be slim, but none the less both may be a type of youthful Goddess associated with new life.

Winifred Hodge on the other hand sees Eostre as being the same as the Goddess celebrated at Walpurgisnacht (Hodge, Winifred, "Waelburga and the Rites of May" *Lina*, 1996). The problem with this is while both Walpurgis and Easter have many of the same customs associated with them, there are also many customs associated with Easter one does not see associated with Walpurgis. Eostre has shining maidens at dawn associated with her, whilst the Goddess of Walpurgis has witches in the middle of the night. If we look to German folklore, the Walpurgis Goddess seems to be Holda. Holda is a rather motherly Goddess with some darker associations. She is at times the kind and lovely mother, and other times seen as the fierce leader of the Wild Hunt. This is quite unlike the symbolism we see at Easter, which seems to be a time of virginal young maidens, or gentle young wives at least.

Nonetheless, parts of the Scandinavian countries celebrate Easter as a time of witches much as their southern kin do Walpurgis. Witches in southern Sweden were thought to fly to the mountain Blåkulla, much like the Walpurgis witches flew to the Broken in Germany. Personally, I prefer to think that, the Swedes were celebrating Walpurgis at Easter (which they do not call the holytide) and Easter on what they referred to as Disting. It could be too that both Walpurgis and Easter were indeed once the same holytide. The shining Goddess Eostre was celebrated in the day while the dark Holda took the night before. Holda and the witches symbolizing winter would make their last assault on Mankind on Walpurgis Eve. Then at dawn Eostre and her maidens would appear to bring in the spring. In extreme ancient times this may have been seen as a battle between the death Goddess Holda and her crones and the Eostre, Goddess of rebirth and her maidens. Grimm in Teutonic Mythology mentions several plays called ôsterspil. These plays portrayed a battle between the forces of Winter and the forces of Summer. Often they involved a sword-dance with twelve men. In other areas of Germany, an effigy of Winter was beaten or burned.

Now in all probability the two Goddesses Holda and Eostre do not do battle. However, the duties of Holda, Goddess of Yule and household work (thus indoor work suited for winter) would largely be over, whilst Eostre's would just be beginning. It could be that if Walpurgis and Easter were the same holytide, the dual imagery seen is a reflection of that shift from winter work to spring work, from the weaving and spinning of winter to the sowing fields of spring. Holda as a household Goddess would be inappropriate for the spring, just as Eostre would be for the winter. Easter therefore would be seen as a holyday of transition.

## Gearde/Gerðr

Gerðr's name is thought related to garðr "enclosure" thus her name in Old English would be Gearde. Gearde is wife of Fréa (Frey) and her wooing is portrayed in the Skirnismal of the *Elder Edda*. Skirnir, servant of Fréa tried to bribe her with Wóden (Odin)'s ring, Freda's sword, and apples, but finally threatened her with a curse. She then consented to marry Fréa in the grove the grove Barri. Not a few scholars have seen the name of the grove as possibly be related to the word barley, a reasonable thought considering Gearde's name, and Freda's attributes as a fertility Goddess. Her name meaning "enclosure" was used also of farm enclosures in both Norse and Old English (a survival in English is "barn yard"). She should probably be seen then as a Goddess of the fields. Gearde does not appear in other myths, outside the Skirnismal.

## Hel

"Hel he cast into Niflheim, and gave her power over nine worlds, that she should appoint abodes to them that are sent to her, namely, those who die from sickness or old age."(Terry translation, Poetic Edda)

Whatever appearance the Goddess Hel may have originally taken in ancient Heathenry has been lost amongst the letters of Christian hands. Some modern Heathens based on folk etymology link her to the Goddess Holde. But High German Hölle and Helle will never equate High German Holle no matter how you twist the sound shifts. And the subterranean domain of Holda/Holle are as often found under ponds as in mountains (which it might be good to add Thor's followers were said to enter a mountain after death as well). Grimm notes that "Hel, the death-goddess, does not destroy, she receives the dead man in her house, and will on no account give him up. To kill a man is called sending him to her. Hel neither comes to fetch the souls fallen due to her, nor sends messengers after them." in Teutonic Mythology. This further dispels the idea Hel is Holda, as Holda regularly lead the Wild Hunt taking the unsuspecting with her.

*Nifolham (Niflheimr) or *Nifolhel (Niflhel) is her home. It seems to be a pleasant place in some areas, in others a dark and foreboding place of shades. Beneath it is *Neostrand (Nástrønd) the abode of punishment where snakes forever drop venom on the wicked. She is according to the *Eddas*, a daughter of Loki by Angrboði. She is half black and half of human colour, sometimes described as half living human and half corpse. Outside the *Eddas*, continental and Anglo-Saxon sources seem to portray her as a greedy, hungry, female deity. A poem in Middle High German ascribes gaping yawning jaws to her as does the Christian Anglo-Saxon poet Cædmon. This view may be why the giantess Thok refused to weep with the added words of "Let Hel keep what she has!"


## Helith/ Heil/Heile

Helith is a goddess mentioned in a few very late sources as a God or Goddess associated with an idol destroyed by Augustine near the Cerne Giant (a chalk drawing in Dorsetshire, England). The earliest of these sources is a thirteenth century biography of Augustine by William of Coventry. In it he states that Augustine destroyed an idol called Helith. Was it not for the area this myth is connected to, it could easily be shrugged off as Christian propaganda. However, the site of the idol was near the Well of Cerne, an ancient holy spring whose creation is attributed to St. Augustine and the Cerne Giant, an ancient chalk drawing is also nearby. Finally, Augustine established an abbey here as well, perhaps indicating an earlier Heathen cultic presence. John Leland writing in the sixteenth century associated Helith with the "Saxon Æsculapius, or preserver of health." The fact the names do resemble known Middle and Early Modern English words for health also adds some credence to this possibility this God or Goddess existed.

## Hreða

Hreða was a goddess mentioned by Bede for whom Hreðmonað (roughly March) was named for. Grimm feels her name Old High German hruod and Old Norse hroðr both which mean "glorious." She would therefore seem to be a warrior goddess of some sort.

## Mona/Mani

Mona is the son of Mundilfari, and brother of Sigel. His horse is named Alsvider. Bil and Hiuki travel the sky with him. There is almost no evidence of moon worship in Anglo-Saxon materials. That is not to say it was not done, simply that there is no evidence.

## Sceadu/Skaði

Some scholars feel Sceadu "shadow" is the Old English cognate of Old Norse Skaði. Others feel it is cognate to modern English scathe. Sceadu appears in the Old Norse lore as the wife of Njördr. In recompense for the death of her father, the Gods allowed her to choose one of them as a husband. However, she could only do so based on their feet. According to Snorri in the rose Edda, she chose Njördr thinking he was Balder. But Sceadu found the sea noisy and Njördr did not care for the mountains, so they live apart. Her home was Þrymheimr, which she inherited from her mountain. Snorri refers to her as the "shining bride of gods."

Like Ullr, place names show her worship was widespread, but she is not mentioned often in the lore. In "Bragi inn gamli's Ragnarsdrápa", she is called öndurdís "Dis of the snow shoe," while the poem Haustlöng also links her to snow shoes. According again top Snorri she hunts animals on skis and shoots with the bow. By all appearances she is a female version of Wuldor in many regards. In the "Lokasenna", Loki does not have anything really bad to say of her, merely referring back to the death of her father. Nonetheless, she is the one that places the snake over him to drop venom when he is bound. Sceadu therefore would seem to be a very beautiful stern huntress and Goddess of the winter snows. Despite this, she is not foreboding and cold, in the "Skirnismál," she expressing concern for her stepson Fréa (Frey).

## Seaxnéat

Seaxnéat is only mentioned in a couple of sources, and therefore is very much an enigma. He is recorded as an ancestor of kings in the genealogies of Essex. When the Heathen Saxons on the continent were forced to renounce their religion and accept baptism, Seaxnéat or Seaxnéat was one of the Gods they had to renounce. It is thought the Saxons took their name from the seax, a short sword, not unlike a large Bowie knife. It would therefore go that the God's name means something like "sword god" or "sword friend." Many have taken him to be either Tiw or Ing, but it is entirely possible Seaxnéat is a God in his own right.

## Sigel/Sól

Sigel is the sun goddess of the Germanic peoples. Her name is cognate to Latin Sol, although most modern Heathens seem to refer to her as Sunna, Sunne, or Sun. Sun worship does not seem to have been widespread, but in *Laxdæla saga*, it would appear Guðrún made an offering to Sigel at sun up. In *Landnámabók*, Þórkell Þórsteinsson had himself taken out into the Sun. The Old Norwegian Rune Poem also has evidence of Sun worship, "

(Sun) is the light of lands; I lout (bow) to the holy deeming."

According to the *Eddas*, she is said variously to have one horse or two, Árvakr and Alsviðr, or Skinfaxi. Mundifaeri was said to be her father.

## Wéland/Völundr

Wéland is portrayed in myth and folklore as a mortal hero, one with a great gift for blacksmithy. However, he appears so often in Anglo-Saxon literature that he would almost appear to be a God. In addition, if he was not worshipped as such then, he certainly is now. He appears in the Old English "Beowulf," " Deor," and the Waldere fragment as well as elsewhere. Many places are named for him including Wayland's Smithy in Oxfordshire, England, an ancient barrow grave that has become connected to the ancient smith. To this day, Englishmen leave gifts for the great blacksmith. There is also Wayland Smith's Cave near Lambourn, Berkshire, England. Which Sir Walter Scott said of, "Here lived a supernatural smith, who would shoe a traveller's horse for a 'consideration.' His fee was sixpence, and if more was offered him he was offended."

Vollund as portrayed in the "Völundarkviða" of the *Elder Edda* had two brothers Egil, and Slagfidur and dwelled in Wolfdale (Ulfdal). In *Þiðrek's Saga* his father is said to be the giant Wade (who has many sites named for himself in England). The "Völundarkviða" is the only work specifically dedicated to Wéland (although there are many mentions of him throughout the lore). In it he and his brothers spend their time hunting on snow shoes, and meet three swan maidens and make them their wives. When the swan maidens leave after eight years, Wéland's brothers go in search of their wives. But Wéland stays, making beautiful jewellery and no doubt swords, awaiting his bride's return. Then King Nidud had him seized and imprisoned to make jewellery and weapons alone for him. While imprisoned in Sævarstad, Wéland's anger brews each time he sees his sword with Nidud or the ring he made his wife on the hand of Nidud's daughter Bödvild. Therefore Nidud had him hamstrung. Wéland then tricks Nidud's young sons into visiting him, and when they bend over to look in a chest for a surprise he chopped off their heads. He then made their skulls into ornate drinking bowls which he gave to the King, and various other body parts he made to gems and gave to the Queen. Shortly after, Bödvild broke one of her rings and came to Wéland to have him fix it. He then got her drunk and seduced her. Finally, he escaped, having made wings. Throughout it is clear Wéland is calculating, and has a very keen mind. At the same time, he is clearly capable of great emotion (devotion to his wife, hatred for Nidud).

Throughout the "Völundarkviða" he is referred to as the "elves' chieftain," an interesting title since he is himself of giant descent.

Modern Anglo-Saxon Heathenry has developed an affinity for Wéland, often conducting blóts in his name as if he were one of the major Gods, and in minds, of many he is.

# Chapter IX Wights

If the beliefs of the Norse and Anglo-Saxon works like *Beowulf* are any clue, in addition to the Gods and Goddesses, the ancient Anglo-Saxon Heathens also believed in many various beings, some of which they accorded worship, others were seen as enemies of the Gods or Man. A few are covered here.

## Álfar (ON)/Ylfe (OE)

The Ylfe are the elves of Northern European mythology. Generally divided into different races, the term elf usually refers to the Ljosalfar (ON), the "Light Elves", beings of great beauty that often associate with the gods. They are said to be quite powerful and have been known to give aid to men and gods alike. They live in Alfheimr which was given to the god Fréa (Freyr) as a gift for his first tooth and it could be the god is seen as their ruler. They had close associations with the gods and seem to be creatures of light and good.

The other variety of elves are the Dokkalfar (ON) and the Svartálfar (ON). The Dokkalfar or the "Dark Elves" are dark beings and many link them to the Niflungar of the Sigurd lays and many hold they dwell in Niflheimr, although this is also said of the Svartalfar by many today. Others feel the Dokkalfar may be the souls of dead men dwelling in mounds. It is difficult to say as even the ancient lore seems confused on the point. There may be no confusion at all however, as it could be that the dark elves dwelling in Niflheimr are nothing more than dead souls. The Svartalfar on the other hand may not be elves at all, but dwarves.

They are said to dwell in Svartalfarheimr and to be ruled by Dvalin, who gave them the runes. One should be wary of calling on any of these creatures' aid as they may be temperamental or seeking their own aims. They are also thought to cause illness as many old terms for disease like elf-shot show. Elf shot was essentially darts shot into a person by the elves to cause illness, presumably for some affront the human had made to the elves.

## Cofgodas (OE)

A group of spirits friendly to humans that help around one's house. Generally they are seen by those with second sight as small humans. Sometimes they are mischievous, but rarely dangerous. They generally dislike lazy humans as they themselves are hard workers. Some cofgods do become nuisances hiding things, making noise, and knocking things over, but generally a simple spell will rid the house of such pesky types.

## Disir (ON)/Idesa (OE)

The *idesa* or as they are called in Old Norse the *disir* are ancestral women of great power that often help the families they belong to. Many are of nearly goddess level although even a few living mortal women were counted amongst their number in ancient times. They were afforded worship in ancient times and in the "Ynglinga Saga" a feast held in their honour is described. The disir often appear to members of their families to help or often punish and are said to appear in dreams. They should not be confused with the *wælcyrgen* (valkyriur) who are handmaidens of Wóden (Odin). The *idesa* of one's family may be called upon in some spell workings esp. those dealing with family matters. They are esp. helpful with childbirth and also attend deaths.

## Dvergr (ON)/Dweorgh (OE)

The dwarves may be one and the same as the black elves of Norse myth. They appear throughout Northern European folklore as small stocky humans with thick beards and an ugly appearance. Everywhere they are associated with subterranean realms, often with mining and the working of precious metals. The dwarves of Norse myth were not at all kind creatures, two of them being responsible for the death of Kvasir. Other places they appeared more benevolent and were always considered the greatest of smiths, crafting some of the Gods' jewellery and weapons. It is said Fréo (Freya) slept with four dwarves for her necklace, the Brósingmene and that they made such things as Þunor (Thor)'s hammer. Apparently, like the elves the dwarves were also seen as causing illnesses as two Anglo-Saxon charms appear in the *Lacnunga* to rid one of dwarves.

## Huldrufolk (Norwegian)

A group of woodland spirits that have the fronts of men, but the hollowed out backs of trees. They are basically one and the same as the wood wives of Germany. In Germany they are often linked to the goddess Holda. A special variety the Elle of Denmark are said to guard the Elder Tree. Generally all these beings seem to be the same type. They appear as beautiful children from the front but have a tree trunk for the back. They generally shy away from Mankind.

## Jöttnar (ON)/Eotnas (OE)

The ettins are a type of powerful being on par with the gods and elves. Usually they are thought of as giants, though not all of them are so large; they can be human sized. Many ettins are friendly to the gods such as the sea ettin Ægir who regularly had the gods as his guest and on a par with them. Others seem to oppose the gods at times. Generally they are wise and quite powerful. Meomer, counted as the wisest being of all, numbers among them as does the Norse god Njörd's wife Skaði. Still it is unwise to use them in spell working.

## Landsvættir(ON)/ * Landwihta (OE)

The Landsvættir are land spirits, the guardian spirits of the woods, forests, and streams. Usually friendly they prefer not to be disturbed by modern man. They do befriend humans though and have been known to give aid to growing crops and in other such agricultural pursuits. The Land Wights dislike blood and violence in general. They do appear in a variety of forms and this may be due to shape shifting abilities. They seem strongest in the untamed wilds and this may be because they shy away from civilized areas.

## Mare (OE)

A mare is a type of wight responsible for causing men to have nightmares. Mares are the most powerful of demons and are to be avoided at all costs. Said to ride humans to death and cause night terrors, the mare has no redeeming qualities. They are generally viewed as hideous creatures with rough features.

## Nykr (ON)/Nicor ( AS)

A Nixie is a water spirit usually associated with rivers and believed responsible for drownings and floods. The nixies are generally thought of evil creatures preying on human flesh. Like the mare they should be avoided. Many areas of Europe once felt these powerful water demons demanded a sacrifice each year, least they flood the fields or drown someone.

## Púki(ON)/Púca (OE)

A small demon similar to a goblin with the habits of a poltergeist. This concept, though somewhat diluted, survived into the Middle Ages to become the "Puck" familiar to us from Shakespeare and other English writers. In parts of England, they sometimes left out bowls of curds and cream for the puck. In most ancient times however they were on par with the mare and thought quite evil. It could be that Loki was in truth a púca. The earlier views of the puck as an evil being are most likely the most accurate and fall in accord with Loki's character perfectly. In Christian Anglo-Saxon texts the Devil is often referred to as the Puck, and this could be a memory of a being in Heathen beliefs on par with or perhaps even Loki himself. The other obvious choice would be Surtr, but then this great fire demon has little in common with the Puck's abilities.

## Rísi (ON)/Hrisi (OE)

A word for a type of giant for described as fair to look

upon and not to be much greater than human stature. They are said to be of low intelligence though and to like throwing boulders at each other. Generally, however they seem helpful to Mankind, but due to this low intelligence that usefulness isn't much good.

### Þurs (ON)/Þyrs(OE)

The thurses are a type of giant not to be confused with the ettins. They often aren't very intelligent (though there are exceptions like Surtr), tend to be ugly, and are usually associated with some elemental or natural force (fire, ice, frost, etc.). Generally they seem to be in opposition to the gods and to Þunor (Thor) in particular.

### Unholda (OE)

A group of evil wights whose names are parallelled by one in High German. The Unholden seem to be a group of evil wights in opposition to the goddess Holda. They may be evil dead or a variety of other wights, the folklore is unclear. At any rate the beings are quite evil and should be avoided.

### Valkyrja (ON)/Wælcyrgie (OE)

The "Choosers of the slain." The Valkyries are Wóden (Odin)'s hand maidens said to protect his heroes through life and to choose amongst the dead who goes to Valhalla. They serve as purveyors of wisdom, protection, and at death to help the fallen hero make the difficult journey to Valhalla. The Valkyries are often associated with the Norns and this may be due to their role at death. In myth they have been seen as both very fierce ugly hags relishing in blood shed and as beautiful young women living to serve the hero to which they are assigned. Both aspects are most likely true. The former view seems to go back to an earlier time when they were seen, like their god, as beings of rage and wind, the fury of battle. However, this does not stop them from taking on other aspects of Wóden which are much gentler. Wóden was also seen as an agricultural god in Germany, known for the giving of gifts and even a great degree of kindness. His advice in the "Hávamál" reveals the god to be much more concerned

112

with common sense than necessarily uncontrolled rage. It could be that the Valkyries who also imbued wisdom carried these kinder qualities as well, and that the separate views of their personalities are only a reflection of a more complex figure.

## Wild Hunt

Legends of the Wild Hunt are found throughout Europe and in Germanic countries the leader of the Hunt is usually held to be Wóden. The Hunt is seen as souls of the dead riding the wind of winter storms often on horse back with their hunting dogs in pursuit of whatever gets in their path. Legend holds that if one sees the Hunt they must join it or else go mad. The only defence against this being to ask the Hunt master for a sprig of parsley. In Germany there is a second version of the Hunt lead by the goddess Holda which consists of the souls of dead infants.

# Chapter X The Holy Tides

It is unclear how many holy tides the ancient Anglo-Saxon Heathens actually celebrated. It is known from Anglo-Saxon records that the Anglo-Saxon witanagemót met most often on St. Martin's Day (November 10th), Christmas, and Easter or Whitsunday (Liberman, *The National Assembly in the Anglo-Saxon Period*). These dates correspond to when Anglo-Saxon kings are reported to wear their crowns (Chaney, *Cult of Anglo-Saxon Kingship,* p. 65). They also correspond roughly to the ones mentioned by Snorri in the *Heimskringla*:

> þâ skyldi blôta î môti vetri til ârs, enn at miðjum vetri blôta til grôðrar, it þriðja at sumri, þat var sigrblôt

> "On winter day there should be blood-sacrifice for a good year, and in the middle of winter for a good crop; and the third sacrifice should be on summer day, for victory in battle." (*Ynglinga Saga Chapter 8*)

These dates come out as roughly sometime in October, Yule (Dec. 21st), and Eostre. That there may have been more Anglo-Saxon holy tides are known from Bede and his description of the Anglo-Saxon pagan calendar in *De Temporum Ratione*. Bede starts the Heathen year with Modranect, the "Mothers Night." It falls between Ærra Geola, our December and Æfterra Geola, or January, and is the period today we know as Yule (which is now no more than a synonym for Christmas for most people). Of Solmonað, roughly our February, Bede says the Anglo-Saxons offered cakes to their Gods, and thus it was named the month of cakes; he also mentions Hreðmonað, roughly our March as when the Goddess Hreðe was worshipped, followed by Eastremonað when the Goddess Eostre was worshipped. He does not name Liða as a sacred month, however, that it falls on Midsummer, there may have been a holy day corresponding to Mid-Winter or Yule. This is pretty much confirmed by Midsummer celebrations that survived into modern times in England. Bede then mentions Háligmonaþ, roughly our September, which was called "holy" as in Bede's words "because our ancestors, when they were heathen, paid their devil tribute in that month." The next potential holy tide mentioned by Bede is Blótmonað, roughly our November. The name its self means "sacrifice month" and was the time when animals were slaughtered for the coming winter. It follows Winterfylleð which corresponds to the Norse Winter Nights. That All Hallows, St. Martin's Day, and Guy Fawkes Day all important English holidays fall in these period would seem to indicate the actual holy tide took place at the junction of the two months. The three great holy tides of Anglo-Saxon paganism, Yule, Easter, and Winterfylleth can be thought of as High Holy Days, while the others as simply holy days. Modern Heathens have added to and changed this list. Those listed here are the ones celebrated by most adherents of the Anglo-Saxon troth.

### Yule/Géol

Yule was according to Bede when the Anglo-Saxon new year began. In the words of Gale Owen:

> The winter festival which Bede called Mothers' Night marked the pagan New Year and was held on 25 December. It is likely that this Yule festival (the pagan name for December and January, we may remember, was giuli) involved the bringing in of evergreens, the burning of a Yule log and a feast centred round a boar's head. Since these non-Christian features became associated with the Christmas festival celebrated at that time. (Owen, *The Rites and Religions of the Anglo-Saxons* p. 48)

Most of the activities connected now to Christmas such as gift giving, the hanging of everygreen boughs, and wassailing probably survived from the old Yule celebrations. *Módraniht* or "the night of Mothers" was perhaps the Anglo-Saxon equivalent of the Norse *Dísablot* sacred to the *Dísir* or ancestral women (*Idesa* in Old English). As such ancestral women would have been celebrated on this night.

Modern Heathens therefore have at their disposal centuries of customs concerning Yule. Many of these date back to the time when it was the ancient Heathens who celebrated the tide of the ancestors, frith, and gift giving. Many of these can be used to enhance the *blóts* and *symbels* done during this period, and therefore are presented here with a brief description.  By using the rites designed for each of the Twelve Nights of Yule, as well as the traditions here it is hoped you can have a fuller holiday experience.

Dreams
One ancient belief is that dreams during the Twelve Nights predict the events in one's life for the coming year.  An interesting activity would be to keep a log of one's dreams for each of the Twelve Nights.

Gift Giving
The tradition of gift giving goes back to Heathen times when gifts were exchanged throughout the Yuletide and not only on one day of the tide. Therefore, it is fitting Heathens do this as well. Gifts need not be expensive and often handmade gifts are better than something purchased at a store. Ideal gifts are those relating to our religion, books, ritual gear, art, tapes, and of course drinking horns.

Holly, Ivy, and Yule Décor: At Yuletide the Elder Heathens decorated their homes with ivy, holly, and boughs of evergreens. Ribbons were also used and the entire home covered with garlands and wreathes.  Modern Heathen should do no less in an attempt to capture the Yuletide spirit. Below are three of the more common house decorations.

  Yule Tree: The tradition of the Yule tree comes from Germany.  Originally it is believed the trees were decorated outside and gifts left for the land wights. This custom can still be observed in other parts of Northern Europe. With Christianity, the trees were brought inside to hide from the church. Modern Heathen trees can be decorated with Heathen symbols as well as the commercial lights, glitter, and ornaments. If one wants, they can decorate a tree outside instead as the Heathens of old did.

Yule Wreaths: Modern tradition uses a Yule wreath at the Mothers' Night symbol as an oath ring. This wreath is oathed upon as well as wished upon, and then burned at the Twelfth Night blót. Therefore these wreathes are best made out of natural substances such as cedar branches.  Other wreathes can be used as decorations around the house.

Lights:  In the more northern countries, Lucy Day which was a festival of lights is celebrated and seems an ancient holiday in connection with Yule. Candles, torches, and other forms of light were left burning to light up the night skies. Today we can use electric lights for the same purpose.

Hoodening: A tradition well recorded in England, but probably beyond the means of most Heathens to perform is Hoodening.  The tradition of dressing in animal skins and performing plays, dances, and processions are practices observed throughout all of the Germanic area, but is recorded particularly well in parts of England and Scandinavia.  As early as the fifth century this practice was condemned by the Church.  Archbishop Theodore condemned  those "who on the kalends of January clothe themselves with the skins of cattle and carry heads of animals". While St. Augustine condemned the "filthy practice of dressing up like a horse or stag" in the 5th century. Men in skins with animal heads are a common theme in early Heathen art.

Hoodening is a practice that was observed in Kent and the Isle of Thanet on Christmas Eve... areas that have remained Anglo-Saxon since the initial invasion of the tribes. Hoodening consisted of carrying either the skull of a real horse or a wooden one from house to house on a pole. The jaws of the horse head were rigged to snap by a string being pulled. The head was then carried by one of the Hoodening party, who was covered in furs or hides. The rest of the party, also dressed in furs, carried handbells ringing them while singing songs. For this they are given gifts usually in the form of money. It was considered bad luck not to give to the Hoodening party. There were several reports in the 19th century of folks being extremely frightened by this, though those from the area seem to have been amused. In the modern era, Hoodening has taken on many aspects of the hobby horse plays and mumming. Below is one of the songs from a modern Hoodening party:    Boy and horse are friends once more

Head and eyes no longer sore
Dobbin now is all submission
Having learned his hardest lesson
Half starved he is now, poor nag
Something please to fill his bag
Do not burst out the door
Give us something, good friends, for ...
If ye the Hooden horse do feed
Throughout the year ye shall not need.

Morris Dancing: Not quite as impractical as Hoodening is Morris dancing. Morris dancing, particularly the variety consisting of sword play also took place during the Yule tide. Morris dancing to quote Linetwigle, former member of the Ealdriht in her paper, *Dance in Northern Tradition* consisted of "stamping, leaping and hopping, rapping of swords or planting rods against the ground (these denoting a connection to fertility of the land), and the wearing of bells, plus a plethora of regional variations." Morris dancing also consisted of blackening of the faces (as did often mumming and hoodening) to either scare off evil spirits, or to mock the Wild Hunt.

Mumming: Something more practical for Heathens, than Morris Dancing or Hoodening,is mumming. Mummer plays take place in all of England, usually in pubs, and like Hoodening seem to date back to the Heathen Era. All of the plays consist of five to twelve cast members and follow the same basic plot. 1) A hero returns from a distant land. 2) The hero is challenged and killed. 3) A doctor is called and revives the hero. 4) All hostilities are ceased. Some see this as a ritual reenactment of the birth and death of a sun god. This is highly unlikely, as Heathen lore seems to have preserved no myths of this particular type. More likely the plays were for entertainment value alone, and if anything to celebrate the healing powers of the gods, particularly Wóden as a healer, and to educate that Yuletide is a time for frith and wishes that come true. Day 8 of the Yule rites presented here consists of a Mummer Play.

Sword Dancing: Another form of dance performed at Yule tide besides the Morris Dances were the Sword Dances. These were at one time performed with the long sword and seem to be quite ancient. Most of the dances consist of a procession and the clashing and leaping of swords as well as the formation of various patterns with the swords. Often the dance ends with a mock death and revival by a "doctor" as with the Mummer Plays.

Wassailing : The wassailing of Victorian times resembled carolling more than it did its earlier counterpart, and is the form most are familiar with. Ancient wassailing consisted of making the drink wassail, originally mulled ale, curds, apples, and sometimes nuts. A group of wassailers would then go out with bowls filled with wassail from house to house and wassail the apple and cherry trees with songs and loud noises to ensure a good crop from the orchards the next year. A few wassailing songs survive, but these seem to be of a later variety.

Yule Log : The Yule log has not survived into modern celebrations for the most part, and for most modern Heathens would be difficult to do without a fireplace or wood burning stove. You may therefore wish to set up a symbolic Yule log. You can carve it with wishes for the New Year, garland it, do what you wish. If you have a place you can burn it outside during Yuletide, you may wish to do so.

Traditionally, the Yule log was brought in on Mothers'

Night, it was then set ablaze and hoped to burn all Twelve Nights (remember this log was nearly an entire tree to be burned in the long pits of a long house). Different areas had different customs concerning the Yule log. Everywhere the log was garlanded and decorated with ribbons prior to the procession to the longhouse. The procession was, as most procession during the holidays, a joyous one. Once burning no one could squint in the presence of the log, nor were barefooted women allowed around it. In Yorkshire, England, they practised what is called mumping or gooding. Children would go begging and singing from house to house as the log was brought in. In other areas, the children were allowed to wassail the log the first night and drink to it.

## Solmonaþ

At the time of Solmonað in the Middle Ages, plow blessing ceremonies took place. Bede also tells us this was the time when cakes were given to the Gods. A ritual honouring the goddess Eorðe and another name Erce (which may be another name for Eorðe or another goddess) was preserved in the Old English document called the *Lacnunga* or "Leech Cunning." It is called variously Æcer-Bót, "Field Remedy," and "For Unfruitful Land" by scholars, but it is apparent part of it is a pagan prayer, and in another part one is instructed:

> Nim þonne ælces cynnes melo and abacæ man innewerdre handa bradnæ hlaf and gecned hine mid meolce and mid haligwætere and lecge under þa forman furh.
> Take all kinds of meal and bake a loaf as broad as a man's hand, and knead it with milk and with holy water and lay it under the first furrow.

This ceremony while a bit Christianized has references both to a plow and the cakes mentioned by Bede. It is fairly apparent that it may have been the sort of rite performed during Solmonað.

Solmonath appears to have been one of the tides most

120

persecuted by the Christian church. Of its rites, only the blessing of the plow was allowed to continue along with the observation of the ground hog's habitual looking for his shadow. According to the *Heimskringla*, "In Svithjod it was the old custom, as long as heathenism prevailed, that the chief sacrifice took place in Goe month at Uppsala." The Old Scandinavian month of Goe falls in our month of February. These sacrifices were offered frith ok sigr, for frith and victory.

Solmonath was the time when the ewes first began giving birth to their lambs, and ewe milk was thus available. It was also when the thaw began and ground could first be broken for the spring planting. Tied to the first tilling of the year, were the various plow rites. It was possibly this time of year when the goddess Nerthus was taken around to villages, as this is when plows were decorated and taken from village to village in medieval England. Drawing on the Æcer-Bót and the activities of the medieval celebrations, these plow processions may have taken the following form:

Two nights before the blessing, a torch processional would have collected the necessary sod from the corners of the farmstead, probably by proceeding sunwise around the bounds of the land. Those familiar with the Icelandic "landnama" rite should see the original purpose of the torch processionals. By going around the bounds of the land sunwise with torches, and taking the soil of the four corners, the land is being reclaimed for its owners. Then before sunset the next day, this soil mixed with the products of the livestock (milk, honey, tallow) would be set back in the earth. That night a housel may have been held, and at sunrise the plow would have been blessed and used to dig its first furrow (into which was buried the first seed and a cake), probably after a processional through the streets of the village. Such rites may have been accompanied by plays depicting the marriage of Heaven and Earth (Fréa and Gerðr or Wóden and Eorðe), as the lines of the "Æcer-Bót" imply. Ewemeolc was the first fertility rite of the year, and so these rites must have played an important role in the lives of the Elder Heathens. It is also possible that this is when the masked dances took place (dancers dressed as animals), though they may well have taken place at Easter. A thoroughly English holiday, this holiday as it comes down to us has strong Celtic influences. Many features however such as the charming of the plow and groundhog festivities appear on the continent, and seem wholly Germanic. Some believe the Dísablót of the Norse also took place at this time, and celebrate it January 31st instead of during Yule.

Charming of the Plow: This was also the time when the plows were blessed. Originally in Heathen times this would have been done in the fields. With the Conversion, of course, farmers still feeling this need brought their plows to the village priest.

Groundhog: Watching to see if groundhogs saw their shadows started in Germany, but there it was badgers or bears. Over the years it shifted from the observation of those animals to the groundhog. Heathens that have a groundhog handy (which are probably quite few) could go out to observe them early morning, perhaps even create rites to go with it.

## Hreðe

The only mention of Hreðe is in Bede. He says that during her month sacrifices were given to her. Grimm has suggested her name means "glorious," but with no other clues as to her worship we are nearly at a loss as to her holy tide. The only Christian holiday that falls during the month of Hreðe is Fasnet as it is called in the Black Forrest area of Germany or Fasching celebrated in Bavaria. Both involved the use of costumes and disguises as if in a Mummer's Play, not dissimilar to Carnival which also takes place at this time. Fasnet seems to have preserved older elements than Fasching with its costumes tending more towards witches and demons. It also has the odd tradition of allowing women to rule for a day, as well as fools wandering around. The celebration ends with an effigy being burned. Of course following this is the fast of Lent in the Christian calendar.

Whether any of this was a part of Hreðe's worship is not known. There appears to have been no obviously pagan customs connected with any of the holidays at this time in England, except for the eating of pancakes on Shrove Tuesday.

## Eostre

Easter is the celebration named for the goddess Eostre, whom we know little about. She is only mentioned by name once, and that is by Bede. However, her name survived as a native month name in both German and English, and in connection with a holy festival at that time. Her name is believed to be cognate with our word east so that she may be she was goddess of the dawn as well as spring.

Folklore surrounding Easter holds that water gathered at dawn is particularly holy, and it is said maidens in sheer white can be seen frolicking in the country side. In England, Easter was the time when the boundaries of farmsteads were beaten with besoms and birch sticks. The young folk along with the procession were also switched lightly. This "beating of the bounds" was probably done to drive away ill wishing wights. Besom and birch were the traditional material for which illness causing wights were driven out of those with illnesses, and that they are used to beat the bounds implies similar purposes. It is to be noted much of Easter seems linked to purification. Water from brooks collected on Easter morning as well as the dew was considered "holy water," and Easter saw bonfires which at other times were used for purification. Young women in early times would go to brooks or streams to wash at dawn, as the water then was thought particularly holy. Below are a few Easter traditions the modern Heathen can use to enhance the holy tide.

Bonfires: Easter like Wælburges and Midsummer saw bonfires being lit atop hillsides. And like Wælburges and Midsummer many rites such as fire leaping were associated with the fires.

Cross Buns : As far back as Easter customs have been recorded have appeared cross buns. Traditionally eaten at Easter, we know not truly what their significance are.  In England, it is believed they had healing powers, while other places believed that is they were hung in the kitchen, they would keep away evil. The cross in the buns may be the rune Giefu. As Giefu is the rune of gift giving and one of exchange, this could be the true meaning behind them.

Decorations : The ancient Heathens decorated for every holy tide.  They garlanded trees, houses, ritual items, and themselves. Easter was no different and saw wreathes of wheat and ribbon.  In Germany, even now, eggs are blown out and hung on trees. Today, in America, this custom of decorating trees for Easter is coming back, and certainly worthwhile for us Heathen folk.

Easter Bunny :The Easter Bunny or Hare was first recorded in Germany as bringing eggs to children, and there children built nests, for the hare to lay its eggs in.  The hare is a symbol of not only fertility, but also somewhat of parenting as hares and rabbits in general tend to be attentive to their young. In parts of England, they held hare hunts. The hare would had to be caught alive and brought into the priest, who would then serve a breakfast of eggs.

Easter Eggs: Ideally the creation of Easter Eggs should be done the night before the celebration. This is so the eggs can be used the next day in various games and customs.  Of course, there is nothing to keep parents from entertaining children with egg colouring Easter day either. Many customs are connected with the eggs. Egg tossing was done in many parts of Northern Europe.  If you caught the egg unbroken, it was thought a sign of good luck. Egg rolling was customary in parts of England.  They would take eggs to the top of a hill and roll them down. This could be adapted into a race if one so desired. Of course Easter egg hunts can always provide entertainment for the children. At one time eggs were exchanged on Easter, much like Yule gifts to symbolize friendship.

Easter Parade: Easter was also the time of processionals when everyone dressed in their very best clothes and in Heathen times probably proceeded to the hof or ritual grove. Most likely these would be summer clothes newly woven and sewn during the winter.

Easter Play: Easter was also a time when a ritual battle between the Winter and Summer took place. These mock fights were much like the Mummers' Plays of Yule. The opposing sides one representing Winter, the other Summer would face off in a sword dance. Other times the plays involved a battle between the hag of Winter versus the maiden of Summer.

Vigils: In many areas it was custom to keep a vigil the night before Easter to watch the rising sun. This could be worked in with bonfires ceremonies by modern Heathens, or even with the collection of holy water.

Winter Effigy: Other places an effigy of Winter would be beaten and burned. This custom can be seen in both England and Germany. This effigy could be a corn dolly or a stuffed dummy.

## Wælburges or Sumerdæg

Sumerdæg was another spring festival for the ancient Heathens. Wælburges Night was thought the night when witches ride by many ancient Heathens and this may reveal a link to the German goddess Holde (who may indeed be Frigga). Holde was considered the goddess of witches by medieval Germans. Many areas saw this as the time when witches and other wights rode thru the air, and thus a time when the gods needed to be invoked. On this night prayers were said for the cattle, sheep, and goats, with special reference to keeping ettins away. And in many areas it was the time for a great feast as well as bonfires. Many of the celebrations took place atop mountains and hills (which in Germany were connected to Holde and witches).

Love and courting seems to be a central theme amongst many of the folktales surrounding Wælburges. Many customs relate to courtship rituals; the gathering and giving of flowers from young beaus to maidens, the Maypole Dance the next day, as well as the frocking in the woods of Wælburges Niht.

Early morning saw children gathering flowers, and in many areas the Maypole dance. In Germany, new trees and saplings were transplanted and nearly everywhere houses were decorated with fresh flowers. In some parts of England, this is when the Hobby Horse plays took place. Other areas crowned a May Queen who would declare winter to finally be defeated (going back to the ritual battles of Easter between Summer and Winter).

Hobby Horse: The Hobby Horse is a tradition practiced in some parts of England to this day. It resembles in many ways the Hoodening done at Yule tide in Kent, and may be one and the same thing performed at different tides. For more information read the article on Hoodening under Yule Traditions.

May Carols: Song played an important role in the festivals of the medieval Germanic peoples, and therefore we can only assume it did with the ancient Heathens as well. Like Yule, Wælburges seems to have been a time of songs and singing.

Maypole: In areas where there were not permanent Maypoles, one would be erected on the morning of May Day. The poles were always made from straight sturdy trees, usually close to 9 feet tall, though later permanent ones go up to over 100 feet. The Maypole is in many ways similar to the Irminsul of the Saxons and one has to wonder if the Old Saxons danced about it come May Day morning.

Maypole Dance: There were a wide variety of Maypole dances some involving ribbons, others not. The earliest sources seem to indicate the dances were done without ribbons.

May Queen: In nearly all areas where Heathendom once thrived, a May Queen was selected from amongst the maidens of the village.

Morris Dancing: In some parts of England, Wælburges was the time when Morris Dancing took place.

## Midsummer/Litha

The showcase of Midsummer was its bonfire. Presumably these were lit in the method known as "Need Fire" using only a fire drill or fire bow (never flint and steel). Need Fires were used in times of need to drive pestilence away from cattle, and this was done at Midsummer as well. On the Eve of Midsummer, folks would gather and build bonfires, drive cattle through the smoke and then conduct a "watch," that is they tried to stay up all night. Lovers would leap through the fires, presumably to encourage the crops to grow, others would leap through them for good luck or health. Flowers were thrown into the fires and folks danced and made merry about them. Midsummer Eve was also a time of courtship. Young couples that had met at Waelburga would continue their courtship, or get married.

Also, on Midsummer Eve folks would gather flowers to decorate the homes the next morning. Many medicinal herbs were also gathered. Among the favourites were St. John's Wort, Vervain, Mugwort, Feverfew, Rue, and "Fern Seed." Worts harvested on Midsummer were thought very powerful, and not a few had special properties. Roses picked on Midsummer Eve were thought to last until Yule, and Mugwort placed in a grain bin on midsummer was thought to keep mice away. Yarrow hung up at Midsummer was thought to keep all healthy for the year. Other herbs were used in love divination. Supposedly if a young maid scattered fern seed on the ground before her, and then looked back over her shoulder on Midsummer Eve, she would see her future husband. There were many other forms involving Orpine and Thistle as well.

The next day, all the wells were cleaned and decorated with the flowers gathered the night before. In addition to the flowers, Rowan and Birch were favoured for decorating for their beautiful branches. Wreathes made of Nine worts or woods were said to be esp. powerful. Some of the worts used were Wolvesbane*, the English Daisy, Mistletoe, Mugwort, Oak leaves, Rowan, Birch, Orpine, Thistle, and Yarrow. There were many others no doubt, now forgotten, or remembered only in local customs.  All of the homes and wells were decorated and birch branches laid around the flax fields. Wells were thought particularly holy at this time and water drawn from them said to heal all sorts of ailments.

*Very poisonous and NOT to be used!

Bonfires: As stated above the bonfires were probably lit using a fire bow or fire drill, and more than likely consisted of nine woods.  Processions would form to go to the place of the fire, with everyone carrying a torch, and every house would be lit. Once at the fire and it was started, folks would dance and sing about it, leap thru it, and throw flowers into it. Many would stay up all night and in England this was called the "watch." To stay awake all night was thought to give one good luck and health.

Burning Wheels: Another Midsummer Night activity was to send burning wheels and barrels down hillsides.

Processions and Warding: Many would wonder from bonfire to bonfire bedecked in garlands and accompanied by Morris dancers or a hobby horse procession carrying torches. Other folks would circle their homes and buildings to ward them for the coming year.

## Hlæfmæst/Freyfaxi

The holy tide appears to be a modern one, although based on Medieval festivals. Hlæfmæst is an Anglo-Saxon reconstruction by Garman Cyning of the Winland Ríce. It means "loaf feast." Modern Ásatrú sometimes calls it Freyfaxi, but there is no evidence it was sacred to Frey or of an ancient holiday with that name either. Nonetheless, in Scandinavia, Germany, and England a festival took place near or on the first of August. In the Anglo-Saxon calendar one of the names for this month was Thunormonath "Thunder or Thor month." It could well be that this festival to celebrate the start of the harvest was sacred to Þunor. In Iceland, it took place near the time of Thingstide. Þunor (Thor) is one of the gods of Thing.

Hlæfmæst or Lamass was the first harvest of the year, when the wheat and first apples were gathered. As such, it has much in common with Harvest Home, and many of the rites are analogous. The last load would have been brought in with a harvest doll proceeding it, and then would have come the threshing. Many rites must have accompanied the threshing because it would have to be a community project. Possibly there were threshing songs that were sung as the work got d one. The first loaves of bread would have then been baked and blessed. No doubt some of these were offered to the gods. The common lands of the village were opened for winter pasturage at this time and remained open until Feb. 2. Bondsman generally paid their rent at this time as well. Even though our society is no longer an agricultural one, no one could deny we must still eat. Therefore, it is fitting that perhaps we go to the store, and buy some flour, and make bread the "old fashioned" way to give to the gods.

## Harvest/Háligmonaþ

Háligmonaþ, today often called Harvest Home in England, falls on the fall equinox. Harvest falls in the middle of harvest in some areas, for others it is the end. For this reason, it and Winter Nights share some customs like the Last Sheaf. Harvest home also shared many customs with Lamass. Again a procession with the last sheaf as the harvest doll took place. Other Harvest customs are unique to it alone such as its version of the Mummer's Play called "Rise Up, Jock." It has much in common with the Yule mummer's plays in that a young king dies and is brought back by a healer with a bag of tricks much like Saint George. In

England songs like Harvest Home were sung when the last load came in, as songs similar to John Barleycorn would have been sung while harvesting. It was at this time beer was started brewing, while the barley was still fresh, and a symbel probably would have been in order. In parts of Germany, a goat was slaughtered and roasted at this time, and meant to symbolize the "oats goat."

In modern Germany, Erntefest is their Thanksgiving taking place on the first Sunday in October. Several customs survived. One very strange one in Cottbus, Germany involved building an oak leaves gate, on the gate was hung a dead cock. Mean would then race for the gate and try to tear a wing off the cock. The one that got a wing and made in thru the gate was the Kral.

Falling near Erntefest is Michaelmas which takes place on Sept. 29th. Ironically this date was also cited by Grimm as Zisa's Day, a day sacred to Tiw's (Tyr's) wife. It is therefore reasonable to think may of Michaelmas's customs were originally Heathen in origin. Such customs are giving water to wolves, letting cattle into the wood was no longer allowed until the end of winter (as the wood belongs to the wolf after Michaelmas), and that the winter fodder for the cattle must be collected by then.

The Last Sheaf: As the festival closing harvest, Winter Nights has many customs connected to the last sheaf. In areas as varied as Sweden and Germany, the last sheaf was left for Woden's horse. Often this was done at Winter Nights, though it could be the three harvest festivals, Hlæfmæst, Harvest, and Winter Nights celebrated the harvest of three different kinds of crops. Wheat, barley, and other grains do not all ripen at the same time. Therefore there could easily be a Last Sheaf for each grain crop.

### Winter Nights/Winterfylleth

Winter Nights was the Icelandic name for this festival, Winterfylleth was the name of the Anglo-Saxon month it fell in. Many modern Heathen combine it with the modern

Halloween, and refer to it as All Hallows. The date of Winter Nights is uncertain. It would seem that it fell around October 15th. From the name of the Anglo-Saxon month, it could have fell on the first full moon after the autumn equinox. Two very important blóts are thought to have taken place at this time. The dísablót and the alfarblót are both mentioned in Icelandic sagas and thought by many to be a part of Winter Nights. This would make the festival one dedicated to the ancestors, and explain how Anglo-Saxon areas quickly adopted the Celtic festival of the dead, Samhain, in the guise of "All Hallows Eve." It is also sacred to Fréa (Frey). In Gisla Saga, it is stated Thorgrim conducted a Frey's blót at Winter Nights in thanks for the harvest. Winter Nights would seem to be the most important of Icelandic festivals, maybe even more so than Yule.

In other Germanic areas neither Winter Nights or Winter Fylleth are mentioned. However, this may be because the holiday was moved by the Church. St. Martin's Day (November 11) is widely celebrated in Germany, and may have been the continental German version of Winter Nights. Also falling at this time is Bonfire Night in England. Although this holiday is said not to date before the Guy Fawks plot to blow up the English government in the 17th century, it seems to be much older. Like Bonfire Night in England, St. Martin's Day involved the building and burning of bonfires. Much like Halloween, children in Germany would go from house to house on St. Martin's, reciting verses, and being rewarded with sweets. The Netherlands also burns bonfires on St. Martin's Day, with processions of lights going to the bonfires. Both in Germany and Scandinavia, geese are killed and eaten, their feathers saved for pillows and other uses. Winter Nights was also when the fall slaughter began. The month immediately following Winterfylleth in the Anglo-Saxon calendar was called Blótmonath for perhaps that reason.

The Last Sheaf: As the festival closing harvest, Winter Nights has many customs connected to the last sheaf. In areas as varied as Sweden and Germany, the last sheaf was left for

Woden's horse. There are many ties to the last sheaf being given to Wóden and the Wild Hunt as well. The general thought being that the Wild Hunt began to ride at this time and stopped riding at the end of Yule. In some areas, it was made into a corn dolly, and paraded through the village.

"Trick or Treating" or Souling : Both modern Halloween in England and America, and the St. Martin's Day celebrations in Germany involve children going house to house getting treats by either threatening  a trick (in America and England), or reciting verses as in Germany. This custom dates back to an older one called "souling."  On All Hallow's Eve, folks would go from house to house begging for "soul cakes." These were little square cakes with currants. In exchange for the cakes, the "soulers" would say prayers for the dead kin of the cake givers.

Apple Bobbing : Bobbing for apples also seemed to have been practiced on the various holidays that was made up Winter Nights. In England a sixpence was often also put in the tub with the apples. Of course, the person that got the sixpence got to keep it. Apples were used in other ways, often being set out with the last sheaf for the Hunt. And of course cider is the drink of preference.

Feasts of the Dead : Both the Celtic holiday Samhain and Winter Nights were festivals to the dead. Therefore the fact they merged to become the modern holiday Halloween should not be alarming. As Heathens, such Celtic practices as Jack o Lanterns fit well with Germanic customs such as bonfires and trick or treating. Primary though, should be an effort to honour the Idesa (Disir) and Ylfe (Álfar) with blóts and feasts. This can be conducted as any blót to the gods would, perhaps followed by a feast, and then a minne drinking (a special symbel in memory of the Dead).

# Chapter XI Ritual Tools

Every worshipper needs equipment to help him or her in his gifts and prayers to the Gods, and this is especially true of a heargweard or other priest. Barring a full fledged ealh or hof, the following list of items may come in useful. 1) Blowing horn 2) Blótorc 3) Hlaut-teinn 4) Húselfæt 5) Oath Ring 6) Récelsfæt 7)Seax 8) Symbelhorn 9) Wéofod. Additional items may be necessary depending on one's patron deity such as a spear for worshippers of Wóden, a hammer for those of Þunor, and so forth.

Blowing Horn

If one is the leader of a kindred or expects to host large blóts and symbels often, they will want a blowing horn to summon folks at outdoor gatherings. A blowing horn is very easy to make or may be purchased from a craftsman.

Blótorc

A *blótorc* (OE) or *blótbolli* (ON) is the term used for the bowl that holds the mead for the blessing. It is also called the blessing bowl. It generally sat on the *wéofod* or altar, and should be made of copper or wood. In it sat the *hlaut-teinn*.

Hlót-teinn

Old Norse *hlaut-teinn* (also called a *störkkull*), was the term used for the aspergum or "sprinkler of holy liquid." *Hlót-tan* is an Anglo-Saxon reconstruction of the term. It was usually a fresh oak branch or a branch of a similar holy tree.

Húselfæt

Anglo-Saxon *húselfæt* was used of the cauldron the feast was prepared in or the kettle in which it was served. It should be of stoneware, although iron could be substituted (do not use copper as it can cause copper poisoning).

## Oath Ring

The oath ring was an arm band containing at least 20 ounces of silver worn by the wéofodþegn at special occasions, and at all other times resting on the wéofod . Oaths were sworn upon it at Thing and on other occasions.

## Récelsfæt

An incense burner in which one can burn dried herbs or incense. It is also called a *stórfæt*, and in Old Norse, a *glóðker*) in which to burn incense (called in Anglo-Saxon récels or stór). It should be of the fire-pan variety, and be made of stone.

## Seax

The seax was the standard knife of the Elder Heathen, and was used by nearly everyone. For religious use, the blade must be kept clean and sharp, and never put to mundane use.

## Symbelhorn

A drinking horn to use at symbel, and in personal rites. Wéofodþegns will want a great horn.

## Wéofod

Anglo-Saxon *wéofod* was the term used for altar, along with the less common term *hearg*, which was usually used of a temple or grove. Its Old Norse cognate *hörg*, however generally meant any altar. Modern practice tends to use *hearg* for outdoor altars, Old Norse *stalli* for indoor altars, and *wéofod* for both. Altars outdoors were almost always of stone, while we have no idea what those used indoors were like, though wood was the most common building material by far for everything.

The *wéofod* can be engraved with holy signs, or left plain. It should be in an enclosed area, or at least covered when not in use. On the *wéofod* should set the blótorc and oath ring. *Wéohas* "idols" of one's patron gods should be set facing it. Outdoor *wéofods* can be constructed by piling up stones. In such a case, an area needs to be marked off around it as the *vé* or *friðgeard*, if possible with rope (in Old Norse called *vébönd*), or a planted hedge.

Other tools
A fire drill or a fire starter kit for starting need fires, a cloak to meditate under, and a set of runes tines also come in useful. Ropes of a natural fibre (flax or cotton if possible) along with staves of hazel or oak come in handy for vébönd. Most of these items can be made by hand, and there are articles on how to make many of the ritual items in books such as Gundarsson's *Teutonic Religion*.

# Chapter XII Sacred Space

## *The Hof or Ealh*

Our spiritual forebears first worshipped in groves as stated by Tacitus and revealed by the original meanings of the meaning of the words for "temple." Anglo-Saxon *bearu* and *hearg* were both used for "grove," long before they came to mean "temple." Gothic *alhs* and Anglo-Saxon *ealh* are also related to Indo-European words meaning "grove." Heathens continued to worship in groves until the conversion to Christianity was complete. The Elder Heathens treated these sacred sites, whether grove or temple, as separate from the outside world, and fenced them off with ropes, hedges, or fences. Such an enclosure, was called a *vé* in Old Norse. *Vé* derives from Old Norse *vígja* "to make sacred, separate from the mundane." These sites were also called *stafgarðr* in Old Norse and *friðgeard* in Anglo-Saxon. Such enclosures surrounded sacred sites like temples, sacred wells, mounds, trees, and so forth. No violence could be done within them, and to commit violence could result in death for the violator.

The enclosure was an important part of an *ealh*, and this probably explains why hedges seem to have played such an intricate part in Heathen belief. The Anglo-Saxon word hæg "hag" derives ultimately from the same word as Anglo-Saxon *haga* "hedge or haw." The *ealh* at Yeavering had an enclosure about it, as did the one described in *Kjalnes Saga*. The *ealh* itself at Yeavering was of long house design, about 35 feet long and 17 feet wide. The interior of it is not clearly known, although there is a pit of oxen skulls by one door, and at the southern end are three post holes that have been filled in with gravel. It is believed this is where the wéofod may have stood as the area seems to have been enclosed in a small apartment. Bede says the *ealh* at Goodmanham in Northumbria had such enclosures and evidence suggests the one at Harrow Hill in Sussex may have. This parallels the description of Thórólf's hof in the *Eyrbygga Saga* and that of Ingmundr's hof in the *Kjalnes Saga*. The hof at Yeavering had buttressed outer walls and inner walls lined with wattle and daub. There were two doorways in the centre of the long walls, and the main pillars which supported the roof was one at each end of the short walls. Directly north and in line with the hof is what appears to have been a dining hall of similar long house design and size. To the west of the hof, was a kitchen/slaughter house where the sacrifices were prepared for the feasts. Northwest of the *ealh*, on a Stone Age burial mound, stood a rather large pole, reminiscent of the Old Saxon Irminsul. Unfortunately, for all this information from the archaeological digs at Yeavering, we know little detail of the interior of the hof.

Fortunately, we do have a few descriptions of hofs in Iceland and Norway, of which we will look at the two most detailed. The *Eyrbygga Saga* gives a good description of Thórólf Mostrarskegg's hof. There was a doorway nearer to one end than the other, and inside were the main pillars, in which *reginnaglar* "holy nails" were driven. At one end, was an enclosure or apartment containing the wéofod upon which the oath ring and hlautbolli (the blessing bowl) sat, around the wéofod were arranged the idols. In *Kjalnes Saga*, we are given a description of an *ealh* built by Ingimundr. The hof was 100 feet long, and inside it had a circular sanctuary which contained the wéofod, and before which stood an idol of Þunor and idols of two other gods. On the wéofod sat the oath ring and the hlautbolli which was made of copper. Outside the door of the hof was a blótkilda, a sacred well in which men were drowned. The *ealh* was surrounded by a fence too high to see over.

What is clear from these descriptions and the archaeological evidence is that in addition to a hof's high pillars, there was a wéofod at one end enclosed in an apartment, around which the wéohas "idols" stood. Upon the wéofod sat the blótbolli and the oath ring. The hof itself was surrounded by a fence or a hedge, and it was very likely a sacred well lay outside its doors in the friðgeard. In numerous Icelandic sources, it sounds as if the feasts were held within the *ealh*, so there must have been benches, and tables.

## Other Holy Sites

Many of the words for "holy site" or "altar" come from words that originally meant "grove" or a wooded area. Old English *hearg* and *bearo* both refer to groves and holy sites. The trees within such groves were held to be sacrosanct and could not be stripped of boughs, and were never to be cut down on the penalty of death. According to Groenbech, around such groves, or any holy site would be a fence of staves, which served as a sacred enclosure. Other sources tell us of hedges about such sites. Within the grove would be a *hearg*, a heap of stones serving as an altar and were from the tress hung the hides of sacrifices, and in the grove, placed the various votive offerings of individuals. It can be assumed that *wéohas*, images of the gods would also set near the altar.

Within the groves were often sacred trees or poles such as the Old Saxons' Irminsul. A tree was said to stand near the temple at Uppsala, and throughout the lore are references to trees thought to be holy. In the Middle Ages, such trees were still garlanded, even though they no longer received Heathen sacrifice. Thought particularly holy were oaks, sacred to Þunor; ash, which resembled Yggdrasil; hazels, whose wood served as the fence for a thing or other sacred/legal site; elders and elms, which represented the feminine principle. Other trees such as birch and yew also received much reverence. The yew in particular appeared in ancient grave yards and was also thought to resemble Yggdrasil, while the birch has a rune named for it.

Other natural sites served as holy steads, particularly those of great beauty. Thingveillr in Iceland was chosen in part for its great view of the country and its wondrous beauty. Waterfalls, mountains, springs, and rivers have all served as holy sites. Finally, the mounds of the dead also served as sacred sites. There were barrows near the temple at Uppsala and near the hof at Yeavering in Northumbria.

One may with relative ease create their own sacred site or ve even in their own back yard. To do so, one will need the following things: 1) A hearg or altar. 2) A form of enclosure for the site such as a privacy fence. 3) Wéohas or idols of the gods if desired. The layout of such a friðgeard is largely up to the individual, but the hearg should be in the north. It may be a pile of stones, or a wooden table, and may be inscribed with holy signs or runes. It may be surrounded by wéohas or allowed to stand alone. Sacrifices may be allowed to remain on it for the gods to consume. The site itself may be surrounded by a fence, traditionally made of hazel, although a natural enclosure of trees or a hedge may do as well, or even a temporary one of rope (called in Old Norse, *vébönd*). One may want to add other features, such as a fire pit, or one's own sacred tree. During times of the holy tides, one may wish to decorate the area with garlands and wreaths made of biodegradable materials, tie ribbons to the trees, or set out candles. Such decor can be timed to the season; Easter eggs for Easter, Yule wreaths for Yule, and so forth.

If one is fortunate enough to have property of their own other than their own backyard to set up a *friðgeard*, they will want to go about a selection process. Groves are the most desirable sites if one is fortunate enough to own a wooded tract of land. However, nearly any natural site will do that gives off a feeling that is mystical and spiritual. One will want to select such a site first on the feeling it conveys, and second on whether or not the land wights are friendly. One can win the friendship of the land wights by performing simple rites to them, giving gifts of bread, milk, or porridge. Such a site can be set up in the same way as a *friðgeard* in one's backyard, only more elaborately. One may want to use a natural enclosure such as a blackberry bramble or construct one of wood. The *hearg* and firepit can be larger and be permanent features, and one can choose one of the larger trees as the sacred tree. If at all possible, such sites should be as secluded as possible.

There are a few rules regarding such holy sites. No weapons that have not been blessed for religious use should be brought into the enclosure. Only sacred speech should be allowed within the *friðgeard*, and no tree within the enclosure can be harmed in any way.

Having one's own holy stead gives one a place to

worship the gods on a daily basis, hold small gatherings, and brings one nearer the gods. If one has a backyard, or a farm or other piece of property to establish a small holy site, they by all means should do so. If no such site is available, a room in one's house or apartment dedicated to the gods will do. A table or desk can serve as a small altar and one can keep their *wéohas* of the gods close by. Like the outdoor holy site, the indoor altar room can be decorated to fit the occasion or holy tide. Finally, temporary holy steads can be created using a portable altar, rope of a natural fibre, as poles made of hazel or birch. One will want to rope the area off and set the portable altar up in the north. A gift needs to be given to the land wights of the area, but after that, one can perform any rites needed. The ancient Heathens worshipped in groves, at river banks, and under waterfalls. It should be no different for ourselves today, and having one's own site can lead to years of joy and pleasure in worshipping the gods.

# Chapter XIII Blót and Húsel

## *History and Background*

None of the ancient rites whose descriptions have been handed down to us from the lore have been so embraced by modern Heathens as blot. Nearly every modern Heathen has attended a blot, performed a blot, or know what one is. The origins of the rite are lost in the mists of time, but the word survived in both Old English and Old Norse. Old Norse *blót* meant a "sacrifice" or "feast" while the verb, *blóta* meant both "to worship" and "to sacrifice." Old English blót simply meant "sacrifice" while Old English *blótan* and Old High German *blozan* both meant "to sacrifice." Old English *blót* seems related to Old English *blétsian*, modern English bless. All of these words seem to derive from the word blood. In *Hákonar Saga goða* from *Heimskringla*, Snorri described how blood was sprinkled on the altar and on the temple walls and such ancient practices may be the origin of the word *blót*. Mythically it was Odin that ordained men to blot. Snorri says in the *Ynglinga Saga* from *Heimskringla*, that Odin decreed:

> "þâ skyldi blôta î môti vetri, til ârs, enn at miðjum vetri blôta til grôðrar, it þriðja at sumri, þat var sigrblôt."

> "On winter day there should be blood-sacrifice for a good year, and in the middle of winter for a good crop; and the third sacrifice should be on summer day, for victory in battle."

## *The Purpose of Blót*

The Elder Edda contains some material that may give the purpose of blot. In "Fjölsvixmál," it is said:

> Tell me, Fjolsvith, for I wish to know; answer as I do ask do they help award to their worshippers, if need of

help they have?
Ay they help award to their worshippers, in hallowed
stead if they stand; there is never a need, that neareth
a man but they lend a helping hand. (Fjölsvixmál,
Hollander translation 39 and 40)

In "Hynduljóx" the idea of men being rewarded for
blot is touched upon as well:

He a high altar made me Of heaped stones-all glary
have grown The gathered rocks-and reddened anew
them with neats' fresh blood; for ay believed Óttar in
the ásynjur. (Hynduljóx, Hollander translation verse
10)

Similar statements appear in the sagas as well. In
*Víga-Glúms Saga*, Þorkell states Frey had "accepted many
gifts from him" and "repaid them well." The Anglo-Saxons
appear to have held similar views as the Norse, the Old
English word *gield*, (modern English yield) meant not only
"payment, tax," but also "sacrifice." Old English *gieldan*
meant "to pay for, reward, requite," and also "to worship, to
sacrifice to." One of the primary purposes of blot then was
and is to give gifts to the Gods and Goddesses in return for
the help they give us.

This exchange of gifts between Man and the Æsir, the
Vanir, and other sacred beings, no doubt was seen as
forming bonds, much like gifts between friends. Such
bonding is referred to in the "Hávamal":

Not great things alone must one give to another,
praise oft is earned for nought; with half a loaf and a
tilted bowl I have found me many a friend.
("*Hávamal*" 53, Bray translation)

Hast thou a friend whom thou trustest well, from
whom thou cravest good? Share thy mind with him, gifts
exchange with him, fare to find him oft. ("*Hávamal*" 44 Bray
translation)

Vilhelm Grönbech furthers this idea of gifting as a form of bonding:

"When an article of value is passed across the boundary of frith and grasped by alien hands, a fusion of life takes place, which binds men one to another with an obligation of the same character as that of frith its self." (Grönbech. *The Culture of the Teutons*, Vol.2, p. 55)"

There is no reason that ancient Heathens would have changed the rules of giving because the Gods and Goddesses were involved. Giving meat and mead to the Æsir, Vanir, and other holy beings therefore not only ensured their help, but also made them a part of the human community, and in a sense one with the folk.

Blot may also have served as a form of communion with the Gods and Goddesses Discussing passages on blot Turville-Petre notes:

"The meaning of the sacrificial feast, as Snorri saw it, is fairly plain. When blood was sprinkled over altars and men and the toasts were drunk, men were symbolically joined with gods of war and fertility, and with their dead ancestors, sharing their mystical powers. This is a form of communion." (Turville-Petre. *Myth and Religion of the North*, p. 251).

This can be seen in the choice of words for the Christian act of Communion, Old English *húsel* was used both of Heathen sacrifices and the Christians' Holy Communion. Its Gothic cognate *hunsl* was only used of Heathen blot. It is probable then that the first Anglo-Saxon converts saw blots and the Christian rite of Communion as having similar aims, one of those perhaps being communion with the Gods or in their case God or Christ. Communion with the Gods and Goddesses would mean a sense of oneness with them, a sense that the Gods and Goddesses were part of the human community. The sacrificial animal having been given to the Gods or Goddesses may have been seen as containing some of the Gods and Goddesses' mægen or power. The blessing of the temple and folk with its blood therefore may have been viewed as spreading the mægen or power of the Gods and Goddesses amongst the folk. The fulls or prayers offered with the horn may have been viewed as a form of communicating with the Gods and Goddesses. And finally, the sacred feast its self, may have been seen as the folk sharing with the Gods and Goddesses, or perhaps as absorbing some of the Gods and Goddesses' mægen. Turville-Petre noted that vaningi "son of the Vanir" was applied to both Frey and the boar in poetry, and that:

> "This implies that when the flesh of the boar was consumed at the sacrificial banquet, those who partook of it felt they were consuming the god himself and absorbing his power." (Turville-Petre, *Myth and Religion of the North*, p. 255).

While it is doubtful that Turville-Petre is entirely correct in his assessment (ritual cannibalism of this sort seems unlikely amongst the Germanic peoples and is probably drawn from comparisons with Christian Communion), the idea that some of the deity's mægen or power is transferred to that of the folk is one that is in keeping with Heathen ideas seen elsewhere.

In addition to a form of communion, blot also served as a method of conveying the wants and needs of the folk to the Æsir and Vanir. The fulls or prayers of blot probably contained appeals for aid in time of famine, drought, or epidemic. At other times, they may have contained words of thanks. In *Víga-Glúms Saga* Thorkell offers Frey an ox with a request for revenge on the man that had taken his land. In Ibn Fadlan's account of the Rus traders, he told how they prayed to the Gods and Goddesses with requests for customers. The "Æcer-bót" an Anglo-Saxon rite found in the manuscript called the *Lacnunga* may contain portions of Heathen prayers that are basically requests for fertility of the land. Blot therefore served as a means of communicating with the Æsir, Vanir, and other holy beings..

Blots in ancient times and now therefore serves many purposes. Primarily, blot is a form of giving back to the Gods and Goddesses just a little of what they have given us. But Blot is also a form of communication with the Gods and Goddesses, a way of giving thanks, or of asking specifically for help in a certain area of one's life. Finally, blot is a way of bringing the Gods and Goddesses into our community, becoming a part of their community, and in some respects becoming one with them. To understand how this was done we need to look at the accounts of blots in the surviving lore.

## The Blót Description from Hákonar Saga goða

Thanks to Snorri, we have some idea of what an ancient blot looked like. Each step has a specific purpose, and those steps will be outlined here. The most detailed account from *Hákonar Saga goða* follows:

> Það var forn siður þá er blót skyldi vera að allir bændur skyldu þar koma sem hof var og flytja þannug föng sín, þau er þeir skyldu hafa meðan veislan stóð. Að veislu þeirri skyldu allir menn öl eiga. Þar var og drepinn alls konar smali og svo hross en blóð það allt er þar kom af, þá var kallað hlaut og hlautbollar það er blóð það stóð í, og hlautteinar, það var svo gert sem stökklar, með því skyldi rjóða stallana öllu saman og svo veggi hofsins utan og innan og svo stökkva á mennina en slátur skyldi sjóða til mannfagnaðar. Eldar skyldu vera á miðju gólfi í hofinu og þar katlar yfir. Skyldi full um eld bera en sá er gerði veisluna og höfðingi var, þá skyldi hann signa fullið og allan blótmatinn. Skyldi fyrstÓðins full, skyldi það drekka til sigurs og ríkis konungi sínum, en síðan Njarðar full og Freys full til árs og friðar. Þá var mörgum mönnum títt að drekka þar næst bragafull. Menn drukku og full frænda sinna, þeirra er heygðir höfðu verið, og voru það minni kölluð.

"It was an old custom, that when there was to be sacrifice all the bondes should come to the spot where the temple stood and bring with them all that they required while the festival of the sacrifice lasted. To this festival all the men brought ale with them; and all kinds of cattle, as well as horses, were slaughtered, and all the blood that came from them was called "hlaut", and the vessels in which it was collected were called hlaut-vessels. Hlaut-staves were made, like sprinkling brushes, with which the whole of the altars and the temple walls, both outside and inside, were sprinkled over, and also the people were sprinkled with the blood; but the flesh was boiled into savoury meat for those present. The fire was in the middle of the floor of the temple, and over it hung the kettles, and the full goblets were handed across the fire; and he who made the feast, and was a chief, blessed the full goblets, and all the meat of the sacrifice. And first Odin's goblet was emptied for victory and power to his king; thereafter, Niord's and Frey's goblets for peace and a good season. Then it was the custom of many to empty the brage-goblet; and then the guests emptied a goblet to the memory of departed friends, called the remembrance goblet."

This account can be further fleshed out with other accounts of blots from *Hákonar Saga goða*.

En bændur töldu að því er hann sat eigi í hásæti sínu þá er mestur var mannfagnaður. Sagði jarl að hann skyldi eigi þá svo gera. Var og svo að konungur sat í hásæti sínu. En er hið fyrsta full var skenkt þá mælti Sigurður jarl fyrir og signaðiÓðni og drakk af horninu til konungs. Konungur tók við og gerði krossmark yfir. Þá mælti Kár af Grýtingi: "Hví fer konungurinn nú svo? Vill hann enn eigi blóta?" Sigurður jarl svarar: "Konungur gerir svo sem þeir allir er trúa á mátt sinn og megin og signa full sitt Þór. Hann gerði hamarsmark yfir áður hann drakk."

"The king accordingly sat upon his high-seat. Now when the first full goblet was filled, Earl Sigurd spoke some words over it, blessed it in Odin's name, and drank to the king out of the horn; and the king then took it, and made the sign of the cross over it. Then said Kar of Gryting, "What does the king mean by doing so? Will he not sacrifice?" Earl Sigurd replies, "The king is doing what all of you do, who trust to your power and strength. He is blessing the full goblet in the name of Thor, by making the sign of his hammer over it before he drinks it.""

And finally:

En er Hákon konungur og Sigurður jarl komu inn á Mærini með her sinn þá voru þar bændur komnir allfjölmennt. Hinn fyrsta dag að veislunni veittu bændur honum atgöngu og báðu hann blóta en hétu honum afarkostum ella. Sigurður jarl bar þá mál í millum þeirra. Kemur þá svo að Hákon konungur át nokkura bita af hrosslifur. Drakk hann þá öll minni krossalaust, þau er bændur skenktu honum. En er veislu þeirri var lokið fór konungur og jarl þegar út á Hlaðir.

"Now, when King Hakon and Earl Sigurd came to More with their court, the bondes assembled in great numbers; and immediately, on the first day of the feast, the bondes insisted hard with the king that he should offer sacrifice, and threatened him with violence if he refused. Earl Sigurd tried to make peace between them, and brought it so far that the king took some bits of horse-liver, and emptied all the goblets the bondes filled for him without the sign of the cross; but as soon as the feast was over, the king and the earl returned to Hlader."

From these accounts it is fairly clear that blot consisted of blessing of the horns or goblets, blessing the folk with the blood of the sacrifice, fulls or prayers to the Gods and

Goddesses, and finally a feast. Whether Snorri presented the events of blot in the order they were performed, we cannot know for certain, but at least we do have the events that took place during a blot. Some parts of blot were left out by Snorri; obviously the sacrifice had to be slain, and rituals must have attended the slaying as well. Nonetheless, a rough outline of events taking place at blot can be somewhat reconstructed.

1) Pre-Feast: Prior to the feast, the sacrificial animal would have had to been slaughtered and butchered. In *Helgakvida Horrvoardssonar*, a boar is lead out to swear oaths on, but it is not clear whether this boar was later slaughtered for blot. In *Heiðreks Saga*, a boar or sonargöltR (the "leading boar," the same term used in *Helgakvida Horrvoardssonar* of the boar) was brought before the king at Yule that was intended for blot, and apparently later slaughtered. Garlanding and swearing of oaths on the animal may have taken place as a regular part of the blot ritual or pre-ritual then. While we are not told by Snorri what events took place at the slaying of the animal, and shortly thereafter, he does tell us that the blood of the animal was drained into the blot bowl. Hlautteinar or "lot sticks" were also made then, and these later used to sprinkle the folk. The Hlautteinar we are told were like brushes.

The slaughter its self was likely to have been fairly humane. Some scholars feel the ancients saw the animal as a representative of a God or Goddess. Temples did keep sacred animals, and this is mentioned several places in the lore. *Flateyjarbók*, described a temple where horses were kept, while *Hrafnkels Saga* told how Hrafnkell Freysgoði kept a stallion dedicated to FreyR. These animals may have been seen as containing the mægen of the God or Goddess they were dedicated to. In Snorri's account though, the folk are portrayed as bringing the animals for blot. After the slaughter, the feast its self would have been prepared. Snorri tells us that the meat was boiled and this is confirmed by words for sacrifice such as Gothic *sauþs*, cognate to Old Norse *sjóða* and Old English *séoþan* "to seethe, boil."

2) Sprinkling or Blessing the Temple and Folk: The temple walls, altar, and folk were then sprinkled or blessed by the priests. This act is also mentioned in *Eyrbygja Saga* in the description of Thorolf Mostrarskeggy's hof. Vilhelm Grönbech in *Culture of the Teutons* felt that the blood of the sacrifice transferred some of the power of the Gods and Goddesses to the folk.

> The blood of the victim was a means of communicating the power of holiness. It was poured over the stone or heap of stones -*stallr* or *hörg* - in the sacred place. The chieftain's ring which reposed in the sanctuary was reddened on solemn occasions, and we learn in one place about two Icelandic claimants to the rank of priestly chieftain (*goði*), that they procured themselves the holy power by reddening their hands in the blood of a ram (Grönbech. *The Culture of the Teutons*, Vol.2, p.211)

Recalling what Turville-Petre had to say on this matter in the quote above about the blood symbolically joining the folk with the Gods and Goddesses, along with Grönbech's passage, it seems fairly certain that the purpose of the blessing was to convey upon the folk some of the power of the Gods and Goddesses. This power may have been thought to take the form of good health (i.e. holiness), prosperity, and frith; or perhaps just sheer luck (in the form of *hamingja*, an Old Norse term referring to luck and/or spiritual strength).

3) Hallowing the Horns or Goblets and Meat: The horns or goblets of mead and meat were then passed over the fire. It is not clear in Snorri's account whether this had ritual importance or not. In the *Landnámabók*, both Thorolf and Jorundr used fire in their land takings for temple sites, while other land takings not involving temples seem to omit this step. It is possible then that the passing of horns or goblets over the fires may have had a ritual connotation of some kind, the most likely being to hallow them. The chieftain then blessed the horns and we are told in one of the later

accounts in *Hákonar Saga góða* that "Earl Sigurd spoke some words over it, blessed it in Odin's name." It is also at this point that King Hakon signed the cross, and Sigurd covered for him by saying he was making the hammer sign.

We do not know what words Jarl Sigurd spoke over the horn. The lore is very sparing with such things and so we can only guess that perhaps it was something similar to the *Þórr uiki* formula found on some rune-stones. The phrase literally means "Thor make sacred." This may be somewhat confirmed by the way Jarl Sigurd covered for the king by saying he was making the hammer sign. Whether or not the hammer sign is authentic Heathen practice or not has been hotly debated in Heathen circles. Many feel it was merely Sigurd's way of covering for Hakon, and the Heathen jarls' unfamiliarity with what Hakon was doing confirms this. Others feel that the jarls perhaps knew what the hammer sign was, but realized Hakon was making the sign of the cross. It is interesting to note that the verb signaði is used to indicate Jarl Sigurd hallowed the horn or goblet. While the verb usually is taken to mean "bless" in Old Norse, it is ultimately related to English sain and sign, both meaning "to sign." Sigurd may therefore have made some sign symbolic of Odin in his blessing of the goblets. Unfortunately, we have no other examples in the lore to go by, and so, the modern Heathen is left to his or her own discretion as to using the hammer sign in blot. The closest example of the hallowing of a horn in the lore is in *Egil's Saga*. Egil scratched runes on a horn he suspected of containing poison, blooded them, and then spoke a verse. How similar this act of rune magic was to the blessing of horns in blot, we cannot say. What is clear though is that the mead, ale, or other drink was somehow blessed at this point in blot either by fire, with words, or with signs, or some combination thereof. The purpose of blessing or hallowing is no doubt to fill the mead or ale with the power of the Gods and Goddesses, and perhaps drive off any thing that might potentially cause illness.

4) The Fulls: The word full simply meant a drink or a drinking vessel in both Old Norse and Old English, but in the

sense of blot it is connected to the words said with that drink. The fulls as seen in this account by Snorri are to Odin for victory, Njord, and Frey for peace and plenty. There is no reason to think these were simple toasts, and indeed probably were not toasts at all, but prayers. We know from other accounts of sacrifices such as Thorkell's in Víga-Glúms Saga that these may have been petitions or prayers. That is, victory was not toasted in Odin's name, nor did the chieftain make a boast to achieve victory in Odin's name, but, that they asked or petitioned Odin for victory. Prayers such as those that survived in the "Æcer-bót" were not simple affairs, but could go on for twenty to thirty lines and were written in alliterative verse. The purpose of the fulls are no doubt several, and dependent on what type of blot is being performed. Nonetheless, they can probably be broken down into words of praise for the Gods or Goddesses, and petitions for help from the Gods or Goddesses. All variations a prayer or full could have taken would be of these two. Both Old Norse and Old English words for prayer are related to modern English bid. Old English *biddan* meant "to pray, entreat, ask," while Old Norse *biðja* carried similar connotations.

5) Bragafull: The bragafull has usually been taken by scholars to mean the "leader's cup" and appears variously in the lore as a toast to a dead leader, or as a boast by a leader to do some deed. In the *Ynglinga Saga*, of the *Heimskringla*, Ingjald boasted at his father's funeral feast to double the size of his kingdom. The bragafull served perhaps much the same purpose as the God fulls, in that perhaps the Gods and Goddesses were expected to help the leader fulfill whatever vow they made.

6)Minni: The *minni* was the remembrance cup, a toast to the memory of departed friends and family. Its purpose is clear when one recall passages from the "Hávamál" and Beowulf about a person's good name after death:

Cattle die, and kinsmen die, Thyself eke soon a wilt die; but fair fame will fade never: I ween, for him who wins it. (Hollander translation, verse 76)

> Grieve not, wise warrior. It is better to avenge one's friend than mourn too much. Each of us must one day reach the end Of worldly life, let him who can win glory before he dies: that lives on after him, when he lifeless lies. (Beowulf lines 1384-1391)

The *minni* was a way of keeping alive the glory of friends that had passed on. In addition, it perhaps was a way of worshipping one's ancestors, and seeking favour from them much as they did the Gods and Goddesses.

7) Feast: At this point the feast probably started. Going by accounts in the sagas, these feasts may have been elaborate affairs lasting for quite a while. The meat for sacrifice for blot was according to Snorri boiled in a broth. This is apparent from the accounts in the *Heimskringla*. Whether this was the only way of preparing the meat for sacrifice is not known, but it seems the preferred way for the Jarls of Norway under King Hakon.

From this we can reconstruct a rough outline of the blót ritual for modern usage:
1) The Blót: In ancient times, an animal would have been slaughtered. Today we just go to the supermarket. Still, there must have been rituals associated with slaying the animal. We are told in one saga, the boar was garlanded and lead to the king to have oaths sworn upon it. This shows the sacredness that took place before the slaughter, and probably during the food preparation. Therefore if preparing food for a feast, every item should probably be passed over a flame and have the hammer signed over it. A few words can be said like *"Thunor weoh"* which in reconstructed Old English means "Thor make this sacred." The food served for the feast should be garlanded and decorated as if for a lavish dinner party. Everything should point to the sacredness of the meal. If merely doing a libation with cheese or bread, much of this can be dispersed with. But nothing beats a feast together in creating community unity.

152

2) The Sith (optional) - The ancient Heathens seem to have enjoyed processions, complete with garlands or wreathes for the particular time of year. Garlands were hung on trees, and the hall decorated with fresh boughs and flowers. Therefore, the food when the food is brought out it should be done with much revelry and with as much decor as possible. The feast table should be decorated to fit the season, as well should the settings. All participants not serving the food, should be already seated. Plates should be set for the ancestors and the Gods as well. Once the food is set upon the table, the servers should take their places, and the weofodthegn can proceed with the ritual.

3) The Wéonde -*Wéonde* is an Anglo-Saxon reconstruction based on the Old Norse word *vigja* "to make sacred, to separate from the ordinary and mundane and make a part of the gods' realm." This corresponds to Edred Thorsson's "Hallowing" in the Blessing outline in *A Book Of Troth*. Its purpose is to make the site of the feast sacred and to ward it against unwanted intruders of the spiritual kind. It is here that the Hammer Rite of the Ring of Troth would be performed, or the *Wéonde Song* of the Englathod. In the Elder Era, this may have been unneedful as they had their own permanent holy sites that had been used for thousands of years. The purpose of the *wéonde* is to call on Gods like Þunor and ask them to separate the area from the ordinary, and the mundane. A formula in Old Norse used to accomplish this was *Þórr uiki* "Þunor make this sacred!" In Old English, this would be *"Þunor wéoh!"*

4) The Hallowing - The weofodthegn or the group leader then hallows the food and drink by passing it over a flame, usually a candle or fire in a fire pot or fire pit. Appropriate words like "Hallow this food and make it whole should be said."

5) The Blessing - As seen above, the blood of slain animals was sprinkled on the walls and altar in ancient times. Today, we instead of blood can use mead that has been specially

blessed for this purpose, blessing the folk as well. The mead is poured into the blót bowl, and then carried by one of the weofodthegn's assistants. The weofodthegn dips the twig into the mead and sprinkles each person there saying some words like "May the Gods bless you."

6) The Fulls - The bedes are then said to the Gods. It is perhaps best to dedicate the prayers to the Gods of the holy tide on hand, or if no holy tide is being celebrated to the Gods of those gathered. The bedes need not be elaborate, and it is best if they are no more than three in number. Too many prayers can make folks get impatient and restless and spoil the ritual atmosphere.

7) The Bragafull - Here the leader of the group can boast of the group's past accomplishments and future plans. Again, this need not be elaborate. It can be in poetic form or prose. In many respects it should resemble the boasts of symbel.

8) The Minni - The dead of all present are drunk to, preferably one at a time, although if too many are present a collective toast might be made. Ideally, one round should go around the table with each person being allowed to toast their dead ancestors. In large groups this may not be possible however, so a collective boast could be done by the weofodthegn.

9) The Housel - The food and drink are consumed. Usually for blots this may just be a morsel of bread and a drink of mead. Often only mead is used. With a housel, this would be the time the feast is consumed.

10) The Yielding - Some of the leftover food plus those plates laid aside for the Gods and ancestors can then be taken outside and given to them. By no means should it be thrown away or put in the garbage compactor.

11) The Leaving - The rite is formally adjourned, with folks retiring to general merriment, or a symbel could be arranged to follow. Experience has taught it is often best to allow a

period of relaxation after eating, and then conduct a symbel an hour or so after the meal is finished. Of course if a simple blót is done with no feast, then there is little reason to wait, and a symbel can be started immediately following the blót.

## Conclusion

Nearly all modern blot outlines have been drawn either directly or indirectly from the *Heimskringla* accounts. However, there are differences. As ancient Heathens probably nearly always used space that had been thought sacred for centuries, or spaces they had made permanently sacred, such a step as is commonly called Hallowing, or the misnomer Warding, was not a part of an ancient blot. When ancient Heathens needed to create sacred space, they did so for permanent usages such as the taking of future temple sites such as in the *Landnamabok*. Therefore, modern blot outlines have added the step of Hallowing with the intention of creating temporary sacred space. Another major difference between an ancient and modern blot is animals are no longer used, except in rare circumstances. Mead has therefore taken the place of meat as the preferred gift to the Gods and Goddesses. It is now used for the blessing, fulls, feast, and gift parts of blot. The modern blot outlines has remained in principle the same however, and therefore study of how ancient blots were performed is of help to the modern Heathen.

# Chapter XIV Symbel

## *Introduction*

No rite is preserved in the Elder Lore quite so well as *symbel* (also know by the Old Norse *sumble* and modern *sumbel*). It appears in the Sagas and *Eddas*, and even in such Christian sources as *Judith*. Even a ritual formula seems to have been preserved in the Anglo-Saxon phrase *sittan æt symble* (*sitia sumbli at* ON) "We sit at symbel (now)". Symbel probably ultimately derives from Indo-European libation rites, but it is very different from the libations of the ancient Greeks, Celts, and Romans. There is no "pouring out" of drinks to the Gods, all of the alcohol is consumed, by the symbel participants. And secondly, while there are toasts to the Gods, these seem almost a secondary aim of symbel. Paul Bauschatz, in his scholarly work *The Well and the Tree* holds that the purpose of symbel was to place one's self into the flow of Wyrd. This purpose is best shown by the gielps and béots or "boasts" of symbel. Symbel is best preserved in the Anglo-Saxon poem, *Béowulf*, mainly lines 489- 675 and 1491-1500. Although it is also seen in the *Heimskringla* in the form of a funeral ale held by King Svein when he boasted to take England, the *Fagrskinna* where it is mentioned memory drinks were made to Thor, and other sources.

The speech made at symbel revolved around deeds, past and present. In the first Béowulf symbel for example, Béowulf tells who his father is and states that in his youth he has undertaken many great deeds. This is a gielp, a boast of one's ancestry and past deeds. Béowulf then makes a sacred oath to slay the sea ettin terrorizing Héorot. This is his *béot*, a sacred oath to complete a specific action. Unferþ the þyle challenges this and Béowulf responds with a more detailed *gielp*, this one about his swimming contest with Brecca, a task similar to one at hand, in that it too, dealt with sea ettins. Between the *béot* and *gielp*, Unferþ makes a flytung "insult, derogatory remark" about Béowulf's ability, testing Béowulf's resolve, and his ability to keep his oath. Béowulf responds with a flytung of his own at Unferþ, questioning the þyle's integrity. Béowulf then reiterates his béot.

This entire ritual sequence seems to serve one purpose, and that is to call up the successful results of Béowulf's past actions so as to influence the present in the same direction. Results of actions of the present are based on the results of actions of the past according to Wyrd. In part this is why Béowulf's béot ends with *Gað a wyrd swá hío sceol* "always goeth Wyrd as she shall." The Elder Heathen's world view was based on deeds as was their concept of Wyrd and their philosophy of law. Results of deeds were based on the results of similar deeds in the past, unless enough mægen were invested to set a new precedent, a new standard of results for one's deeds.

*Béots* and *gielps* were not the only significant speech made at symbel. Symbel began with the same fulls as those at housel, and throughout symbel, there was entertainment in the form of scops "poets" telling poems based on the ancient tales, *gléoman* "minstrels" singing songs, and others throwing in their own little anecdotes. All of this was based on past action though, bringing the past into the present. The scop, according to scholar Dwight Conquergood, may have made the collective gielp for the entire þéod by telling of exploits of past kings and heroes. Even the *gléoman*, with his much lighter fare, probably sang of exploits of the past, though admittedly they would have been of a less serious nature (though they could have been *flytungs*, belittling enemies and such). The seriousness of the béots and gielps and the scop's *ealdgesagen* "old tales" can be shown in that they also occurred before battle, such as in those done prior to battle in "The Battle of Maldon."

The scop, þyle, and *gléoman*, all served a purpose in symbel, as did the *symbelgifa* "symbel giver, host" and the ale keeper or *ealu bora* "ale bearer." The scop's purpose, as already stated, was to say the *gielp* for the þéod, and to entertain the folk, perhaps reminding them of the seriousness of the boasts with his tales. The *gléoman*, on the other hand, was there to largely entertain, but no doubt being a minstrel and sometimes jester, he may have poked fun at the þéod's enemies, making unflattering gielps for them, and also making sure that happier, lighter deeds like courtship, play, and childishness were not left out.

The þyle seemed to have had a much more serious position, for it was his duty to challenge those he felt had made false boasts. This perhaps is why Unferþ challenged Béowulf, Béowulf's childhood having been unpromising. The *symbelgifa* too was a rather serious office, usually held by the residing king or lord. His place would be to serve as host, and make the béot for the þéod, and also to judge whether one's béot was serious and likely to be fulfilled. This would not be like a court judge saying yea or nay, but simply a refusal to lend his speed to the deed one oathed to do, and thus not endanger the tribe's *mægen*. Finally, the *ealu bora* was perhaps the most important position. The *ealu bora* was always a noble woman, often a queen, and it was her hand that poured the first drink thus sacralizing it in the ways of the Norns, *Waeliglcyrgien*, and *Idesa*; something, no werman could do. When doing so she might pay a compliment to those being served as a form of encouragement to do great deeds. She also probably served as the peacemaker when quarrels broke out, no one wishing to offend the likes and power of a queen. Noble women in the Elder Period were the most powerful of men. It was they that actually made many of the political decisions and ensured that the thews were kept. It was Guðrún that charged her sons with avenging their sister's death, and Latin sources make it clear that elderly women made many of the political decisions concerning the Germanic tribes. Many a warrior might offend a king, few sought to offend his king's queen. Within the Englathod there are three forms of symbel that are performed, these vary only in their outlines, the basic premise behind the three forms nonetheless are the same.

## Symbel

Most symbels follow the pattern, Eric Lord Wódening set forth in his article An Anglo-Saxon Symbel. This rite is usually referred to as symbel, and can be seen with only slight variation amongst Þéodsmen and Asatruar alike. His outline has only been slightly modified here, but follows the same general pattern:

1) Seating - Celebrants should be seated according to their rank and seniority in the mæþel, officers should be at the symbelgifa's table, and the symbelgifa in the high seat. In many cases this seating is discarded with, and nearly always is amongst Asatruar.

2) The Wéonde -*Wéonde is an Anglo-Saxon reconstruction based on the Old Norse word *vigja* "to make sacred, to separate from the ordinary and mundane and make a part of the gods' realm" This corresponds to Edred Thorsson's "Hallowing" in the Blessing outline in *A Book Of Troth*. Its purpose is to make the site of the feast sacred, and to ward it against unwanted intruders of the spiritual kind. With symbel this is largely optional. Ideally, if the mood for symbel is right, time and space should lapse as celebrants enter the flow of Wyrd's Well. Few wights would be willing to violate such, or the *frið* that even Loki would not break.

3) Forespeech - This is a speech made by the *symbelgifa* or host of the symbel to sit everyone down to symbel. It should be simple, but eloquent, and its only purpose is to get people ready. Wednesbury þéod, used to use a paraphrase of lines 489-490 in Béowulf.

> Sit now to symbel and unseal thy mettes
> Siges rethe say as they soul whets.

4) Pouring - The *ealu bora* or horn bearer pours the ale for each symbler in turn as they make their boasts. First is the *symbelgifa* as he or she must make the fulls. With each celebrant the *ealu bora should* say something favourable, preferably in alliterative verse.

5) The Fulls - The *symbelgifa* wassails the three most popular gods of the mæðel, followed by a wassailing of the mæðel's *mægen*, and finally the bregofull, a boast of the mæðel's plans. Alternatively, the host can merely hail their own god or goddess and every participant can boast a god or

159

goddess of their choice.

6) The Minni - Each celebrant speaks of and drinks to their dead kinsmen and friends.

7) Gift giving (optional) - Gifts can then be exchanged, beginning with the *symbelgifa*. Gifts to the kindred are given to him first, followed by gifts to him personally. Then each person is given a gift according to their station and rank.

8) Gielps and Béots - Each celebrant, according to rank and station within the kindred, or according to honour amongst guests may make a *gielp* and or *béot*. They may also wish to tell jokes, lead a song, or recite a poem. From here on, symbel usually takes a life of its own. It is not unusual, at least in the Englathod, for symbels to run well over their allotted times, and for even non-drinkers to feel an other worldliness. It must be stressed here though, a gielp is not a simple boast or the false bragging of Shakespeare's Falstaff, it is a truthful recitation of one's past accomplishments that did something good for one's self or the folk, preceded by a statement of whose one's forebearers were. Similarly, a *béot* is not a simple promise, but a holy oath enforced by Wyrd with the most powerful of obligations to complete. Even the gods participate in symbel and they are held to their words by Wyrd just as we are. If the gods cannot escape Wyrd with false oaths or idle boasts, then how can we? It is best to be truthful in such matters.

Once a boast is made, the þyle may challenge it if he sees due cause and the symbelgifa may wish to lend his speed to the deed to help the celebrant if it is a great deed that benefits everyone. If the þyle challenges, the celebrant may respond with another gielp, and reiteration of the béot, and this may continue until both are satisfied with having made their points, or the *ealu bora* or *symbelgifa* intervene. The *symbelgifa* can then lend his speed, say it is a good *béot*, or simply but tactfully say that the deed may not be successful. Whatever is said must be carefully worded so as to not affect the celebrant's *mægen* if he is being truthful.

160

The béots and gielps continue in rounds until all has been said that can be said or the "officers" (the scop, *symbelgifa*, þyle, and *ealu bora*) deem it should end. At that time the *symbelgifa* should say a suitable endspeech and close the rite.

## High Symbel

High Symbel is only preformed by Þéodsmen for the most part, and rarely seen in the general Heathen community. It is intended only to be performed by those of high arung, i.e. a leader of the folk. The rite presented below is a consolidation of research done by Eric Wódening in his article *An Anglo-Saxon Symbel*, Steve Pollington in his academic work *The Mead-Hall*, and Paul Bauchatz's academic work *The Well and the Tree*. The only major difference between High Symbel and Symbel is in the opening rounds. Otherwise, everything that applies to Symbel applies to High Symbel. The outline for these opening rounds is drawn from Pollington's work, *The Mead-Hall* pages 42 to 47 with additional elements added from Eric Wódening's outline seen in *An Anglo-Saxon Symbel*.

1) Summoning - The guests are summoned to the hall by a horn. Pollington notes that on the Bayeux Tapestry, a horn blower is shown.

2) Entrance of Guests into the Hall - The guests enter and wash their hands. Pollington points to a verse from the "Hávamal", "Water and handcloth and friendly word, a chance to speak, guest friendship will he gladly find, kindness and attention" (Pollington, p. 42).

3) Seating - The symbelgifa as in regular symbel seats each person according to arung. The symbelgifa then takes the position before the high seat.

4) Symbelgifa Forespeach -The symbelgifa opens symbel with words similar to those from Béowulf lines 489-490: "*Sitaþ nu to symle ond onsælaþ meoto, sigehreð secgum,*

*swa þin sefas hwettaþ* (Sit now to symbel and unwind your measures, victory hearted heroes)," and then sits down. If folks are not already seated they should do so at this point.

5) Ealubora Forespeach - The *Ealubora* then enters with the horn and mead. She greets all present, and then presents the symbelgifa with the horn. According to Pollington, Enright, and others this may have involved a ritual formula much like Wealtheow's words in Béowulf lines 1169-1175:

> *"Onfoh þissum fulle, freodrihten min, sinces brytta!*
> *þu on sælum wes, goldwine gumena, ond to Geatum*
> *spræc mildum wordum...*
>
> Take this full, my lord dryhten, hoard sharer, you be happy, warriors' gold friend, and speak to the Geats with mild words..."

6) Bregofull - The symbelgifa then performs the boasts to the three gods and goddesses worshipped by his or her household, followed by a minni to the ancestors, and finally, the bregofull, a boast of what his or her folk will do in the coming year.

7) Guest Speech - If there is a guest of arung close to the *symbelgifa*, they are then given the right of guest speech. The *ealubora* will take the horn to them, and they will greet the *symbelgifa*, and make a béot (which may be a boast to help the *symbelgifa* or his or her own folk in some way, a *minni* in praise of the gods, or simply a toast of some sort). The þyle may of course challenge (as they may anyone save the *ealubora* and *symbelgifa*).

8) The First Full - The ealubora then takes the horn to each person by arung. They may make a béot, boast to the Gods, or ancestors. The *ealubora* then takes their seat, and the task of carrying the horn about is taken over by others.

9) Gift giving (optional) - The *symbelgifa* may then give gifts to those present. Theoretically this can be done at anytime

during symbel however

10) Léoð (optional) - The Scop may then sing a song, either in praise of the gods, the folk, or the *symbelgifa*.

    11) The Fulls - From here on High Symbel follows the same pattern as Symbel does with the ritual rounds. People may make a gielp and béot, sing a song, toast someone, recite poetry, even tell jokes. The þyle, of course, can challenge any boast. The *ealubora* may also decide to pour mead for anyone at any time along with flattering speech.


# Gebeorscipe

    *Gebeorscipe* is the term that the scholar Pollington uses to refer to other forms of drinking rounds seen in the lore. They are, what in modern Heathenry would be called an "impromptu symbel;" the sort that happen around a camp fire when one Heathen says to another, "Hey lets symbel." As such, it will have many of the same elements of symbel such as boasts, the rounds, gielps and béots. However, it is likely to be very less formal. As such there are no hard and fast rules for *Gebeorscipe,* the only one perhaps being that it goes in rounds, and there perhaps be initial boasts to the gods and ancestors. This may be the most common form of symbel in modern Heathenry due to its simplicity.

## The Roles in Symbel

Symbelgefa - The *symbelgefa* is the host or hostess of the symbel. This may be the owner of the house it is held at, or the leader of the group hosting the symbel (in the case of a þeodisc group, their hláford or hláfidge). It is the *symbelgefa* who has final approval on boasts if the þyle challenges, and also sees that the frith of the hall is maintained (though this is primarily the role of the ealubora).

Ealubora - The "ale bearer" is usually going to be a woman. This is not some sort of sexism, but based in ideas held by the ancient Heathens about the sanctity and high status of women. In ancient times, it would have been the lady of the hall. Her purpose was to maintain the frith of the hall, however she saw possible. Enright in *Lady with a Mead Cup* theorized that in many cases, she may have even used her abilities as a seeress in judging boasts. As such she may have been the antithesis of the þyle, but instead of ridiculing those that made bad boasts, she flattered those that made good ones. She also served to advise her husband and others as the symbel went on. In ancient times, much business was conducted during symbel, and with her words, she could ensure the best for her tribe. In essence, she was a lady of decorum, regal in bearing, and wise in words. In addition to this, Bauschatz in *The Well and the Tree*, felt that because Wyrd was seen as feminine (as were the Norns in the *Eddas*), that perhaps the mead had to pass through a female's hands to make the sacred connection to Wyrd. If that is the case, the ealubora may be the most vital of all positions in symbel. Many in Modern Heathenry have continued this tradition by at least having a woman pour the mead into the horn, even though a werman may bear it about. The *ealubora* therefore should be the highest ranking woman of a group.

Þyle - In ancient times, a þyle was a sort of wiseman, ritual poet, orator, and judger of men's words. In symbel, the þyle serves one purpose, to challenge boasts he or she deems false, and thus antagonize the boaster into being truthful. The þyle only uses blunt honesty to accomplish this, but they can be, as Unferth was in Béowulf, brutal with words. Enright saw the þyle as a balance to the *ealubora*, one chiding, the other flattering. There is no reason a þyle should be much different today in their duties.

Scop - In ancient times a scop would tell the old tales of the tribe's ancestors, heroes, and gods and goddesses. As such they played a role in making the link to Wyrd in a very important way. Today, modern poets can do the same in symbel.

Gléoman - The *gléoman* was not much different than the scop, save they would not have been likely to hold an official position. *Gléomen* were musicians and sang songs, played the harp and pipes to entertain folks during the symbel. The same, of course, can be done by musicians today.

Byrele
- The *byrele* was the cupbearer, a position which was usually filled by a female (esp. since they would be assisting the lady of the hall), but often filled by young males (in the same sort of role of pages in the Middle Ages) in ancient times. Today, a *byrele* would be any cup bearer other than the official *ealubora*.

Duruþegn - In ancient times, the duruþegn's duty was to guard the door, welcome guests as they enter, and not permit the unwanted to enter. The same role can be used today, and indeed, is helpful in keeping a rite from being interrupted.

## A Few Rules For Symbel
Symbel is a sacred rite, and it therefore should not be abused While it is a solemn occasion, it is solemn in the sense of a funeral for your dog that always bit you. Therefore, it should be filled with a good share of laughter and happiness and even rowdiness. However, rudeness should not be allowed, or drunkenness. A few simple rules for symbel are as follows:
1) The frið of a symbel is sacred, no one should be allowed to break the peace or commit violent acts in the symbel hall. Violators should be immediately removed, no questions asked, physically if necessary.
2) Celebrants should not get dead drunk. Symbel should have its share of drinking, but it is not a "beer bust," a wild party (though at times symbel may seem that way), or a place to suicide via alcohol poisoning. And NO ONE, absolutely NO ONE should be allowed to drive home drunk. If you feel you've had too much, make small sips of the ale instead of larger ones, extending your drinking time. If all else fails, stop making béots and gielps, and simply yell "wassail!" to others' boasts. And then find a place to sleep at

165

the site or someone sober to drive.

3) If, in a state of drunken zealousness you make a boast the *symbelgifa* or þyle feels you cannot keep, try to prove them wrong and do what you oathed to do. DO NOT hold a grudge against someone for doing their religious duty in symbel, even if they allowed personal prejudice to affect their judgment. In such a case, by your behaving honourably, it is their honour that is lessened not your own, and they are not likely to challenge you again in symbel. Too, remember that a symbel's frith is rigidly enforced. Open debate is welcome, and even pointing out flaws in someone's honor with insults, but half truths, flat out mockery of honourable actions, and lies are not. And few true Heathen would have a problem with someone expounding such being asked to go outside, as Þunor did Loki in the "Lokasenna."

4) Do not make passes at married ale bearers or the spouse of another. Causal flirting is okay, but it might be good to keep this line of the *"Hávamal"* in mind: "Be especially wary of ale and of another man's wife." This goes for ladies too. Alcohol and anything beyond flattery can bring on jealousy and a fight.


**Conclusion**

Symbel along with the housel is one of our most sacred rites and should be done often. A few conventions concerning symbel might be mentioned. The greatest of symbels is at Yule tide, when the dead are closest, and we are more in touch with our past. Some kindreds hold several symbels throughout that holy tide. As for the ale, a keg of beer is always good to have on hand, as are non-alcoholic drinks for non-drinkers (preferably juices high in vitamin C). The fulls however should be made with homemade mead or beer properly hallowed, and most kindreds prefer to exhaust their home made supply before touching anything from a brewery. Symbel can be done with any type of alcohol, though mead is preferred by many and it seems to have been preferred in the Elder Period as well. Theoretically though, even mixed drinks or plain water could be used.

For non-drinkers, something high in vitamin C like orange juice seems to work best. A vitamin C high can, like alcohol help one achieve an altered state to go into the flow of Wyrd more easily. Also, it is best if a great horn is used for the fulls and boasts while each celebrant has their own horn for wassailing a well done boast or performance of a song by the scop, gléoman, or other celebrant. And finally, if you have no boasts to make at symbel, tell a joke, sing a song, or entertain the crowd while others are contemplating what to say. If you have the skill to do so, the poetry of the Elder Tongues is quite beautiful, and never fails to impress, and gives you the advantage of adding to the tribe's boasts.

# Chapter XV Rites of Life

Rites of life are rites of passage through life. The ancient Heathens marked such times as birth, naming, marriage, and death with rituals. Many of these are unfortunately forever lost, or can no longer be performed as they once were. Nonetheless, many of them were documented in the Icelandic sagas and other sources, and therefore can be reliably reconstructed.

## *Ceremonies of Birth*

Not much information survives on birth rituals. Going by Germanic folklore, the father was definitely expected to be present at the birth of a child, and to provide the mother moral support and help ease the pain during the birth its self. This is seen especially in the Scandinavian countries. An old German practice that has been preserved was for the midwife to lay the newborn after birth, on the floor or ground, where upon the father picked it up. This seems to have meant that the father claimed the child and it was not to be exposed. In the Norse areas this seems sometimes to have been incorporated into the naming rite, and done on the ninth day.

Within the lore its self, most birth rites deal with the goddesses and Idesa (Disir). "Sigrdrífumál" verse 9 advises:

> "Biarg-(help-) runes thou must know, if thou wilt help, and loose the child from women. In the palm they must be graven, and round the joints be clasped, and the Dísir prayed for aid. (Thorpe Translation)"

And in "Óddrúnargrátr" verses 7 and 8 we are advised:

> "Then speech the woman so weak began, Nor said she aught ere this she spake: "So may the holy ones thee help, Frigga and Freyja and favouring gods, As thou hast saved me from sorrow now." (Bellows translation).

168

Modern Heathens therefore should be ready to pray to Fríge (Frigga) and Fréo (Freya) during the birth, and invoke the Idesa (Disir) prior to it as well.

## Name Giving

After the birth, the primary activity of an infant's early life took place on the ninth day after the child was born. This was the day the child was formally named and brought into the family. The *Vatni Ausa* is well preserved in the sagas, and may well be the most mentioned Heathen rite in the lore.

> Mærin var vatni ausin og þetta nafn gefið. Hún óx þar upp og gerðist lík móður sinni að yfirlitum. Þau sömdust vel við Glúmur og Hallgerður og fór svo fram um hríð.

> So the maiden was sprinkled with water, and had this name given her, and there she grew up, and got like her mother in looks and feature. Glum and Hallgerda agreed well together, and so it went on for a while. (Njal's Saga Chapter 14, DaSent translation)

> Þórsteinn þorskabítur átti son er kallaður var Börkr digri. En sumar það er Þórsteinn var hálfþrítugur fæddi Þóra sveinbarn og var Grímur nefndur er vatni var ausinn. Þann svein gaf Þórsteinn Þór og kvað vera skyldu hofgoða og kallar hann Þórgrím.

> Thorstein Codbiter had a son who was called Bork the Thick. But on a summer when Thorstein was five-and-twenty winters old, Thora bore him a man-child who was called Grim, and sprinkled with water. That lad Thorstein gave to Thor, and said that he should be a Temple-Priest, and called him Thorgrim. (Eyrbyggja Saga, Chapter 11, Morris and Magnusson translation)

> Þóra ól barn um sumarið, og var það mær; var hún vatni ausin og nafn gefið og hét Ásgerðr.

Thora bare a child in the summer; it was a girl. She was sprinkled with water, and named Asgerdr. (Egils Saga Skallagrímssonar, chapter 35, Green translation)

By comparing the many different accounts of the Vatni Ausa, Edred Thorsson reconstructed the naming rite in an article in the compilation work *Green Runa* as follows:

"Ek verp vatni þetta barn a, ok gef honum nafnit _____(name) (eptir afa/ommu sinum/sinni.)"

The English translation: "I throw water on this child and give it the name _____ (after its grandfather/grandmother) (or some other ancestor).

One can do an Old English translation of this. For a boy this would be as:
Ic weorpe wæter on bearne, ond giefe hine naman _____ (æftre his Ealdfæder). or for a girl: Ic weorpe wæter on bearne, ond giefe hí naman _____ (æftre híre Ealdmodor).
One would of course want a longer ritual than this though, so it is suggested one add a *blót* and perhaps a symbel to the naming ceremony, not to mention flesh out the naming rite its self. An outline for such a ritual might go as follows. Items needed for the naming rite its self are a blót bowl, and some water:

**The Naming**
1) The Opening: The folk are called to stand around the altar, the mother holds the child.

2) The Naming: The mother hands the father the newborn, and then picks up the blót bowl filled with water. The father then dips his fingers in the water, and says the following for a boy: Ic weorpe wæter on bearne, ond giefe hine naman (name). Or for a girl: Ic weorpe wæter on bearne, ond giefe hí

naman (name). He then sprinkles the water on the baby's forehead. 3) The Closing: The father then hands the mother the baby, and invites all to take part in the húsel to follow.

## Baby's First Blót or Baby's First Húsel

The goddess Fríge should be invoked for the baby's first *blót* as she is the guardian of the newborn. Also invoked should be the ancestors especially the Idesa (Dísir). For a basic *blót* outline see Chapter IV. The first to be blessed during the blessing part of the *blót* should be the baby. Immediately, following the *blót*, all should be seated to feast. By now, baby should be ready to nurse, although he or she may need to go to sleep. If the babe needs to sleep, that is fine. He or she would not be the first to sleep through a feast in their honour!

## Baby's First Symbel

Following the feast should be a short symbel in the baby's honour. The rounds would begin with the traditional first three, but the fourth round would be toasts to baby, or lullabies in the baby's honour. Following the fourth round, would be gifts to the baby. After the fourth round, the symbel may precede as usual (see Chapter XV).

A baby's naming rite is its first public ritual and therefore should be conducted with much joy and honour. It could well set the tone for the rest of the baby's life.

## *Oath Brotherhood or Sisterhood*

Oath brotherhood also called blood brotherhood or in Old Norse, *fóstbrœðralag* (though this term could also refer to the fostering of a child and not oath brothers) is not seen in the Anglo-Saxon lore. That is not to say it did not form a part of the Heathen religion. After the conversion of the Scandinavian countries, it disappeared there as well. The ritual is preserved in *Gisli's Saga*, and is quoted below:

> Þeir skildu þar fjórir undir ganga, Þorgrímr, Gísli, Þorkell ok Vésteinn; ok nú vekja þeir sér blóð ok láta renna saman dreyra sinn í þeiri moldu, er upp var

skorin undan jarðarmeininu, ok hræra saman moldina ok blóðit; enn siðan fellu þeir allir á kné, ok sverja þann eið, at hverr skal annars hefna sem bróður síns, ok nefna öll goðin í vitni

The four then went under the spear, Þorgrímr, Gísli, Þorkell and Vésteinn; and now they draw their blood and let drain together in the earth, which had been cut open under the strip of earth, and mixed together the earth and the blood; then they all fell to their knees, and swore that oath, that each shall avenge like a brother, and named all the gods as witnesses.

Similar rites are described in the Fostbrædra Saga, Fornrnanna Sögur, and Egils saga einhenda og Asmundar saga berserkjabana (Egil and Asmund's Saga).

## *Wedding*

### **The Proposal in Ancient Times**

There is no surviving manuscript that details an Anglo-Saxon wedding, we can only assume that through references in the Anglo-Saxon lore, it must have resembled the Icelandic ceremony in many respects. By borrowing elements from the Icelandic sagas, and incorporating many elements from medieval, and even modern weddings that may be Heathen in origin can reconstruct a reliable wedding ritual. The following ritual outline is drawn in part from an article by Gunnora on Viking weddings, an unpublished article by Eric Lord Wednesbury of the Winland Rice of Theodish Belief on Anglo-Saxon weddings, and two articles byWinifred Hodge on weddings within Ásatrú and Heathenry.

Marriage amongst the ancient Heathens was an important institution. It meant a financially stable environment in which children could be raised. And it essentially was thought of as a contract between two families. Many prenuptial rites were done to ensure that the future wife and any children the marriage produced were cared for. Even the vastly romantic Anglo-Saxon poem "A Husband's Message" refers to the fact he can now provide for her. Thus marriages were negotiated by all the parties involved, the bride's parents and siblings as well as the bridegrooom's friends and family. A werman wishing to have a woman in marriage would approach her family with prestigious friends to negotiate for her hand. If an agreement was struck, these friends served to witness *on hana sellan*, the handshake that sealed the agreement that the couple should wed. At this time the morning gift was agreed upon as well as the *handgeld*, and other specifics. The prospective bridegroom had to come up with the *brýdcéap* paid to her family to completely seal the pledge to marry. The *brýdcéap* also called the *mund* or *handgeld* was to prove the groom could support his future wife and any children they had. However, it also had many and varied spiritual connotations. The concept of *mund*, which is very similar to ideas about frith appears in common association with weddings in ancient Heathen belief. *Mund* meant not only the *handgeld*, but also could refer to "protection." This not only meant physical protection, but also spiritual protection as well. The *handgeld* carried the mægen or in Old Norse, *hamingja* of the groom, and its intent was to reimburse the bride's family for the loss of the *mægen* or spiritual luck the bride carried within her.

Women were seen as very powerful carriers of the family *mægen*, and more intimately connected to the kinfetch as well as the ideas (the female ancestral spirits) of the clan than wermen. They served as head of the household, and did many of the chores that ensured the community would survive. Therefore when they left to marry, the family suffered a great loss. To a lesser degree, the *handgeld* was to reimburse the family for the loss of labour, but in no way should it be seen as purchasing a bride. Instead it was an attempt to equalize gift for gift. This gift for a gift scenario is seen throughout the ancient marriage process, and was a way of exchanging *mægen* between the couple and their families. It was in essence, fusing members of the two clans into one family. The exchange process continued from the start of the proposal throughout the wedding ceremony. In various Heathen areas such customs existed as exchanging rings, swords for keys, drinking mead together, or eating cake together. Such customs are very old and dated at least to the time of Tacitus' writing of *Germania*. In it he says that brides were obtained by payment of a dowry by the groom in the form of sword and shield, cattle, and a bridled horse. On the morning after the wedding, the groom also had to give his bride a morning gift, the *morgengifu*. This was hers to keep and use the entirety of her life. Finally, in addition to the groom paying the handgeld and *morgengifu*, the bride's family had to pay the *brýdgifu*. This was the bride's dowry, forever hers, and untouchable by her husband. It was to ensure, in the event of the husband's death or a divorce, that the bride and any children she had would be cared for.

The following ritual is broken into three parts. The first is the agreement on the handgeld, morgengifu, and *brýdgifu*. This is to be performed before the wedding, at the beginning of the "engagement." Since modern views on marriage differ a great deal from those of ancient times, the negotiation is likely to be between the bride and groom and not necessarily their families. The second part is the wedding ceremony its self, and finally there is the *brýdeala* or "bride ale," the "wedding feast" or *húsel*.

1)The Handsel or Handfæstung  After the proposal had been accepted, ancient Anglo-Saxons negotiated the *handgeld, morgengifu, and brýdgifu*. These negotiations were called the *handsel* in Old Norse, *handfaestung* in Old English (as the hands were shook to bind the agreement). These negotiations included setting the amount of the bride price or in Old English *brýdcéop*. In Old Norse, this consisted of two payments from the groom and his family the *mundr* and *morgengifu* in Old Norse, or *handgeld* and *morgengifu* in Old English. The bride and her family would provide a dowry called *heiman fylgia* in Old Norse (Gunnora, *Courtship, Love and Marriage in Viking Scandinavia*), the *wituma* or *brýdgifu* in Old English. The *handgeld* was a payment to

174

ensure the bride's protection by her family, and that no other suitors were promised her hand. In addition, it proved the groom's ability as a provider. It was to be paid at the time of the agreement. The *morgengifu* was to be paid the morning after the wedding. The dowry or *wituma* was a sizable payment by the bride's family. However, it remained the bride's, and not considered part of the communal property of the couple. It was to remain in case of the husband's death, divorce, or disability. Once all was agreed upon, the two parties would shake hands in front of witnesses.

The *handfæstung* or "hand fasting" can be done by modern Heathens in fun with the exchange of engagement rings or other gifts symbolic of their love and the *mægen* being exchanged. Once all is agreed upon, they can conclude the negotiations with the following words spoken by the bridegroom (adapted from one done in Iceland) and a hand shake with witnesses present:

"We declare ourselves witnesses that thou, (bride's name), bondest me in lawful betrothal, and that with a handshake thou pledge me marriage in exchange for the handgeld and morgengifu promised, and engagest me to fulfil and observe the whole of the oath between us, which has been said in hearing of witnesses without wiles or cunning, as a true and honest oath."

Following this the date of the wedding could be set. Fridays seem to have been a favoured day in Scandinavia and in England as well. Folklore has long dictated June as the best month for weddings with May being counted one of the worst. Many superstitions surround the sitting of the date.

2)The Wedding Ceremony
Items Needed: The wedding rings The groom's ancestral sword A new sword to be given from bride to groom A sauna or sweet lodge The bridegroom's house keys

Prior to the wedding the bride should go to the stánbaþ (a sauna or sweet lodge), if one is available, attended by her bride's maids. This was a step perhaps in ritual purification for the wedding ceremony. There she sweats and then bathes. Her and her attendants would then dress her in her wedding gown and crown her head with the wedding wreathe or bridal crown. This whole time she should not be seen by the groom. The groom too attends to the act of purification, going to the stánbaþ, and bathing. Once done with bathing, he dresses in his wedding attire and straps on his ancestral blade.

a) The Wedding Trip
The bride with her attendants goes to the site of the wedding at the appointed time. She is preceded by a young kinsman bearing the new sword to be given to the groom. The groom likewise, bearing his ancestral blade is accompanied by the groomsmen to the site. The families also come together at a preassigned spot. They then form a procession to where the wedding will take place.

b) Hallowing the Site
The wéofodþegn or priest hallows the site and opens the ceremony with a few words, and confirms that the two have gathered to take oaths to be werman and wife.

c) Exchange of Handgeld and Brýdgifu
The handgeld and brýdgifu are then exchanged. This may be done with the following words:
Wéofodþegn to groom: "Do you have the handgeld as you oathed to have?"
Groom: "Yes"
Groom to father of bride:
"I give you this, the handgeld as I oathed to do."
A few words may be added describing the handgeld.
Wéofodþegn to father of the bride: "Do you have the brýdgifu as you oathed to have?" Father of the bride: "Yes." The father of the bride then gives her the brýdgifu with these words: "I give you this brýdgifu to have and hold all of your days."
Wéofodþegn:
The brýdgifu and handgeld have been gifted and given. The holy oaths have thus been held. Now let the bridegroom and bride wed."

176

d) The Exchange of Swords
The groom gives the ancestral sword to the bride with some
words that it is to be held in trust for their first born when of
age. The bride then gives the groom a new blade, so that he
never be unarmed and be able to defend the family.

e) The Exchange of Rings, Oaths, and gift of the House Keys
        The couple should then exchange vows and rings.
These oaths are best written by the couple and should
involve any premarital agreements that were made. Both
oaths should, but need not, have to invoke the goddess Wær
(Vár) as keeper of oaths. Both the groom's oath and the
bride's should end with something like "With this ring, I thee
wed," with the placement of the ring upon the other's
wedding finger. The bride's ring may be offered her on the
hilt of the new sword symbolizing the groom's trust in her.
Finally, the groom's house keys are given to her, as she
becomes the new head of his household.

f) The Pronouncement The wéofodþegn witnessing the vows
then pronounces the couple werman and wife and states
whatever else may be needed to meet with the laws of the
state or country the wedding is being performed in.

3) The Brýdeala Ideally the *brýdeala*, or "bride ale," the
marriage feast should take place immediately after the
pronouncement with no apparent break in the ceremony.
However if this is not possible, it is permissible to break the
wedding and *brýdeala* into separate ceremonies. Regardless,
all should be seated at the start of the rite. A *brýdeala* is little
different from a standard blót. The following is an adaptation
of the standard Englathod *húsel* outline for the purpose of a
wedding:

        Items Needed: A "Loving Cup," a bowl of kasa (ON)
with handles Feast gear Blót bowl Blót tine

a) Hallowing of the Bride-The wéofodþegn hallows the bride
by laying the hammer in her lap, and says something like
"Þunor bless the bride, hallowed by hammer in sacred hall."

The wéofodþegn then helps the bride to her feet, and proceeds with the *blót*.

b) The Hallowing-The bride takes the blót bowl, and the "loving cup" and fills them with mead. The wéofodþegn then passes the drink and food over a flame, and sains the hammer over them. He or she may wish to say something like "wassail this food!" The flame and the words are intended to ensure the food and rink brings health by driving away illness causing wights.

c) The Blessing-The bride blesses the groom and the groom her. The bride then assists the wéofodþegn in sprinkling the gathered folks by carrying the blót bowl around as he or she blesses the folk.

d) The Fulls-The bride and groom use the loving cup to make their toasts to the Gods. Fríge and Fréo are the most important to toast as they are the goddesses to ensure a good marriage. When their toasts are made, both drink from the loving cup at once. If not, the other holds the cup as the other drinks.

e) The Housel-The food and drink are then consumed by all gathered. Following the feast, one may hold *symbel* or dancing or any number of activities. Eventually, however, the *brýdhlóp* should take place. This was the journey to the new home. In ancient times, this was a race by the separate parties to the new home. The party that lost had to serve the other at the next feast. Regardless of who gets there first, the groom blocks the door, and then carries or leads the bride over the threshold.

 The month following the wedding was called the *hunigmonaþour* or "honeymoon." For the next month, the couple should drink mead daily. The next morning, the groom should present the bride with the *morgengifu*. Under Icelandic law, where marriages were often arranged for reasons other than love, witnesses to the consumption of the wedding were required. However, this does not appear in Anglo-Saxon law codes, where most married for love. In today's law, even those of an Icelandic Heathen bent should probably waive this requirement.

## *Funeral*

Modern Ásatrú and Heathenry in general seem to have no set way of performing funerals. Yet the funeral rite is one of the best preserved in the lore. In the *Eddas*, we are treated to Balder's funeral, Béowulf contains three funerals alone, and then there is Ibn Fadlan's account of a Rus funeral. Most of the funeral rites preserved are cremations, of these, three are ship cremations in, or on the edge of water. This seems in contrast with the archaeological record which shows mounds were often built away from water, and that inhumation as well as cremation was practised. For Anglo-Saxon Heathens, reconstructing a funeral rite based on ancient principles is fairly easy. We need look no farther than the funeral of Béowulf:

> Then the bairn of Weohstan bade command, hardy chief, to heroes many that owned their homesteads, hither to bring firewood from far -- o'er the folk they ruled --for the famed-one's funeral. " Fire shall devour and wan flames feed on the fearless warrior who oft stood stout in the iron-shower, when, sped from the string, a storm of arrows shot o'er the shield-wall: the shaft held firm, featly feathered, followed the barb." And now the sage young son of Weohstan seven chose of the chieftain's thanes, the best he found that band within, and went with these warriors, one of eight, under hostile roof. In hand one bore a lighted torch and led the way. No lots they cast for keeping the hoard when once the warriors saw it in hall, altogether without a guardian, lying there lost. And little they mourned when they had hastily haled it out, dear-bought treasure! The dragon they cast, the worm, o'er the wall for the wave to take, and surges swallowed that shepherd of gems. Then the woven gold on a wain

was laden --countless quite! -- and the king was borne, hoary hero, to Hrones-Ness. THEN fashioned for him the folk of Geats firm on the earth a funeral-pile, and hung it with helmets and harness of war and breastplates bright, as the boon he asked; and they laid amid it the mighty chieftain, heroes mourning their master dear. Then on the hill that hugest of balefires the warriors wakened. Wood-smoke rose black over blaze, and blent was the roar of flame with weeping (the wind was still), till the fire had broken the frame of bones, hot at the heart. In heavy mood their misery moaned they, their master's death. Wailing her woe, the widow [footnote 1] old, her hair upbound, for Béowulf's death sung in her sorrow, and said full oft she dreaded the doleful days to come, deaths now, and doom of battle, and shame. -- The smoke by the sky was devoured. The folk of the Weders fashioned there on the headland a barrow broad and high, by ocean-farers far descried: in ten days' time their toil had raised it, the battle-brave's beacon. Round brands of the pyre a wall they built, the worthiest ever that wit could prompt in their wisest men. They placed in the barrow that precious booty, the rounds and the rings they had reft erewhile, hardy heroes, from hoard in cave, -- trusting the ground with treasure of earls, gold in the earth, where ever it lies useless to men as of yore it was. Then about that barrow the battle-keen rode, atheling-born, a band of twelve, lament to make, to mourn their king, chant their dirge, and their chieftain honour. They praised his earlship, his acts of prowess worthily witnessed: and well it is that men their master-friend mightily laud, heartily love, when hence he goes from life in the body forlorn away. Frances B. Grummere translation)

While Béowulf's funeral consisted of a cremation with the building of a mound, there is no reason we cannot use some elements of it for a modern funeral, be it cremation or inhumation. Ibn Fadlan's account of the Rus shows a slightly different outline, most of the elements being of a sort we cannot use. However, only the Béowulf account really needs concern Anglo-Saxon Heathens. The parts that can be easily used should be clear. Wiglaf spoke some words, Béowulf's men placed the grave goods on the pyre with the body, Béowulf's queen sang a dirge. Then once the mound was built 12 warriors circled the mound on horse back singing songs of praise for Béowulf. This can be broken down into an outline usable for a modern funeral: 1) A eulogy. 2) Placement of grave goods. 3) A dirge sang by a female relative. 3) The burial of the body or ashes or spreading of ashes. 4) Songs of praise for the deceased done by 12 people circling the grave. This would have all been preceded in probability, by a wake where the relatives would sit with the body as was the custom to do until recent years even in the USA and most of Northern Europe. We also know from the Icelandic sagas, and Anglo-Saxon sources that a funeral feast would have followed, although it may occur months after the funeral. The *Laxdaela Saga*, portrays the funeral feast of Hoskuld as a rather lavish affair, several months after the funeral.

This feast was referred to as *erfi* or *minni* in Old Norse, the *ierfe húsel* or *\*ierfealu* (a reconstruction based on Old Norse *arvöl* "heir ale" and Old English *byrdfealu* "bride ale") in Old English. The funeral feast served two purposes. The first was to honour the dead, and the second was to give the heirs a chance to exert their rights to inherited property. Several funeral feasts are seen in the Lore. We know from the Lore that they generally followed the same pattern of a *blót*. However, a few funeral feasts seem to have been more like a symbel, or consisted of a feast and a symbel, for instance the Funeral feast of King Harald Gormson in *Heimskringla*:

> The first day of the feast, before King Svein went up into his father's high-seat, he drank the bowl to his father's memory, and made the solemn vow, that before three winters were past he would go over with his army to England, and either kill King Adalrad (Ethelred), or chase him out of the country. This

181

heirship bowl all who were at the feast drank. Thereafter for the chiefs of the Jomsborg vikings was filled and drunk the largest horn to be found, and of the strongest drink. When that bowl was emptied, all men drank Christ's health; and again the fullest measure and the strongest rink were handed to the Jomsborg vikings. The third bowl was to the memory of Saint Michael, which was drunk by all. Thereafter Earl Sigvalde emptied a remembrance bowl to his father's honour, and made the solemn vow, that before three winters came to an end he would go to Norway, and either kill Earl Hakon, or chase him out of the country. (Samuel Lang translation)

At the funeral feast, the *minni* of the deceased was made by the heir. The heir would then do a *béot* as one would in symbel, a vow to do something. In King Svein's case, he drank to his father's memory, and then vowed to take Ethelred the Unready's kingdom. Each heir in turn would drink to the respective deity of that round, and then one of them would drink to the deceased's memory and follow this with a vow. Following this, the rounds seem to have proceeded as that of a symbel.

Using this information, we can reconstruct the funeral rites to some degree of certainly. There would be the funeral its self, followed some months later by the feast or *húse*l, with a *symbel* immediately following.

**The Funeral Rite or Lícthenung**

1) Preparation of the Body: In ancient times, the women of the family washed and prepared the body for burial or cremation. Today, this is taken care of by a funeral home (largely due to laws in the various states that dictate this be so). However, modern funeral homes have several practices not in keeping with the Lore. Nails of women are not trimmed as we are told the nails of all corpses must be in the ""Völuspa"." Too, bodies are not buried with shoes on now. Since Christians do not believe in grave goods, and clothing is merely for the benefit of the living when viewing the body,

182

shoes are seen as not needed.  However, the ancient
Heathens sent their dead off with "Hel shoes" so that they
could walk to the afterlife in relative comfort. Heathens
therefore need to request of the funeral director that nails be
fully trimmed and that shoes be placed on the body.

2) The Wake or Wæcce: There is little information on what
form wakes took in ancient times. Judging from what
information survives on the funeral its self, Germanic wakes
were probably a time of lamentation. It is doubtful they were
seen as joyous occasions as is the case with Irish custom.

3) The Funeral or Lícthenung: As noted above, a funeral
ceremony can somewhat be reconstructed from Béowulf.
a) The Eulogy or Minni: This is best done by a close friend of
the deceased. In all the surviving descriptions of Heathen
funerals, none seem to indicate that a priest was present or
even necessary.  The exception being the "Angel of Death" in
Fadlan's account. Even then she seems only to be present to
dispatch those wishing to enter death with the deceased.
Eulogies are not easily written.  Modern ones typically state
the person's date of birth, their parent's names, the names of
survivors, and note major events such as marriage. They
then go on to talk about accomplishments of the individual,
or favourable personal traits. There is no reason this cannot
be done with a Heathen eulogy or minni.

b) Placement of grave goods: The heirs should then place
anything they wished buried with the deceased by the coffin
or in it. Ancient grave goods ranged from simple to
elaborate. Regardless, they nearly always included a toiletry
set, jewellery, and tools of the deceased's trade. Egil's Saga
speaks of smiths being buried with smithing tools and
archaeology has shown this to be true. Warriors were buried
with their swords, spears, and shields.  Women were often
buried with spindles, and other items involved with house
holding.

c) A dirge sang by a female relative: We have no idea what
kinds of funerary songs were sung. They were no doubt
mournful as every description in ancient times from the

Roman accounts to the Sagas portrays them as mournful in the least, wailing at their worst. Probably, for the sake of the survivors' ears, something sorrowful, but beautiful should be sung. This may mean a new song must be composed in short order, as we have no songs surviving from the ancient era (and modern Heathen songsters do not seem too keen on composing funeral songs just to be ready for when needed). Some of the Skaldic eulogy poems may serve as a guide, or such items in the Lore as Ragnar Loðbrok's death song.

d) The burial of the body or ashes or spreading of ashes: In the Béowulf account, it took ten days to build the mound. Today, it would not take nearly as long to bury a body, even if a mound were being built. No special ceremonies seem to be connected with the burial or burning of the body. With the cremation funerals portrayed in the Lore, folks seem to have just stood and watched: e) Songs of praise for the deceased done by 12 people circling the grave.

Following the completion of the mound, at least in the Béowulf account 12 horsemen circled the mound singing songs in honour of the dead king. This is probably impractical now, and indeed this part of the funeral account may be a borrowing from Homer's *Illiad* (though it may be common Indo-European practice too, the Hittites also seem to have circled the grave mound of the newly buried). Nonetheless, it could be incorporated as the last act of a funeral rite. While one could probably not get 12 horsemen, and they probably would not be allowed in a public cemetery regardless, one could have 12 singers circle the grave singing songs in praise of the deceased. We are not told what direction they circled, though it was probably clockwise given most rites preference for that. Again, a look at many of the Skaldic poems might give one an idea what these songs may have consisted of.

4) The Funeral Feast or Ierfe Húsel

a) Húsel: The funeral feast is likely to have consisted of a *húsel* followed by a symbel in ancient times. It is not known what Gods the feast is likely to have been dedicated to. However, the patron Gods and/or Goddesses of the deceased are a likely guess. This can be performed as a standard Husel as outlined in the chapter on the *blót*. b) Minni: The Minni seems to have differed a great deal from the standard symbel in its initial rounds. The first round was to the deceased followed by a vow by an heir, this is likely in ancient times to taken the form of a *bragafull*. The second to a diety followed by one to the deceased and then by a vow by an heir. The third followed this pattern, being first to a diety, then the deceased, followed by yet another vow by an heir. Thereafter, the order seems to have followed that of an open symbel, although no doubt, plenty of toasts were made to the deceased. The opening rounds can be roughly outlined as below:

i) Closest Heir (the spouse or eldest child)

a) Minni: The *minni* is the primary boast of the deceased given by the eldest and closest of the heirs.

b) Bragafull: An oath made on behalf of all the heirs by the eldest as the new head of the family. Once this is done, the eldest heir may step up to and sit in the High Seat of the deceased (in modern times this would probably be the deceased's favourite chair).

ii) Second Closest Heir:

a) The God Full: This full is to one of the deceased's patrons made by the second closest heir.

b) Minni: The second closest heir then drinks a horn in memory of the deceased.

c) Bragafull: An oath is then made by the second eldest. This should be a personal endeavour that would benefit the entire family.

iii) Third Closest Heir:

a) The God Full: A toast is made to another of the deceased's patrons or favourite Gods by the third eldest heir. b) Minni: The third closest heir then toasts the deceased. c) Bragafull: Finally, the third closest heir makes an oath to accomplish some task. iv) Open Rounds

From here on out the Minni takes the form of standard symbels. The funeral feast seemed in ancient times as much to celebrate the succession of the heirs to their inheritance as it was to celebrate the deceased life. At several funeral feasts in the *Heimskringla*, gifts were even given.

185

# Chapter XVI Other Rites

Many rites must have existed that have been forever lost, and there are many we know existed only from brief mentions in the lore with no details as to how they were performed. These rites often fall outside the realm of worship or life rites, or often form a component of the greater rites that can be used on its own as well. Land taking, ritual saunas, need fire, as well as other rites all fall in the realm of "other rites."

## *An Altar or Wéofod Dedication*

For the ancient Heathen, making an area sacred was a simple task. Many of the areas had been used for centuries in the worship of our Gods. Even in Iceland, we know from the sagas that sacred items and even temple pillars were carried from Norway to their new homes by such folks as Thorgrimr (see *Kjalnesinga Saga* Chapter 2). This made their job somewhat easier. Still, we know from hints in the lore that they must have had ways of making items and areas sacred. The "land taking" rite in the Icelandic *Landnámabók* may have been such a rite, as it claimed one's land and separated it from the wilds. We also know from the *Eddas*, as well as rune stone inscriptions that Þunor was often invoked to make an item sacred. Fire was also used in *blóts* to hallow the food and drink (this we are told in the *Heimskringla*). Combining all these items one can produce a simple *wéofod* dedication much like the one below. While not authentic, it is based on ideas seen in the lore.

Items Needed: Blót Bowl Blót Tine Horn wéofod Mead Torch or Candle

1) Set up the altar or *wéofod* as you would to do a *blót*.

2) Circle the *wéofod* bearing a candle or torch while chanting or singling the following in English or Old English. The purpose of this is to make the space around the altar sacred. The concept of circling with fire is taking from the land taking seen in the Icelandic *Landnámabók*. The idea of

"making sacred; is deeply rooted in such concepts as the Norse vé, and the Anglo-Saxon friðgeard, and further supported by phrases found on rune-stones invoking Þunor to make sacred the stones.

> Fyr ic bere ymb friðgearde, Ond béode men frið fremman, Líeg ic bere tó belúcan, Béode ælwihta fléogan aweg. Þunor wéoh, Þunor wéoh, Þunor wéoh þisne ealh. Fyr ic bere ymb friðgearde, Ond béode men frið fremman, Líeg ic bere tó belúcan, Béode utlaga féran aweg. Þunor wéoh, Þunor wéoh, Þunor wéoh þisne ealh. Þunor wéoh, Þunor wéoh, Þunor wéoh þisne ealh. Fire I bear around this sacred site, And bid all men make peace, Flame I bear to enclose, And bid evil spirits to flee Thor make sacred, Thor make sacred, Thor make sacred this holy site Fire I bear around this sacred site, And bid all men make peace,
> Flame I bear to enclose, And bid outlaws fare away. Thor make sacred, Thor make sacred, Thor make sacred this holy site. Thor make sacred, Thor make sacred, Thor make sacred this holy site.

3) Call on Þunor as the hallower to make the altar sacred. These words are usually best your own. However, even a simple phrase such as "Þunor wéoh wéofod," "Þunor make sacred this altar," would work followed by a list of possible threats to the altar, and what would happen to the offender.

4) Do the wéofod's first blót calling on the Gods to bless it and sprinkle it with mead. One should do a prayer to each of the Gods and Goddesses, dedicating the *wéofod* to them, and asking them to bless it. You have already made the altar sacred (separate from the mundane), and hallowed it (made it whole and healthy), now you are seeking the blessings of the Gods upon it.

5) Close the rite with words to the effect that the *wéofod* will be used well in the name of the Gods.

This ritual can be as elaborate as one wishes.

## The Land Taking

Land taking is primarily seen in the Icelandic *Landnámabók*, when new land was being taken as property. It is also seen elsewhere albeit often in Romanized or Celtized forms. The "beating of the bounds" still done in some shires in England is a form of land taking, as is the establishment of land markers. Land taking is in essence the establishment of sacred space, the creation of one's own *innangarð* for their kith and kin to use.

Land taking or establishment of sacred space is seen in several places in the lore, and through a variety of means. Most of these involve the establishment of boundaries of some kind. Within the lore, the following means of land taking were used: 1) Symbols or land markers placed around the area. 2) The building of fires at certain points along with the erection of some sort of symbol. 3) Circling the area with fire. In addition, land taking, at least in the case of temples or other especially sacred areas was also accompanied by bringing soil from another sacred site, or the transporting of sacred pillars from a previous temple to the new site to be used in the new temple. As stated above, land taking ceremonies are fairly common in the Icelandic *Landnámabók*. One such example is that of two brothers, Vestmann and Vemund, who though Christian fell back on pagan principles when taking land:

> Þeir fóru til Íslands ok sigldu fyrir norðan landit ok vestr um Sléttu í fjörðinn. Þeir settu öxi í Restargnúp ok kölluðu þvíÖxarfjörð. Þeir settu örn upp fyrir vestan ok kölluðu þar Arnarþúfu. En í þriðja stað settu þeir kross. Þar nefnduKrossás. Svá helguðu þeir sér allan Öxarfjörð.

> "They set an ax on Restargnúp and called it Öxarfjörð. They set and eagle up in the west and called it Arnarþúfu. And the third they set a cross. They named it Krossás. So they hallowed all of Öxarfjörð

(*Landnámabók*)

This type of land claming is similar to the hallowing seen in the Anglo-Saxon Æcer-Bót:

> Genim þonne on niht, ær hyt daguge, feower tyrf on feower healfa þæs landes, and gemearca hy hy ær stodon .... Nim ðonne þa turf and sete ðær ufon on and cweðe ðonne nigon siþon þas word, Crescite, and swa oft Paster Noster.

> "Take at night, before dawn, four turfs from the four quarters of the lands, and remember how they had stood ... take the turfs and set them down, and say these words nine time, 'Crescite' and as often the "Lord's Prayer."

While heavily Christianized the "Æcer-Bót" account may reflect earlier pagan practices, just as the account of Vestmann and Vemund may also. It is not said whether these actions took place at cardinal points, or at the cross quarters, or even if they were evenly spaced. Accounts of Heathens taking land on a large scale nearly almost always involve fire, quite unlike the Christian accounts. Helgi, a man who practiced both Heathenry and Christianity built fires on his land to claim it:

> Helgi var blandinn mjök í trú. Hann trúði á Krist, en hét á Þór tilsjófara ok harðræða. Þá er Helgi sá Ísland, gekk hann til frétta við Þór, hvar land skyldi taka......... Helgi kannaði um sumarit herað allt ok nam allan Eyjafjörð milli Sigluness ok Reynisness ok gerði eld mikinn við hvern vatnsós ok helgaði sér svá allt herað.

> "Helgi's faith was much mixed. He held troth with Christ, but called on Thor on voyages and hard journeys. Thus when Helgi saw Iceland, he asked Thor, where land he should take........ Helgi took all of Eyjafjörð between Sigluness and Reynisness and made fires at every estuary and hallowed the land."

(*Landnámabók*)

More thoroughly Heathen men portrayed in the *Landnámabók* generally circled their land with fire. This usually seemed to have been involved with the erection of a temple. Jörundr goði carried fire around the land his hof was to be built on to hallow it.

þar er nú heitir á Svertingsstöðum. Hann reisti þar hof mikit.....Þat land fór Jörundr eldi ok lagði til hofs.

"There he called it Svertingsstöðum. He there built a temple.... That land, Jörundr carried fire around where he later laid his temple." (Landnámabók) Thorolf, who also established a temple, carried fire around his land to claim it as well.

Eftir það fór Þórólfur eldi um landnám sitt, utan frá Stafá og inn til þeirrar ár er hann kallaði Þórsá, og byggði þar skipverjum sínum.
Hann setti bæ mikinn við Hofsvog er hann kallaði á Hofsstöðum. Þar lét hann reisa hof og var það mikið hús.

Thereafter Thorolf fared with fire through his land out from Staff-river in the west, and east to that river which is now called Thors-river, and settled his shipmates there.
But he set up for himself a great house at Templewick which he called Templestead. There he let build a temple, and a mighty house it was. (Eyrbygga Saga, Morris & Magnusson translation)

That fire is not needed to perform a land taking is shown by the other examples, not is it specifically associated with hallowing as we see hallowing done without fire (though only in mixed Heathen and Christian contexts). However, it is clear that fire is associated with land taking, at least with the erection of temples.

One can easily design their own land taking ceremony from the citations above, or use the one below. Land taking seems to have consisted of 1) Some symbolic marking out of the land, either by circling with fire, bonfires on the borders, or the erection of symbolic markers. 2) Naming the land as in the case of Thorolf, or Vestmann and Vemund.

Land Taking

Items Needed: A candle or torch

1) Circle the land with an enclosed candle or some form of torch. Be careful that it is not an open flame that will blow out easily or start a fire. While doing this, one may wish to chant or sing some form of land claiming song or boast. An example is given below:

Fótum ic fére --- foldan nim, Ic nim lond --- for min léode, Lond ic belúce --- wiþ eall þæt láþ

By foot I fare --- earth I take,
I take land --- for my people, Land I enclose ---
against all that is hated.

2) Once one had reached the primary living area or the entrance to the property, they may wish to bestow a name upon that place. This can be done by performing a blót and when blessing the place, bestowing a name with words like unto the ones below:

Ic giefe noma (name) --- (name) héht

I give you the name (name)     (name) call you.

## *Making Sacred Space*

The creation of sacred space is also seen (often to the taking of land) in the *Landnámabók* as well as in other places such as the example previously cited from *Eyrbygga Saga*. Generally, when land was taken for a temple or ealh, fire was used. This is seen when Thorolf took his land for a temple, and can also be seen in the *Landnámabók* when Jörundr takes land for his temple.

þar er nú heitir á Svertingsstöðum. Hann reisti þar hof mikit.....Þat land fór Jörundr eldi ok lagði til hofs.

> "There he called it Svertingsstöðum. He there build a temple.... That land, Jörundr carried fire around where he later laid his temple." (*Landnámabók*)

Other methods were used as well. Temporary sacred space could apparently be made using what was called in Old Norse vébond, "sacred space ropes" that were tied to hazel poles. Such space is described in Egil's Saga:

> The place where the court sat was a level plain and hazel poles were set in a circle on the plain linked by ropes. These were called the sanctuary ropes. (Egil's Saga Fell translation)

This type of space was not only seen with law courts, but also duelling sites. Such duelling sites marked by hazel poles and ropes are seen in *Kormack's Saga*. Other ways of making a site sacred are also seen, such as transporting the soil of one sacred site to another, or the temple pillars. Thorolf when he came to Iceland brought the pillars of his temple in Norway with him as did Thorhadd, and Inigimund the Old. Some areas though were thought to be innately sacred, either for their natural beauty such as Thingveillr in Iceland or for their use by other peoples as a sacred site such as Yeavering in England.

Creation of sacred space is probably more important to Heathens in the United States of America and Canada. We are in the position of the Icelanders in many respects, dwelling on land that had never been occupied in some cases, or in the position of the Anglo-Saxon peoples, dwelling on land that was long inhabited by others. We can create sacred space by using any of the methods of the ancients. These can be roughly classed as 1) The use of fire to surround the area in some way. Either by circling the area with a torch or by building bonfires are key points. 2) The transport of parts of a sacred structure and/or soil to the new location. 3) In the case of temporary sacred space, the use of *vébönd* (which can be reconstructed in Old English as *wéohband*). In addition to these, there are also clues the ancients invoked Þunor to make an area or item sacred. Many runestones are inscribed with "Þórr uiki " or in English "Thor make sacred." Þunor as the one who makes things sacred is well attested to in the lore, his hammer or a symbol of it was used to hallow brides at weddings, and he is even referred to as Veurr "the one who makes sacred." From this information, a rite to make a grove, a temple site, or other areas permanently sacred can be reasonably be constructed (minor modifications can easily produce one for temporary space as well).

1) If available, lay items from another sacred site where the altar will stand.

2) Circle the area with fire, and recite something similar to the Englathod's Wéonde Song:

Fyr ic bere ymb friðgearde, Ond béode men frið fremman, Líeg ic bere tó belúcan, Béode ælwihta fléogan aweg. Þunor wéoh, Þunor wéoh, Þunor wéoh þisne ealh. Fyr ic bere ymb friðgearde,
Ond béode men frið fremman, Líeg ic bere tó belúcan, Béode utlaga féran aweg. Þunor wéoh, Þunor wéoh, Þunor wéoh þisne ealh. Þunor wéoh, Þunor wéoh, Þunor wéoh þisne ealh.

Fire I bear around this sacred site, And bid all men make peace, Flame I bear to enclose, And bid evil spirits to flee Thor make sacred, Thor make sacred, Thor make sacred this holy site Fire I bear around this sacred site, And bid all men make peace, Flame I bear to enclose, And bid outlaws fare away. Thor make sacred, Thor make sacred, Thor make sacred this holy site. Thor make sacred, Thor make sacred, Thor make sacred this holy site.

3) The area should then be named (one can use the naming formula from the land taking ceremony above if they wish), and the first blót performed.

## *Need Fire or Níedfyr*

Need fire was a widespread custom amongst the Germanic, Celtic, and Slavonic peoples. It had to be generated by wood drill, fire bow, or other means of producing fire with wood against wood. Flint and steel and other methods never seem to have been used. All other fires in the village had to be extinguished and then relit from the need fire. It was often used to drive away pestilence, esp. amongst cattle who were driven through its smoke (see Frazier's Golden Bough and Grimm's Teutonic Mythology on this topic). Amongst the Germanic peoples it was sometimes made annually. Grimm states that:

> Needfire.---Flame which had been kept some time among men and been propagated from one fire to another, was thought unserviceable for sacred uses; as holy water had to be drawn fresh from the spring, so it made all the difference, if instead of the profaned and as it were worn out flame, a new one were used. (Grimm, *Teutonic Mythology*, Stallybrass translation)

It was thought lucky to leap over the Midsummer bonfires in many parts of Northern Europe, and cattle were driven through the smoke of a need fire to cure murrain. Many hofs or ealhs portrayed in the lore also had temple fires that were never put out. Need fire therefore may be seen much like holy water gathered from springs at Eostre, in some way sacred.

The only surviving element we have from Need Fire rituals is the fact it must be started with a fire bow, fire drill, or other fricative means of producing fire from wood. We have no words from any formulas survived for producing it unfortunately. Nonetheless, one could probably use a rite like the one below:
1) Set up the tender, wood, and other fuel for the fire.

2) Then using a fire bow or fire drill, start the fire while reciting, or have someone else recite the following or something similar:

Sperca, sperca, --- sméoc on smic gléde weorð glæm,
bærn, bærn, --- blaest onblaw brand weorð blæle,
fýre, fýre, --- fýs fácnu bringe frið ond frofre.

Spark, spark smoke and fumigate embers become bright, burn, burn kindle and blow Torch becomes fire fire, fire drive away evil, Bring frith and comfort.

## *Ritual Sauna*

"Sauna-like sweat baths, too so important in Amerindian cleansing rites - were also used by Germanic healers; the technique of bringing water together with heated rocks to produce the therapeutic steam, called stánbaþ "stone bath" by the Anglo-Saxons, is very widespread" (Glosecki, Shamanism in Old English Poetry, p. 128).

Many rituals have been forever lost with little or no information to form a basis for their reconstruction. We know they existed, as they are mentioned in the lore, but that is about it. Such is the case of the sauna or "sweat lodge." We know certain ceremonies were connected with them as they were used in conjunction with weddings and other sacred times. But we know no details. There therefore have been attempts at reconstructing some form of sauna rituals. Most have been based on Native American practices as their sweat lodge rites seem very similar to our ritual of symbel. Even were their rites not similar to one of our own, they still follow a logical pattern the ancient Heathens could identify with.

The ancient Heathens probably did not use structures such as the domed Native American sweat lodge. However, this type of structure is convenient and easy to use. There are several good books that tell how to build one. For the stones, it is recommended you use some form of lava rock or other igneous rock (basalt, red granite, lava rock). Sedimentary rocks like sandstone can explode and break when water is poured on them, though not violently. Rocks with quartz or white granite in them however can explode violently and should not be used whatsoever. Coal and slate too under no conditions are to be used as they will burn in the fire before ever making it into the lodge.

Items Needed: 9 or More Stones (lava rock is best) Large Fire Pit Wood to heat the stones Water Towels Whisk made of bundled birch twigs Sweat lodge Someone to tend the fire (The "Fire Warder") Someone to pour the water (The "Water Tender") Water bucket (preferably stoneware and not metal) Wooden or stone dipper

1) Sacralizing the Area -If one is not using a regular ritual spot, they will want to form a frithstead or ve around the fire pit and the lodge. This may be done by using the Wéonede Song of the Englathod, the Hammer Rite of the Troth, or similar ritual. If using the Wéonede Song, say the following in Old English or English while bearing a torch or candle around the area:

Fyr ic bere ymb friðgearde, Ond béode men frið fremman, Líeg ic bere tó belúcan, Béode ælwihta fléogan aweg. Þunor wéoh, Þunor wéoh, Þunor wéoh þisne ealh. Fyr ic bere ymb friðgearde, Ond béode men frið fremman, Líeg ic bere tó belúcan, Béode utlaga féran aweg. Þunor wéoh, Þunor wéoh, Þunor wéoh þisne ealh. Þunor wéoh, Þunor wéoh, Þunor wéoh þisne ealh.

Fire I bear around this sacred site, And bid all men make peace, Flame I bear to enclose, And bid evil spirits to flee Thor make sacred, Thor make sacred, Thor make sacred this holy site Fire I bear around this sacred site, And bid all men make peace, Flame I bear to enclose, And bid outlaws fare away. Thor make sacred, Thor make sacred, Thor make sacred this holy site. Thor make sacred, Thor make sacred, Thor make sacred this holy site.

2) Placing the stones -In the fire pit build a platform of logs and smaller wood. Make sure to have enough tinder near the edge of the base to ignite the larger wood. Generally it is best to use 4 large logs to build a rectangular platform. Then fill in the platform, with a bit of tinder. Atop the platform, almost like wickerwork lay small sapling size branches. It is on these that the stones will rest. Make sure that you do not pack the wood too tightly, or the fire will not get air and will die out frequently. Once the platform is built, place the stones. Many Native Americans have traditions associated with placing the stones. However, perhaps it is enough to bless each stone by saying something like "Þunor wéoh þisne stan" (Thor make sacred this stone) as one places each stone. The stones should be evenly spread over the "wickerwork" top of the platform.

3) Need fire -Once the stones are placed, one should start the fire. Need fire was a special kind of fire built by friction and whose smoke was thought to drive away disease and pestilence. Many areas in Northern Europe would build these fires and then drive their cattle through them. It is thought that at one time all ritual fires in Northern Europe may have been built this way. Therefore it is fitting to try to start the fire to heat the stones using a fire drill and tender, and to utilize some form of ritual. The following words may be said while starting the fire:

> Sperca, sperca, sméoc on smic gléde weorð glæm, bærn, bærn, --- blaest onblaw brand weorð blæle, fýre, fýre, --- fýs fácnu bringe frið ond frofre.

> Spark, spark smoke and fumigate embers become bright, burn, burn kindle and blow Torch becomes fire fire, fire drive away evil, Bring frith and comfort.

4) Gathering the folk -The folk are gathered to go into the sauna. Due to the intense heat a good lodge can generate, nothing more than skirts and kilts should be worn. Folks can

go in nude if they wish. Absolutely no metal can be worn as it will literally sear your body wherever it touches you. For a similar reason, metal buckets and dippers should not be used. The folk progress to the sauna and enter. Songs may be sung on the way, or it may be done in silence. Seating should be done in order of age and/or arung "honouring." Special guests should be seated nearer the pourer as should be kindred leaders and other notables.

5) The Rounds -In this particular sauna rite nine rounds are done. At the beginning of each round, a stone is brought in by the fire warder (who knows to bring one in when the pourer opens the flap). The lodge is then closed and the Water Pourer then sprinkles it with mugwort (or if one wants they can use one each of the nine herbs of the "Nine Worts Galdor") and says "Wes hal wéoh stan!" or "Wassail holy stone!" He or she then pours water on the stone and begins the prayers for the round. The prayers then proceed clockwise around the lodge. The rounds are to: a. Gods b. Disir c. Álfar (Ancestral males) d. Heroes e. Family f. Friends g. Community h. Oaths i. Closing prayers. During the ritual, the pourer may pour more water on the stones as he or she sees fit. The prayers can take the form of the boasts of symbel. At the close of each round, participants may wish to lightly beat themselves with the birch whisk. This brings the blood to the surface of the skin and aids in purification. Birch, by the way was generally used as a way to drive away illness causing wights, and is seen used in whisks even today in Northern European saunas.

6) Closing the Rite -Once the final round has been completed, the pourer should give a brief prayer to the Gods in thanks for the cleansing of the bodies present. The pourer then should open the flap, and lead to folks to stand by the fire. A very brief blót can then be conducted and the folk dismissed.

Conclusion

Sauna is meant to be a ritual of bodily cleansing. In

ancient times it was done prior to weddings, and even duels. Even though we have lost the way the ancient Heathens may have performed it, through modern innovation we can refine a way appropriate to our times and approved of by the Gods.

# Chapter XIX Social Structure

Within modern Germanic Heathenry there is no definite structure. This was not true of ancient Heathenry which was very tribal in nature. That is it had a class system with democratic assemblies, ancient customs, and elected chieftains. Over time this changed as the tribes evolved into nations. The class structure became more fixed with less chance of advancement, and kings were no longer elected from people thought descended from the Gods. Titles became hereditary. People could no longer advance up and down the social scale freely. The status of women was greatly degraded. In essence, ancient tribalism became feudalism. Modern Heathenry for the most part has not sought to duplicate either of these structures, except in a few cases. In order to make things easier, the social structure of Ásatrú (or Norse Heathenry) will be handled first as a short overview, and then the social structure of Þéodisc Geléafa will be handled in more detail.

## *The Social Structure of Ásatrú*

As stated earlier, Ásatrú or Norse Heathenry for the most part is not tribal, but relies on modern social constructs. The basic organisation of this modern social construct is the kindred. A misnomer perhaps as kindred means literally "reckoned kin," that is those of blood relation (as in a family). However, the term has been adopted by Ásatrú (not Anglo-Saxon Heathenry or Þéodisc Geléafa) to mean any local Heathen group that *blót*s and studies together. For the most part Ásatrú kindreds are run democratically often with an elected leader, sometimes with an appointed priest. The leader can variously be a lawspeaker or goði, some kindreds use both with the lawspeaker handling mundane affairs, the goði handling those connected with worship. Other offices are often added such as a loremaster, treasurer, or secretary, and rarely a þulr (the Icelandic version of the þyle). Offices can vary a great deal from group to group. National organisations usually operate with a corporate structure with elected board members, who then appoint the officers. Both the Troth and Frigga's Web operate this way.

Other national Ásatrú organisations operate using a more tribal structure. The idea behind this to create groups that are more community minded and have a more solid common identity. The Ásatrú Alliance for example meets at an annual Alþing, and membership is only available to kindreds, not individuals. Others such as Nordanlog and Northvergr Felag use an even more traditional tribal structure. They do this to even better accomplish the purpose of creating a more community minded group. Organisations using a tribal structure differ from those that do not in that they usually exclude those that they feel will not work well within the group, or more generally, those they feel may be a threat to its members. The tribe determines who is a member of the tribe. There is very sound reasoning for this.

Within any group, it doesn't matter if it is the Lions Club or the Elks or the Roman Catholic church, there is a chance of attracting the dangerously mentally ill, child molesters, serial killers, and such ilk. A group needs to be able to keep out such people that might be a threat to its members or children. What if, for example, a child molester wanted to join a kindred? Should they be allowed to on the grounds of their rights as a human being? What about someone known to have conducted a smear campaign against an upstanding member of the Heathen community, or a self avowed Nazi?

Tribal organisations only differ from non-tribal in their exclusive behaviour in that they have mechanisms to keep such folks from joining. Tribal groups rarely blackball anyone simply over personal differences and get away with it. But at the same time some non-tribal organisations because of their disclaimers on not excluding people could legally be forced to admit a convicted serial rapist that has served their time. Tribal organisations because they give their groups the right to exclude, cannot be.

Beyond giving members a right to decide who is or is not in the tribe, tribal groups also try to create tribal traditions and rites. Many of these are based on ancient Heathenry, while others may be new innovations. Sometimes they are started by accident. It really does not make much difference. Such traditions are meant to give a stronger sense of common identity. Finally, most tribal groups try to create a uniform moral code based on the ancient moral codes. This along with a strong belief in and understanding of the word frith solidify the ideal of a common identity as a tribe. As yet however, Ásatrú has not embraced the idea of tribalism.

Both Ásatrú and Anglo-Saxon Heathenry have sacred offices in common and these are covered below:

Dröttin (ON)/Dryhten (OE): This office is sometimes used to designate a leader of a kindred or larger organisation. Their functions are usually that of the president of any other organisation. Anglo-Saxon organisations tend to avoid using this title except in its traditional sense.

Goði (male)/Gyðia (female): Goði is the title most often used for a priest in Heathenry in general. Anglo-Saxon groups however use a wide range of other titles the most common seeming to be *wéofod*þegn. Others that are fairly common are *heargweard*, *blótere*, and *\*goda* (a reconstruction of the Norse Goði). This is the person that generally performs the *blót*s and other rites for a kindred or larger group. Duties vary from kindred to kindred. Often the Goði also serves as the group's leader.

**Law Speaker**: Many kindreds opt not to use the title of Dröttin and instead use Law Speaker for the title of their elected leader. The duties generally run the same.

**Loremaster**: Used of the person in charge of educating new comers into a kindred. Often this amounts to be little more to a librarian, although it can also mean being an expert on all parts of the religion. It varies from kindred to kindred. In many kindreds, esp. those of a more Anglo-Saxon background, this office is combined into that of þyle or þulr.

**Spaman (male)/Spakona**: Not usually a kindred office, but a title nonetheless of those that use spae (see chapter XVII).

**Þyle (OE) / Þulr(ON):** A sacred office not often seen outside of Anglo-Saxon kindreds, the þyle is in charge of educating newcomers coming into a kindred. He or she also has final say on issues of the lore, and the right to challenge any false oaths made in symbel. Þyles tend to be combination mystics and scholars, using the runes, mound sitting, and other mystical means along with modern scholarship to search out the truth.

Many other offices can and do exist, and this list is not at all exhaustive. Duties will vary from kindred to kindred, and from national organisation to national organisation.

## The Social Structure of Þéodisc Geléafa

One particular brand of tribalism is Þéodisc Geléafa. Þéodisc Geléafa (Theodisc Geleafa or Theodish Belief as some call it) means in Old English "tribal faith"; it is the "belief of the tribe." Two thousand years ago had someone asked a Germanic tribesman what their faith was, they would have explained their religion as the belief of the folk or tribe. Tribes at that time were social units linked by a common cultural identity, common history, as well as shared customs, traditions, and religion. Often Germanic tribes traced descent from a common ancestor, usually a hero or even a deity. Tribes gave their folk very much a sense of community and identity. Social bonds within the ancient tribes were usually one of blood (tracing back to the common ancestor) or via a hold oath (an oath similar to blood brotherhood in that it bound two people together), and much stronger than those of general society today.

The great sociologist Emile Durkheim, found that loss of social identity or cultural identity within a society generally lead to a decline in morale within the individuals of that society. Such a loss of morale could lead to depression and suicide, and therefore societies that over emphasize individualism, were prone to higher suicide rates than those that emphasized cultural identification while still maintaining individual rights. Societies with little to no regulation of individuals, and with no social structure according to Durkheim were also those that see a decline in morals, an increase in crime, as well as depression and suicide. Ideally, Durkheim thought that the only way to combat this was to reintegrate individuals into some form of social structure. In a similar vein, the great Chinese philosopher Confucius felt that social order came from respecting the custom and traditions of society, respecting humanity (or *Jen),* and proper behavior towards one's ancestors and the living (or the concept of *Li).* Thus Þéodisc Geléafa seeks to rebuild tribal societies in order to create a healthier society, one with social order and harmony.

Þéodisc Geléafa therefore holds that the natural place for Germanic Heathenry and the worship of the Germanic Gods and Goddesses is in a tribal society. The ancient Germanic peoples from time immemorial worshiped the deities as a community; either as families, clans, or tribes. They were social creatures and while individuals had many of the rights they do today, these were often secondary to the concerns of one's tribe. While it would be difficult to form tribes now as they were in ancient times, Þéodisc Geléafa seeks to reform them in such a way that at least some of the benefits of tribalism will be felt. Modern Þéodisc Geléafa had its start in 1976 when Garman Lord began to explore the idea of resurrecting the old religion of the Angles, Saxons, and Jutes, and doing so in a tribal tradition. For the longest time, the only Þéodisc groups were Anglo-Saxon Heathen (dedicated to one of the Anglo-Saxon tribes or the Anglo-Saxons as a whole). Now however, there are several Þéodisc groups dedicated to such various tribal traditions as the Angles, Jutes, Normans, Goths, and Norse. All Þéodisc groups generally believe in certain social concepts. Amongst these social concepts are: sacral kingship, the idea of a sacral ruler that collectively holds the luck of the tribe; a tribal assembly, a place where the folk can make law and discuss problems; a structured society, one which has distinct social classes in which one has to earn their position; that all have freedom of conscience, and finally, that folk can be bond together by oaths and blood into a tribe.

Every large Anglo-Saxon Heathen organisation today

is tribal or þéodisc in nature, no other social structure is used. Generally, inherent in this þéodisc structure are 1) an elected head or chief.  2) An advisory board or tribal council appointed by the chief at the head of the organisation. The chief can be elected for a term or life, and the council can take the form of a representative council elected by the membership, one appointed by the chief, or the entire adult oathed membership. This is the true core of tribalism. Nothing else needs be added to the structure of the organisation to make it tribal. In theory, any local kindred whether Anglo-Saxon Heathen or Ásatrú that uses a tribal council, has its own traditions, and an elected chief, could be thought tribal. If that is the case, many Ásatrúar are already practising tribalism.

Within tribal societies however, for that matter, within any group of any numbers, a hierarchy soon develops. This happens in any organisation or group and seems almost to be instinctive. Usually when such hierarchies develop however, they are not based on service to the group or wisdom and experience.  Often they develop merely because of popularity. To keep this from destroying the tribe's democratic structure, some Anglo-Saxon Heathen groups have instigated *árungas* or ranks.  These are not like military ranks or noble titles, their purpose is to give more influence to those that have proven their worth through hard work and wisdom.

All within the þéod or tribe remain equal, and if not considered equal, are considered to have the same rights.  In this way they are closer to grades in High School (Freshman, Sophomore, and so  forth) or college degrees. Not all tribal organisations handle it this way. In some groups, they may be closer to military ranks, others, noble titles. But all tribal groups have rights that are granted to all full members regardless of station. That is all have basic rights that cannot be violated as these rights were and are a core belief of Germanic Heathenry.

In essence, ranks are a way of telling who has more experience.  It does not mean they have necessarily more say in the running of the organisation per se, but simply that some folks have been around longer. Ideally such a hierarchy or anti- hierarchy would be organic.  Realistically however favouritism would creep in and ruin the system.  Whether or not a group has ranks however, does not determine if it is or is not a tribal organisation.

## Árungas

There are as many different forms of *árungas* as there are Þéodisc organisations. Englatheod, (whose social structure is based on that of the ancient Anglo-Saxon kingdom of Mercia) is divided into three different primary classes of *árungas* or "honorings." In the Dark Ages, the majority of people in Mercian society were *ceorls* (modern English churls). They were the working class, the individuals who farmed land and made crafts. It was not unusual for *ceorls*, particularly those who owned land, to be wealthier than the members of the nobility. In the Englathod, the *ceorls* are the common members responsible for nothing more than their own home and family. In ancient Mercian society, the class above the *ceorls* were the *thegns* (also spelled *thanes*) or *gesiðas*. The thegns owned more land than the *ceorls* (at least 5 hides--a hide being enough land to sustain one family). They also owed such duties to the king as military service and the maintenance of bridges and fortresses. In the Englathod, it is the *thegns* who form the civil service, who hold the various offices, and generally ensure that everything in the Ríce runs as smoothly as possible. Above the *thegns* are the *ealdormen*, thegns appointed to run a *sæte* of the Ríce. It is they who provide the administration for the Englathod, it is they who oversee the running of things. It must be pointed out that the class system of Dark Age Mercia was flexible. *Ceorls* can and did become *thegns*. And *thegns* did become *ealdormen*. It was in some respects very much an upwardly mobile society. As such, so is the Englathod. Other Þéodisc groups use similar *árungas* numbering between three to six.

These *árungas* serve two primary purposes. One is to inspire and maintain members' willingness to dedicate themselves to religious self-development, hard work, and taking responsibility for the well being of the community as a whole. The *árungas* recognize and reward such willingness. The second is the idea that a structured society with clearly defined roles, responsibilities, and expectations for each member helps promote the long-term stability of our community, and encourages the development of frith (peace and good relationships) and troth among the folk, as it did in the past for the ancient Heathens. These levels are conferred upon each person by their local group and their leader as they progress in self-development and service, and show willingness and ability to maintain a higher level of responsibility. Members are not required to progress to another rank, however, if they are satisfied where they are. All Þéodisc groups also have some form of provisional membership. In order to become a member of Englathod, for example, one must first complete a period as a *þéow*. *Þéowas* exchange physical labor at religious gatherings for learning materials, and have fewer rights within the Ríce than *wærgengas*. *Þéowas* like *wærgengas* stay in that position for a year and a day. At the end of a year and a day for both forms of provisional membership it is determined whether one is ready to oath as a full member of Englatheod. If it is determined they are, they then take a hold oath to a member of higher árung, and become a ceorl.

Other þéodisc use similar *árungas,* and these can be summarized as follows :

**Cyning/Þéodan**: Some groups use the modern term king for this *árung*, others avoid the term for the taint it was given by Christianity. Cyning cannot truly be thought of as an *árung*, it is more of a sacred office, roughly equating to High Priest. The kings of the ancient Germanic tribes were nothing like the kings of medieval Europe. The later are probably best termed monarchs as their role had greatly been changed by Christianity. Heathen kings were elected by the people from families thought to be descended from a God (usually Wóden or Ing, although the line of Essex was thought descended from Seaxnéat). The king was therefore thought as an intermediary between the Gods and Man. In addition to being an intermediary, the king was thought to contain the tribal mægen or collective luck. As such, he was thought responsible for good harvests, victories in battle, and the general welfare of his people. Any king that failed in this could be sacrificed. At least a couple of modern Heathen organisations have experimented with kingship, more or less with some success. There is a danger however of organisations confusing Christian principles about kingship with Heathen ones, and therefore most do not.

**Æþeling**: An æþeling was a member of one of the families from which the cyning was elected. In modern Heathen organisations an æþeling is someone that has been identified as having the qualities required to become cyning.

**Ealdorman**: In ancient Anglo-Saxon England an ealdorman was roughly the equivalent of a Jarl in the Scandinavian countries. He was a large landowner with a private army usually in service of the king. In modern Heathen organisations, ealdormen are wermen or women that have worked to further the religion for many years, and holds great respect within the Heathen community.

**Hláford**: A hláford was a smaller land holder that had enough land to have others serving under him. He was usually in service to an ealdorman. In modern Heathenry a hláford is someone that has shown outstanding ability in leading the folk, and working at furthering Heathenry within the world.

**Þegn**: A þegn was the ancient Heathen equivalent of the medieval knight. He usually held a small part of land with peasants working under him, and served a lord in return for it. In modern Heathenry, þegnas form the backbone of any tribal Heathen organisation. They usually serve as the officers of local groups and often in the lesser offices of national organisations.

**Gebur/Ceorl**: In ancient Heathenry, the ceorl was a member of the lowest free class. They could and often did hold a small piece of land, but only served in extreme times of war. Within modern Heathen organisations, ceorlas form the general membership.

**Leornere**: Leorneres are just that "learners." Within modern Heathen organisations they are those just beginning to learn about Heathenry, and therefore are not yet permitted full membership within the organisation. Some groups refer to this *árung* as thrall or other such terms, and have many restrictions.

## The Web of Oaths

The ancient Anglo-Saxon tribes had a common identity and common history by virtue of many forms of bonds, not the least of which were bonds ofkinship. As seen in Tacitus' *Germania*, many tribes traced their origins to a common ancestor:

> In their old ballads (which amongst them are the only sort of registers and history) they celebrate Tuisto, a God sprung from the earth, and Mannusn his son, as the fathers and founders of the nation. To Mannus they assign three sons, after whose names so many people are called; the Ingaevones, dwelling next the ocean; the Herminones, in the middle country; and all the rest, Instaevones.

Further, tribes were made up of families, groups of people that could trace their kinship out to at least third cousins (for the purpose of wergild, amongst theAnglo-Saxons, kinship was traced to fifth cousins). Today's situation is quite different. Most within a þéod would be lucky to claim being 7th cousins of their fellow tribesman much less anything the ancients might recognize as truly close kinship (the inner family of the hælsfang, our nuclear family). However, kinship was not the only way a tribe could create bonds. Men without kin, or simply seeking adventure would often come together in a dryht or "warband." In the Migration Era many lost their kin through warfare, migration, or simply left their kin to earn their worth in battle. These warbands were bound together by thewarriors all having an oath to serve the leader of the dryht. The kin group being the earliest organized unit of society that the ancient Heathens recognized, the dryht mimicked the structure of the family. Its members held the same obligations to each other and their lord as kinsmen would. Were one murdered they had to take revenge (esp. were it their lord), and could seek wergild. The lord or dryhten of the warband was seen as a fatherhood figure with the warband as a sort of band of brothers. The veterans of the warband held more say than the youths as would be the case in a family with the eldest family members having more say than the youngest. For the warband to operate as an artificial family however there had to be some form of bonding. The core of a dryht would often be true kinsmen, and for them no artificial bonds were needed. But for others, there had to be a substitute for the bonds of kinship created by birth into an extended family. This substitute was the hold oath.

The hold oath is often mistaken or confused with the later medieval oaths of fealty, and while they have much in common with these, there are differences (mostly revolving around the obligations and lack of land tenure). At the head of the dryht was the dryhten, its lord or leader. The dryhten was a warrior that had made a name for himself, and shown his ability to lead men into battle. He was obligated to give his men wealth in exchange for service, and often provided them food and shelter. All the men of the dryht were oathed to serve the dryhten (and in turn his lady at whom's command they were also). The wording of none of these oaths has come down to us intact unfortunately. Fortunately we can attempt to reconstruct such oaths from heroic poetry. The hold oath placed certain obligations upon both the lord and the warrior serving him. Should the lord be killed, those oathed to him had to take vengeance. The lord in turn had to be generous with gifts, mead, and weapons.

Within the warband there were various functions but primary amongst these was the lady of the hall who served as an artificial mother, and indeed, had as much command over the dryht as her husband if not more. In Beowulf, Wealhtheow informs Beowulf that:

þegnas syndon geþwære, þeod ealgearo,
    druncne dryhtguman doð swa ic bidde.

> The thegns stand as one a folk at the ready
> warbandmen given drink so they do as I bid.

Within modern Þéodisc Geléafa, hold oaths are used in lieu of ties of blood. Modern Heathens are in a situation very similar to ancient warriors who lost their kin through warfare or migration. We are not related to the people we chose to join in fellowship, worship, and community. Yet to be a þéod or tribe we must have ties that bind, bonds that draw us closer together as a folk and help inbuilding a common identity. It is only natural then that we use hold oaths in the way they were used in ancient times, as a way to create bonds of artificial kinship.These bonds within a modern Þéodisc group are referred to as the web of oaths, and cumulate in the person the group has chosen as its leader. One man is oathed to a lord, who in turn is oathed to another lord, ultimately ending with the ealdorman, dryhten, or cyning of the þéod. The person one is oathed to can be thought of as a kind of foster brother or sister (or if the age difference is sufficient, a father).The purpose of the web of oaths is to build a common identity necessary for a þéod to develop a common history and build a community of individuals and families that share a common goal and welfare.

## The Structure of Hold Oaths

Unfortunately no Heathen hold oath survives from ancient times. And while medieval oaths of fealty survive, these, having been sworn in a Christian context with heavy Classical influences may bear little resemblance to the oaths used in the Elder Heathen Period. Fortunately, while we are not given the exact wording of even one hold oath sworn by a Heathen gesíþa to a Heathen dryhten, we are told repeatedly throughout the literature of the age the duties or obligations of these oaths. In addition, we are given examples of oaths sworn in symbel, the *gielpas* and *béota*s such as Béowulf swore. Using these clues we can attempt to reconstruct a hold oath such as an ancient Heathen may have sworn.

## 1. Gielpas and Béotas

Within the sacred rite of symbel, vows to accomplish something had a definite structure. One would first recite their ancestry, and then follow that ancestry with great deeds that have been accomplished in the past, and end with a vow to do something. Within Þéodisc Geléafa, the recitation of ancestry and past deeds has become known by the Old English word *gielp*, "boasting, fame, or glory;" while the vow to accomplish a great deed has become know as the *béot*, "promise, vow." The prime example of this comes from Beowulf.

> "Wæs þu, Hroðgar, hal! Ic eom Higelaces mæg ond magoðegn; hæbbe ic mærða fela ongunnen on geogoþe.
> Wassail Horthgar! I am Hygelac's kinsman and thegn I have many great deeds, done in youth.

Another example, this one from a battle and not in the context of symbel is found in the poem The Battle of Maldon:

> Ic wylle mine æþelo eallum gecyþan, þæt ic wæs on Myrcon miccles cynnes; wæs min ealda fæder Ealhelm haten, wis ealdorman, woruldgesælig.
> I am willing that my nobility be known to all, that I am Mercian of a great family, my grandfather was called Ealhelm, a wise ealdorman and very prosperous.

This formula is seen again in the *Heimskringla* at the funeral ale of Harald Gormson.

> The first day of the feast, before King Svein went up into his father's high-seat, he drank the bowl to his father's memory, and made the solemn vow, that before three winters were past he would go over with his army to England, and either kill King Adalrad (Ethelred), or chase him out of the country.

(Heimskringla, Gordon translation)

Here while it is only natural that Svein would drink to his father's memory, one cannot help but think he was also doing it to preface his vow to take England as was custom. It is possible hold oaths, like béótas may also have began with the recitation of one's ancestry. The ancient Heathen believed that one's orlæg (karma or "personal wyrd") was passed down from an ancestor. The importance therefore of reciting one's ancestry, especially the more glorious ones, should be clear then. It was an attempt to influence the vow about to be made to have similar ends as the speaker's ancestors' would have. The idea being, "my ancestors never failed, therefore I shall not either." It would be only natural then that such a gielp could proceed a hold oath, if as anything else, as a way the warrior established who they were.

2. Obligations of Oaths as Described in the Lore

The obligations of a warrior to his lord, and a lord to his warriors are mentioned repeatedly throughout the heroic poetry of the Elder Heathen Age. A lord had to give gold, weapons, provide mead, and other gifts for his warrior:

> Ne gefrægn ic næfre wurþlicor æt wera hilde sixtig
> sigebeorna sel gebæran ne nefre swanas hwitne medo
> sel forgyldan ðonne Hnæfe guldan his hægstealdas

> Never have I heard of worthier than were at battle sixty victory warriors so bore themselves, never was such bright mead well repaid than that Hnaef yielded his home dwellers. (Finnsburh fragment)

> He beot ne aleh, beagas dælde, sinc æt symle.
> He (King Hrothgar) his boast leave allay: rings dealt out, treasure at symbel. (Beowulf 80-81)

213

In return a warrior had to fight for his lord, including avenging or dying with him if necessary:

"Ic ðæt mæl geman, þær we medu þegun, þonne we geheton ussum hlaforde in biorsele, ðe us ðas beagas geaf, þæt we him ða guðgetawa gyldan woldon gif him þyslicu þearf gelumpe, helmas ond heard sweord.

I that time remember when we mead tasted, then we promised our lord, in beer hall that gave us rings, and war gear he we would repay, if him these in ever happen in need of, helmets and hard sword. (Beowulf 2033 - 2039)

he hæfde ðeah geforþod þæt he his frean gehet, swa he beotode ær wið his beahgifan þæt hi sceoldon begen on burh ridan, hale to hame, oððe on here crincgan, on wælstowe wundum sweltan; he læg ðegenlice ðeodne gehende.

he had fulfilled that oath he swore his lord, that he boasted ere before his ring giver that either should both ride to the enclosure, whole to home or fall fighting, on the dead home dying of their wounds; he lay nobilly near his king. (The Battle of Maldon)

Looking at the Germanic heroic poetry foremost for a leader of a warband was generosity, for a warrior, loyalty.

## Sibb and the Web of Oaths

Besides the web of oaths, Þéodisc Geléafa also recognizes the natural bonds of family and kinship. Within the Englathod, for example, each individual has bonds to another in some way, shape, or form. The most basic of these bonds is that of *sibb* or kinship. The family or *mægð* was the basic unit of Dark Age Mercian society. It was the *mægð* who cared for individuals when they were ill or fell on hard times. The *mægð* was obligated to either collect wergild or wreak vengeance in case one of their number was murdered. They were also obligated to pay the wergild if one of their number murdered someone else. Women continued to be considered to be part of their families even after they married. A woman's kinsmen were expected to look after her interests and to take action if her husband abused or injured her. Beyond the *mægð,* was the *sibb* or extended family which had similar obligations. In the Englathod, the *mægð* plays an important role as it did in Dark Age Mercia. Family is important to all Þéodisc groups, and most encourage people in maintaining familial relationships even with non-Heathen family members.

## Other Core Beliefs of Anglo-Saxon Þéodisc Practice

Groups within Þéodisc Geléafa for the most part share some common beliefs that help define their version of tribalism regardless of what flavour of Heathenry they take. Below are a few of the more commonly held ideas of various Þéodisc groups.

Innangardhs/utangarths: The idea of innangardhs/utangarths is based on the ancient Heathen mindset concerning the þéod. The tribal group is viewed as an enclosure. This enclosure is made up of smaller enclosures, that is, communities, and family units. The most important group of any tribe would be its families. All outside the enclosure is seen as not affecting its existence, unless it intrudes. If an intrusion is friendly, there is no problem. If it is not friendly, the tribe reacts to defend its self. This core belief in the tribe or þéod as an enclosure is related to many of the other core beliefs in tribal ørlög, "luck", and even frith.

Frith: The word frith derives from Indo-European *priyas,* "one's own." Many other words derive from this root word such as Old English freogan "to love," freodom "freedom," and Old Norse Freyr, the god. According to most Old English dictionaries, the word frith meant "peace, tranquillity, security, or refuge." It also referred to the special protection offered by the tribe and the penalty for breaching that protection. A verb form, frithian meant "to make peace with, cherish, guard, defend, or keep." For the Heathen neo-tribe it means the peace and security that must be maintained to ensure the group's prosperity. A breach of frith can affect the group's luck and ørlög.

Tribal Ørlög and mægen ("luck"): Just as individuals have mægen (hamingja or "luck") that is determined by their deeds, and ørlög that determines the course their lives will take (again based on their deeds), tribal organisations feel as a whole they do too. As such, the ørlög and mægen of a group are determined by its actions as a collective whole. This was the earliest theological basis for Heathen law. Law was seen as that which was laid down in the Well of Wyrd to guide the tribe.

These beliefs along with the standard beliefs of Ásatrú and Germanic Heathenry, in the Gods, wights, and Wyrd form the core of tribalism.

## Geographical Proximity

Ideally a tribe would live in the same area. This helps strengthen the tribal identity, and gives a chance for weekly if not day to day interaction. However, this has not often worked out. The Miercinga Ríce, one of the larger tribal organisations has strove for forming "micro-tribes" if you will with a small degree of success. However, it has not been on a scale to see if it indeed would work any better than members spread across a wide area. Theodish Belief's Frisian Ríce was very localized, and this grew to descent numbers (they are one of the larger Theodish groups). However, its members are now widespread after a few years of existence.

216

# Bibliography

Aswynn, Freya. Leaves of Yggdrasil. (St. Paul, MN: Llewellyn)

Bauschatz, Paul. The Well and the Tree (Amherst, MA: University of Massachusetts Press, 1982)

Blain, Jenny Nine Worlds of Seid-Magic: Ecstasy and Neo-Shamanism in North European Paganism, (Routledge, 2001)

Bosworth, Joseph; T.Northcote Toller. An Anglo-Saxon Dictionary and An Anglo-Saxon Dictionary: Supplement. (Oxford, England: Oxford University Press).

Branston, Brian. Gods of the North (London: Thames & Hudson, 1955)

Branston, Brain. Lost Gods of England (London: Thames and Hudson)

Byock, Jesse (tr.). Saga of the Volsungs. (Berkeley, CA : University of California Press)

Cæsar, Julius; S.A. Handford, tr. The Conquest of Gaul (Penguin Books, 1982).

Chisholm, James, Grove and Gallows (Austin TX: Rune-Gild, 1987).

Cleasby, Richard; Gudbrand Vigfusson, An Icelandic-English Dictionary (Oxford, England: Oxford University Press)

Conquergood, Dwight. "Boasting in Anglo-Saxon England, Performance, and the Heroic Ethos". Literature and Performance, vol. I, April 1991, pp. 24-35.

DaSant, George W.(tr.) Njal's Saga ((London, 1861) Elliot, R.W.V. Runes, (Manchester, England: Manchester University Press)

Ellis-Davidson, H.R. Gods and Myths of Northern Europe. (New York, NY: Viking-Penguin)

Ellis-Davidson, H.R. Myths and Symbols in Pagan Europe. (New York: University of Syracuse Press: Syracuse).

Ellis, H.R. The Road to Hel (Cambridge: Cambridge University Press, 1943; rep. Greenwood Press, 1977).

Gloseki, Stephen. Shamanism and Old English Poetry (New York: Garland Publishing, 1989).

Grammaticus, Saxo; Oliver Elton (tr.) The Danish History

(Norroena Society, 1905).

Grattan, John Henry Grafton. and Charles Singer. Anglo-Saxon Magic and Medicine (Norwood, PA: Norwood Editions, 1976).

Griffiths, Bill, Aspects of Anglo-Saxon Magic (Norfolk: Anglo-Saxon Books, 1999)

Grimm, Jacob; James Stallybrass (tr.) Teutonic Mythology (4 vols). (Magnolia, MA: Peter Smith Publishing) Grönbech, Vilhelm. Culture of the Teutons (London: Oxford University Press, 1931).

Gundarsson., Kveldulf Teutonic Religion (St. Paul, MN: Llewellyn,1996)

Hastrup, Kirsten. Culture and History in Mediæval Iceland (Oxford: Clarendon Press, 1985)

Hallakarva , Gunnora "Courtship, Love and Marriage in Viking Scandinavia" (http://vikinganswerlady.org [Electronic version])

Hodge, Winifred, "On the Meaning of Frith" (Lina, Midsummer 1996)

Hollander, Lee. The Poetic Edda. (Austin, TX: University of Texas Press)

Lang, Samuel (tr.) Heimskringla: A History of the Norse Kings (London: Norroena Society, 1907)

Owen, Gale R. Rites and Religions of the Anglo-Saxons (Dorset Press, 1985)

Page, R.I. An Introduction to English Runes, (London: Methuen and Co.)

Paxson, Diana, "The Matronæ" (Sage Woman, Fall, 1999)

Paxson, Diana "The Return of the Völva: Recovering the Practice of Seidh (Mountain Thunder, Summer, 1993)

Polomé, Edgar C. Essays on Germanic Religion (Washington: Institute for the Study of Man, 1989).

Press, Muriel (tr.) Laxdaela Saga (London: The Temple Classics, 1899)

Schwartz, Stephen P. Poetry and Law in Germanic Myth (Berkeley: University of California Press, 1973)

Storms, Anglo-Saxon Magic (The Hague: Martinus Nijhoff, 1948)

Sturluson, Snorri ; Anthony Faulkes (tr.). Edda. (Rutland VT : Everyman's Press)

Snorri Sturluson; Erling Monsen, A.H. Smith (trs., eds). Heimskringla. (New York, NY: Dover Publications: Inc).

Storms, Dr. G. Anglo-Saxon Magic (The Hague: Martinus Nijhoff, 1948).

Tacitus, Cornelius. Agricola, Germania, Dialogus. Loeb Classics Library ed., (Cambridge, MA: Harvard University Press)

Thorsson, Edred, A Book of Troth (St. Paul, MN: Llewellyn)

Turville-Petre, E.O.G. Myth and Religion of the North. (Westport, CT: Greenwood Publishing Group)

Wilson, David. Anglo-Saxon Paganism (New York, NY: Routledge, 1992)

Wilson, David M. (ed.) The Archaeology of Anglo-Saxon England (Cambridge: University Press, 1981)

Wodening, Eric, "The Meaning of Frith" (Ásatrú Today, December 1994)

Wodening, Eric, We Are Our Deeds: The Elder Heathenry, its Ethic and Thew (Watertown, NY: THEOD, 1998)

Wodening, Swain, Beyond Good and Evil: Germanic Heathen Ethics (Watertown, NY: THEOD, 1994)

Wodening, Swain, Þéodpisc Geléfa" The Belief of the Tribe (Huntsville, MO: Englatheod, 2007)

# Appendix I

Online Resources

Englatheod http://www.englatheod.org The website of Englatheod which contains much information not included in this book on Anglo-Saxon Heathenry.

English Heathenism http://www.englishheathenism.homestead.com/ An excellent resource that concentrates solely on Anglo-Saxon paganism

# Appendix II

Old English Pronunciation Guide

Vowels

**a** as in "baa" (like a sheep) **á** as in 'father" **æ** as in "hat" **ǣ** as in "bad" **e** as in "bed" **é** as in "bade" **i** as in "bid" **í** as in "machine"

**o** as in "body" **ó** as in "boat" **u** as in "pull" **ú** as in "pool" **y** as in French "tu" **ý** as in French "ruse"

Dipthongs

Dipthongs are two vowels that blend together to form one sound such as the ea in "beast" or the oy in "boy." **ea** æ + e **éa** long æ + a **eo** e +o **éo** é + o **ie** i + e **íe** í + e

Consonants

Most consonants are pronounced the same as in modern English. There are a few exceptions:

c before the vowels o, a, u, æ and the consonants r, l, n it is like c in "corn." Before e and i and after i it is pronounced like the ch in "chin." There are exceptions such as OE céne which uses a k sound. If in doubt, use the pronunciation of the modern word as a guide. cg like the dg of "bridge." f at the beginning of a word like the f in "fat." Between vowels it is pronounced like the v in "love." When doubled it is the same as in "offer." g has three different sounds. Before o, a, u, æ and the consonants r, l, n it sounds like the g in "gold." Between vowels and at the end of words it sounds like the ch of Scots "loch." Before the vowels e and i it sounds like the y in "yield." h at the beginning of a word like the h in heart. Between vowels it is much like the ch in Scots "loch." s at the beginning of a word is like the s in "seven." Between vowels it is

like the letter z. Doubled it is like the two ss of "mess ." **sc** like sh in "ship." **þ / ð** þ is pronounced like the th in "thorn," while **ð** comes only between

vowels and is pronounced much like the th in "thine."

# Appendix III
## Englisc Rímbóc
The Anglo-Saxon Calendar

Bede's Account of the Calendar in *De Temporum Ratione*

One of the least studied things in ancient Anglo-Saxon culture is the old pagan calendar. Yet, it is an area of most interest for many. What we know of the calendar was handed down to us by Bede in his work *De Temporum Ratione*. Unfortunately, while Bede gave us much information, he also left us in quite a mystery about how the calendar worked. We know not from his information alone whether the months were reckoned by the phases of the moon, and if so, whether they began on the Full or New Moon. We are perplexed how a fixed solar date could be the start of the year in a calendar that appears to be solar lunar (a calendar using both the Sun to keep track of years and the Moon to keep track of months), and even more so by when that fixed date occurs. Still, the information Bede gave us, along with other clues from Anglo-Saxon culture, the practices of other cultures, and comparison with the Icelandic calendar can result in a reliable reconstruction.

Bede begins his account of the old Heathen calendar by saying

> Antiqui autem anglorum populi (neque enim mihi congrum videturaliarum gentium annalem observantiam dicere et meæ reticere)iutxa cursum lunæ suos menses computavere. Unde et a lunahebræorum et græcorum more nomen accipiuiunt; siduidem apudeos luna mona, mensis appellatur monath.

> The ancient English peoples -- for it does not seem to me proper to explain the yearly observance of other nations, and to keep silenceconcerning my own --

reckoned their months by the course of themoon, just as they were named from the moon in Hebrew andGreek. (Charles W, Jones translation)

Thus the mystery begins from the start of his text. Most have thought that "cursumlunæ suos menses computavere (by the course of the moon calculated)" indicates that the months were determined by the phases of the Moon. However, besides keeping track of time through the phases of the Moon, one can also keep track of time by the path the Moon takes through the sky. Using the course of the Moon to keep track of time results in using what modern astronomers call a sideral month,which is 27 days 7 hours and 43 minutes long. Every 27 days the moon returns tothe same position in the sky it was 27 days before. The scholar Vaster Guðmundsson believed that this was the form of month the Norse used, and used it in his theoretical reconstruction of the ancient Scandinavian calendar (Guðmundsson. 1924, p.88). It is possible then that the Anglo-Saxons also did the same. However, as Bede draws a comparison to the Greek and Hebrew calendars, we may want to assume that the Anglo-Saxons used a synodic month (a month measured from a phase of the Moon to the next time that phase of the Moon occurs). There are other clues in Bede's account, that indicate this was so, and I will touch on those later. Bede then goes on to name the months of the old Anglo-Saxon calendar and further gives the corresponding Roman month.

> Primusqu eorum mesis, quem latini ianuarium vocant, dicitur giuli;deinde februarius, solmonah; martius, hredmonath; aprilis, eosturmonath; maius, thrimilchi; iunius lida; iulius, similiter lida; augustus, vveodmonath; september, halegmonath; october, vvinterfilleth;november, blodmonath; december, giuli eodem quo ianuariusnomine vocatur.
>
> The first month, which the Romans name January, is with them*Giuli*. Then follow February, *Solmónaþ*; *March, Hrédmónaþ*; April, *Éosturmónaþ*; May, *Þrimilchi;* June, *Líþa;* July also *Líþa;* August, *Wéodmónaþ; September, Háligmónaþ;* October, *Winterfylleþ;*November, *Blótmónaþ;* Decemeber,

223

*Giuuli,* the same as for January. (Charles W, Jones translation)

At first this may not seem important, however, it shows that the Anglo-Saxon months roughly followed the Roman ones, enough so that Bede could draw correspondences. This shows what we have suspected, that the calendar was a solar lunar one, not a straight lunar calendar. And while it does not rule out the use of the sideral month, it increases the odds that the Anglo-Saxons used a synodic month. Sideral months being shorter would move more within the solar year. Synodic months being closer in length to the Roman fixed months would make for a closer comparison, and not move as much in relation to the seasons aslong as intercalary (leap) months were used.

Bede then touches on when the year started. Something he has already hinted at by naming *Giuli,* the month corresponding to January as the first month.

> Incipiebant autem annum ab ocatavo kelendarum ianuariarum die,ubi nunc natalem domini celebramus. Et ipasm noctem nunc nobis sacrosanctam, tunc gentili vocabulo modranect, id est matrum noctem, appellabant, ob causam, ut suspicamur, ceremoniarumquas in ea pervigiles agebant.
>
> They began the year with December 25, the day we now celebrate as Christmas; and the very night to which we attach special sanctity they designated by the heathen term *módraniht,* that is, the mothers' night --- a name bestowed, I suspect, on account of the ceremonies they performed while watching this night through. (Charles W,Jones translation)

At that time, under the old Julian calendar, December 25 (or eight days before the calends of January as Bede puts it) was also the winter solstice. The problem with this is that if the Anglo-Saxon calendar was a solar lunar calendar, then it could not have a starting point that was a fixed solar date (at least not have such a fixed date and operate with any accuracy). Bede may have confused an Anglo-Saxon pagan mid-winter festival with a New Year's celebration. Or it is possible the actual start of the new year was on the Full or New Moon near the solstice. It is also possible the Anglo-Saxons used a sideral month and somehow managed to reconcile its differences with the solar year (though it would be as difficult to do this as reconciling the start of a lunar calendar using synodic months in such a fashion). Finally, the most distinct possibility perhaps is the Anglo-Saxon Heathens used more than one calendar for more than one purpose. That is they could have used a solar calendar separate from the one Bede presented, and it was the solar calendar whose new year began on December 25. There have been many theories as to why the year began on December 25, ranging from Roman borrowing to influences of Mithraism, but few have thought it the start of a separate calendar. The possibility is distinct however.

The Icelanders, for example, did use a solar calendar which they established in 930 CE in conjunction with the Norse lunar months (which ceased to be lunar), but reformed again in 955. The core of this calendar consisted of twos easons, winter and summer for a year of 364 days or 52 weeks. Each season was 26 weeks long. To this calendar was added one week every seven years as a "leapweek," to keep it in line with the solar year (much as a day is added every four years to the Gregorian calendar today). New Year's Day was Veturnætur or"Winter Nights," a time near the Fall equinox. While some scholars have attributed the Icelanders adopting a solar calendar as being due to Classical and Christian influence (via trade relations with the then Christian Anglo-Saxons and Irish), one cannot rule out the possibility a solar calendar was a native idea to most Germanic peoples. The Anglo-Saxons like the Icelanders also had only two seasons, Summer and Winter, and this is even stated by Bede (though elsewhere he refers to four, a comment that can be attributed to his Church education which held there were four seasons, not two). It would not be surprising then if they used a separate solar calendar based on the equinoxes and solstices, perhaps even using weeks for time reckoning much like the Icelanders did. Further it would not be farfetched if they saw

Módranect as some sort of marker in this calendar. In Bede's account the start of the year, he notes the start of Winter (while linked to a Full Moon, it would be close to what we know as autumn), the Winter solstice, and the fact months were added after the Summer solstice. It would be difficult therefore to assume that the Anglo-Saxons and Germanic peoples in general could not have kept track of time by the Sun. Bede then goes on to talk about the use of an intercalary month called Þriliða.

cum vero temporibus, hoc est xiii mensium lunarium, annus occurreret, superfluum mensem æstati apponebant, ita ut tunc tres menses simul lida nomine vocarentur, et ob id annus ille thrilidi cognominabatur habens quattuor menses æstatis, ternos ut semper temporum cæsterorum.

When, however, an embolism occurred, that is, a year of thirteen lunar months, they added the intercalated month to the summer, so that in that case three months in succession were called Líþa. Such a year was known as Þrilíþi, having four months of summer, and three of the other seasons. (Charles W, Jones translation)

We know from this statement by Bede that Þriliða was added in some years in the Summer to bring the calendar back in line with the solar cycle. This again is a clue that the calendar was indeed a solar lunar one, most likely using synodic months (using one phase of the Moon to its next occurrence as a way of measuring a month). The Chinese, Hebrews, and even the ancient Romans used similar methods to adjust their calendars.

Item principaliter annum totem in duo tempora, hiemis videlicet et æstatis, dispertiebant - sex illos menses quibus longiores sunt noctinus dies æstati tribuendo, sex reliquos hiemi. Unde et mensem quo hiemalia tempora incipiebant vvinterfilleth apbellabant, composito nomine ab jieme et plenilunio quia videlicet a plenilunio eiusdem mensis hiems sortiretur initium.

The general division of the year was into two seasons,

winter and summer, summer comprising the six months in which the days are longer than the nights, and winter the others. Hence the month with which they began the winter season was called *Winterfylleþ,* a name compounded of the terms for winter and full moon, because from the full moon of that month winter was esteemed to begin. (Charles W, Jones translation)

It is worth noting that the time of *Winterfylleþ* was also the time the Old Norse started their year (Veturnætur or "Winter Nights"), and there has been speculation on whether or not the actual new year of the calendar presented by Bede did not start at this time also, that Bede was mistaken. That Winter could be used of the entire year and not just the season is apparent to anyone that has studied Old English. The Anglo-Saxons counted years by winters and even had such terms as *wintergetel* "a number of years" and *wintersteal* "a one year old stallion." Garman Lord in *The Way of the Heathen* even theorizes that perhaps the name *Winterfylleþ* could have meant something closer to "New Year's Day." More important though, what Bede has to say about *Winterfylleþ* is also a clue that the months began with the Full Moon. Bede goes on to discuss the meaning of the month names, and as such this is his extent of clues on how the calendar operated. For more information on exactly how the calendar worked we must go outside his text to Anglo-Saxon concepts of the day, as well as draw from other cultures with solar lunar calendars. One of the primary problems with the calendar is determining when the months began. Since few ancient cultures used the sideral month in calendars of this type, we can safely assume perhaps that the ancient Angles, Saxons, and Jutes used a synodic month like the Chinese, Hebrews, ancient Romans, and most other peoples in the world. But then we are faced with the question of when did the months begin? The only clue Bede gives us is in the name of *Winterfylleþ,* when he states that Winter was said to start from the Full Moon of that month. If Winter started on the Full Moon of *Winterfylleþ* and each season only had six months (not portions of months but whole months) then we almost must assume that *Winterfylleþ* began on the Full Moon. Then again Bede states Winter began on the Full Moon of that month, meaning that the month its self might not begin on the Full Moon. For a solution to this dilemma we must look to other cultures with similar ways of seeing tides as well as closely related cultures.

A bronze plaque with a calendar used by the Gauls engraved on it was found in Coligny, France, in 1897, and dated to about 50 CE. This calendar consisted of 12 months with names of Celtic origin. Further these months began on the Full Moon. The Gauls had lived in close proximity to the Germanic peoples for centuries. At one point it is possible that some of the Germanic tribes had developed a fascination with Celtic culture (or alternately been subjugated by a Celtic people). Within the Germanic languages there are several Celtic borrowings of great antiquity. These borrowings were words for rulership and warfare. Among them are the modern English word iron, Old English *ríce*, "kingdom;" and Old English *ambeht,* "servant." It is possible then that due to Celtic influence the Anglo-Saxons used the Full Moon as the marker for the start of a new month. Most societies that use a solar lunar calendar however do not use the Full Moon as a starting point for months.

Indeed, there is just as much evidence when we look at other cultures for the Anglo-Saxon calendar beginning its months on the first crescent of the New Moon. Further the evidence is also more convincing when common sense is applied. The first and best argument is that it is difficult to determine precisely when the Full Moon is occurring in Northern Europe. Indeed, it can appear to be full for three days, when in truth, only one of these days is the Full Moon. The New Moon can be almost as difficult to determine, but not quite as difficult. One can always look to the First Crescent of the New Moon, something easy to spot if one is watching for it, and not easily mistaken for another phase. This is precisely the moon phase many cultures such as the Hebrew and Babylonian cultures used. Further, cultures that start their day at sunset, also usually begin their year in the

Winter months and their months (if they use a solar lunar calendar) with the New Moon or the First Crescent. The ancient Roman calendar prior to revisions by the Republic also started its months with the First Crescent as did that of the ancient Greek cultures. Perhaps the best evidence arguing for the Anglo-Saxons using the First Crescent is that of the Lithuanian calendar. The Lithuanian calendar not only started its months on the First Crescent of the New Moon, but also had a midwinter celebration the same time as Yule. Oddly enough though it started its year in April (Straižys and Klimka). Perhaps of all Indo-European peoples the Balts have the most in common with the Germanic. Even their religion is very close to the ancient Germanic one with components such as a World Tree, and deities similar to our own such as the thunder god Perkunas who is not a far cry from the ever familiar Þunor (Thor), not to mention a Sun goddess and Moon god. Unfortunately, especially since it may be the closest comparison to the Anglo-Saxon calendar, not much has been written on the Lithuanian calendar in English. Yet considering the close relationship of the Balts to the Germanic peoples, it presents a good argument for the Anglo-Saxon months starting with the First Crescent, and not the Full Moon. Another clue to the months starting on the First Crescent is when the Anglo-Saxons began their day. Other cultures such as the Hebrew that use the First Crescent as the starting point for their months, start their day at sunset (the Lithuanians seem to be an exception). We find this too with the Anglo-Saxons. Wódenesniht to an ancient Engle was not Wednesday night but Tuesday night; Wednesday began on what we would think of as Tuesday evening. We can also see this start of the day at Sunset with the festivals, for example, Módraniht mentioned by Bede. Modern survivals of this include Halloween (a contraction of "All Hallows Evening"), New Years Eve, and Walpurgis Night. The Old English word *niht*, not *dæg* was used for counting, that is one would say "10 nihtas" not "10 dægas" (a modern survival of this is our term fortnight). This too was indicative of cultures that started their months on the First Crescent. We can therefore probably safely assume therefore that the Anglo-Saxons used the First Crescent as a marker for the start of a month, although we can never be one hundred per cent certain (barring finding a lost document dating from the period detailing such calendar information).

Other Potential Calendars

As mentioned above, a solar lunar calendar may not have been the only way that the Anglo-Saxons kept track of times longer than a day. There were the two seasons called *missera* in Old English. We know that they had two seasons, but we do not know if they were used in such a way as the Icelanders later did. For the Icelanders, the *missera* played a more important role than the solar year. Indeed, their calendar was not based so much on the solar year as it was the half year. As detailed above, their calendar consisted of the two seasons, numbered 26 weeks each. The two seasons were further broken down into weeks. The week has always been a problematic time unit however. Most scholars view it as a borrowing from the Romans, who in turn borrowed it from the Greeks. Ultimately it is seen as having come from the Semitic cultures of the Middle East with its sole purpose being religious. That is scholars feel the week is a man-made time unit with no bearing on astronomical or natural events (unlike the month, the year, the day). The problem is that within the written record of many peoples such as the Celts and Germanics, there is no sign of there not being a 7 day week, or at least a week of some sort. So while scholars can claim that the week is a borrowing, they cannot prove definitively it is a borrowing. This problem is further complicated when one looks at how a week can be used in time keeping. The synodic month is approximately 29 days and 12 hours long. Four seven day weeks could then be used as a rough division of the month (being only a day or so off). This is somewhat confirmed by the origins of the word week which scholars think comes from an Indo-European word meaning "to turn." In other words, the word week might have originally referred to the turning of the phases of the moon (and it also may have been a longer time unit than now). Even there we are on shaky ground as while some consider it a native Germanic term, others see it as coming from Latin *vices* "recurrences." While the week as we know it now may be a borrowing, the concept of a unit of time lasting several days (but only a fraction of a month) may not be. The Lithuanians used a nine day week at one point, which makes for a good division of the the sideral month. As mentioned above a sideral month, is 27 days 7 hours and 43 minutes long. Therefore the week in some form may have always been a Germanic time keeping unit (however, it may not have always been seven days long). Vaster Guðmundsson believed that the Norse used a five day week prior to the borrowing of the seven day week, and used this in his reconstruction of the Norse calendar. However, his week has no bearing on astronomical events either. The solar year is more evenly divided by five week periods though, and there is an Old Norse legal term referring to such a five day period as a *fimmt*. There could no doubt be other time units similar to the week we do not know of that the ancient Germanic peoples, and thus the ancient Angles, Saxons, and Jutes may have used. That information though is unfortunately lost if it ever existed.

Regardless, that they could have used a solar calendar similar to the Icelandic one after Roman contact is a certainty. They would have had the time unit of the week, and had all the astronomical knowledge to use one (which they had well before Roman contact). It could well be that such a solar calendar is seen lurking behind the solar lunar one as presented by Bede. He does after all refer to solar events such as the start of the year on the winter solstice and the seasons in his description of the calendar. The only problem is, we can keep on saying "could," as there is no evidence truly for or against the Anglo-Saxons using a solely solar calendar like that of the Icelanders. What we do know is that *missrera* could also be used to mean years, as its Old Norse cognate *missari* could also. Indeed, the Norse did not even truly have a term for the whole year. If the *missrera* then played a more important part in Anglo-Saxon time keeping, they would most certainly had a solar calendar as well.

Other Methods of Telling Time Shorter than a Day

On quite firmer ground than the possible use of a solar calendar is how the Anglo-Saxons divided the day. It would appear that they, like their Norse cousins divided the day into eight even divisions, or *stundas* (sometimes referred to as a *tíd* in Old English). Early Anglo-Saxon sundials (a *sol-merca* or *dægmæl*) show only four evenly spaced marks for telling time during daylight (these four divisions of daylight are paralleled by four at night). The names of these eight divisions are seen throughout Old English literature. They are: *úht* (roughly 3 am to 6 am), *morgen* (roughly 6 am to 9 am), *undern* (roughly 9 am to noon), *middæg* (roughly noon to 3 pm), *gelotendæg* (roughly 3 pm to 6 pm), *æfen* (roughly 6 pm to 9 pm), *niht* (roughly 9 pm to midnight), and *midniht* (roughly midnight to 3 am). Our usage of such words as morning, noon, and evening to divide up the day are but vestiges of this time keeping method. There is a very good article on how the Norse used these divisions for time keeping at:

hea-www.harvard.edu/ECT/Daymarks/

called *Telling Time without a Clock: Scandinavian Daymarks*. The methods described in it are no doubt the same as used by the ancient Anglo-Saxons

Ritual Times

The earliest calendars of most ancient societies seem to have been established to keep track of religious observances. Agriculture, the other great preoccupation of ancient peoples had no real need for a calendar as the time to plant or reap was fairly obvious by observing the weather. Bede mentions several potential Anglo-Saxon holytides but did not unfortunately elaborate on them. Snorri does say if the Old Norse in the *Heimskringla* that:

þâ skyldi blôta î môti vetri til ârs, enn at miðjum vetri blôta til grôðrar, it þriðja at sumri, þat var sigrblôt

"On winter day there should be blood-sacrifice for a

good year, and in the middle of winter for a good crop; and the third sacrifice should be on summer day, for victory in battle." (Ynglinga Saga Chapter 8)

The ancient Anglo-Saxon Heathens seem to have paralleled these three great holy tides of the Norse. Libermann in *The National Assembly in the Anglo-Saxon Period* notes that the Anglo-Saxon *witanagemót* met most often on St. Martin's Day (November 10th), Christmas, and Easter or Whitsunday. These dates correspond to when Anglo-Saxon kings are reported to have worn their crowns (Chaney, *Cult of Anglo-Saxon Kingship, p. 65*). If we accept Bede's description of the Anglo-Saxon pagan calendar in *De Temporum Ratione* there may have been more Anglo-Saxon pagan holy tides. Bede as stated above started the Heathen year with *Modranect*, the "Mothers Night." It fell between *Ærra Geola*, our December and *Æfterra Geola*, or January, and is the period today we know as Yule (which is now no more than a synonym for Christmas for most people). Of *Solmonað*, roughly our February, Bede says the Anglo-Saxons offered cakes to their Gods, and thus it was named the month of cakes; he also mentions *Hreðmonað*, roughly our March as when the Goddess *Hreðe* was worshipped, followed by *Eastremonað* when the Goddess *Eostre* was worshipped. He does not name *Liða* as a sacred month, however, that Midsummer falls within it, there may have been a holy day corresponding to Mid-Winter or Yule. This is pretty much confirmed by Midsummer celebrations that survived into modern times in England, not to mention much folklore surrounding St. John's Day which falls near the summer solstice. Bede then mentions *Haligmonað*, roughly our September, which was called "holy" as in Bede's words "because our ancestors, when they were heathen, paid their devil tribute in that month."

The next potential holy tide mentioned by Bede is *Blótmonað*, roughly our November. The name its self means "sacrifice month" and was the time when animals were slaughtered for the coming winter. It follows *Winterfylleð* which corresponds to the Norse Winter Nights or Winter's Day, the time the ancients reckoned winter to have started.

That All Hallows, St. Martin's Day, and Guy Fawkes Day, all important English holidays fall in this period would seem to indicate the actual holy tide took place near or at the junction of the two months. One of the problems in reconstructing the Anglo-Saxon Heathen calendar is that we do not know the criteria for dating a holy tide year to year with the exception of *Modranect* (and of course if we accept a similar holy tide on Midsummer). Heathen Easter for example may have been dated by the Spring equinox, the same way the Christian Easter is by the first Full Moon after the spring equinox, or by the first New Moon of Spring.

A Reconstruction of the Heathen Anglo-Saxon Calendar

A reliable reconstruction of the Heathen Anglo-Saxon calendar is possible (though whether it comes close to how the ancient one was truly reckoned is another matter). First we must make some assumptions based on Bede as we have few facts on how the calendar operated. These assumptions are: a. the month began on the First Crescent of the New Moon; b. the month was a synodic month; c. leap months were periodically used to pull the lunar calendar back in line with the solar year; d. the months of *Líþa* and *Giuli* are double months (that is they are roughly 57 days long). The first two assumptions are based on comparisons with other cultures that use a lunar or solar lunar calendar, the last two based on the statements by Bede on the month of *Þriliða* and the names of the months. In addition we have a clue provided by Bede as to how the calendar should operate. *Modranect* is a set solar event that will not change year from year and therefore the calendar must accommodate it in some way. In order to make a solar lunar calendar work, we must first make up for the difference between the lunar and solar years. A lunar year using synodic months is 354 days long while a solar year is about 365. Using straight lunar months with no leap days, weeks, or months would result in the calendar being off by over an entire month in under four years. The Muslim calendar does this, allowing its months and holy tides to float around the year. However, as indicated by Bede (as well as the month names) this does not seem to be the case for the Anglo-Saxons. Therefore one needs to use leap months to keep the two calendars (solar and lunar in line). One method that works for this is to use the Metonic Cycle. The Metonic cycle was discovered by Meton of Athens (about. 440 BCE) who noticed that 235 lunar months made up almost exactly 19 solar years. Thus phases of the Moon fall on exactly the same solar dates every 19 years. By adding Þriliða in the 3rd, 6th, 8th, 11th, 14th, and 19th years of this cycle one can keep the lunar months roughly in line with the solar calendar. Another method developed by Professor Kenneth Harrison involved using the the *octaëteris* or *ogdoas*. The *octaëteris* or *ogdoas* is a span of eight years of 99 lunar months at the start of the Metonic cycle following the pattern of OOEOOEOE where O is an ordinary year and E is a leap year. This method follows roughly the same pattern as the one above only over a shorter period.

John Robert Stone based on Harrison's model created several rules that perhaps are more practical. These are (quoted exactly): 1. The next month is intercalary if the first crescent of the after *Líða* is observed on or before July 4, the eleventh evening after Midsummer Eve (June 23). 2. The next month is intercalary if the first crescent of the after *Líða* is observed before Midsummer. 3. The next summer will contain a third *Líða* if the first crescent of the after *Geola* is observed within the eves of Christmas tide (December 24 to January 4). Stone's method does work but it also has problems. The first is he is working on the idea of an *Ærra Géola* and *Æftera Géola* as well as *Ærra Líða* and *Æftera Líða*. Bede does not mention these month names, and while the names for *Géola* are paralleled in the Gothic month names of *Fruma Jiuleis* and Aftuma *Jiulea*, there is little else to suggest these were separate months and not double months. The primary problem with using *Ærra Géola*, *Æftera Géola* and *Ærra Líða*, *Æftera Líða* is it is near impossible to construct a calendar that will sandwich the solar dates of Yule and Midsummer between their respective months.

This is perhaps only possible if one uses double months for *Líþa* and *Giuli*. The Norse once used a calendar of only six 59 day months (or double months) which indicates the idea was not alien to Germanic peoples. If one makes *Líþa* and *Giuli* double months, one can then ensure that Yule and Midsummer always fall within their respective months regardless of which set of rules one uses. The next problem is reconciling the start of the year with the beginning of the months. Bede clearly states that the year began on *Módraniht* and gives a date of December 25th, the old winter solstice date under the Julian calendar. It is not truly possible for the first month of the year to begin on this date every year as the First Crescent of the New Moon will not fall on December 25th each and every year. Indeed, the majority of the time the First Crescent will not fall on December 25th. We must assume then that perhaps Bede was mistaken, and that *Módraniht* merely fell near the start of the new month (perhaps within 12 days of it). It is also possible that the Anglo-Saxon new year was actually in the Fall, and that it began with *Winterfylleþ*. The Norse started their year at this time and referred to it as *Veturnætur* or "Winter Nights." In closing one can create a reconstruction by considering the following: 1) *Líþa* and *Giuli* are considered double months. 2) *Módraniht* fell within 12 nights of the First Crescent of the New Moon. 3) Intercalatory months were added in the 3rd, 6th, 8th, 11th, 14th, and 19th years of the Metonic Cycle.

Bibliography

Baity E.C. Archaeoastronomy and Ethnoastronomy so far // Current Anthropology. 1973, 14. p.389-449.
Harrison, Kenneth, The Framework of Anglo-Saxon History to A.D. 900 Cambridge: Cambridge University Press 1976
Hastrup, Kirsten, Culture and History in Medieval Iceland. Oxford: Claredon Press 1985
Hutton, Ronald The Pagan Religions of the Ancient British Isles; Their Nature and Legacy
Nilsson, Martin P. Primitive time-reckoning, Lund: C. W. K. Gleerup, 1920 Straižys, Vytautas and Klimka, Libertas (12, Vilnius 2600)  Chapter 5. Natural rythms and calendar, COSMOLOGY OF THE ANCIENT

BALTS Retrieved 2 Sept., 2004 from
http://www.lithuanian.net/mitai/cosmos/baltai5.htm
Stone, John Robert, Observing Bede's Anglo-Saxon Calendar
Retrieved 2, Sept., 2004 from
http://www.kami.demon.co.uk/gesithas/calendar/obs_bede
.html

# Appendix IV Basic Mead Making

This mead recipe is for a "sack mead," a very sweet mead with a high alcohol content. It is a pure mead, in that nothing but honey is added, except for tannic acid or tea as an option. The ratio of honey to mead is high, 5 lbs of honey to 1 gallon of water. This makes it an extremely sweet mead in that some of the sugars survive fermentation. The reason is simple, there is too much sugar for the yeast to covert to alcohol before the sheer amount of alcohol kills the yeast, and stops fermentation. One can expect to produce a mead with anywhere from 16% to 18% alcohol content.

Items Needed ! primary fermenter (a glass carboy), secondary fermenter (a second glass carboy) , fermentation lock, (two, one for the primary and one for the secondary)., siphon hose, bottling valve, bottles, corks, stoneware or enamel pot (to boil in.. DO NOT use metal, it leaches into the mead and can ruin the flavour), wooden spoon (for the same reason as above)

Ingredients:

 10 to 20 lbs. of unpasteurized non-blended honey (clover honey seems to work best)
 2 to 4 gallons of water (preferably spring water like Thor's Spring)
 champagne yeast  (1 to 2 packets)
 tannic acid (2 to 4 teaspoons) or a strong tea like Earl Grey (1 to 2  bags) (optional)

Making the Mead

Prior to starting, sterilize every piece of equipment you are using. This can be done by using chlorine bleach, or boiling the equipment in water. But regardless of how, everything must be washed clean, and sterilized right before use. Once your equipment is ready, put the water in the stoneware pot. Bring the water to a boil in the stoneware, and then allow to cool to a slow simmer. Once the water has cooled to a simmer, add the honey by stirring it in. Stir the mixture of honey and water constantly! If you do not stir it, the honey will settle to the bottom of the pot, and burn. Once the honey is fully dissolved, using the wooden spoon, or a piece of cheese cloth, skim the scum off the top, and keep this up until it is fairly clear (the honey water should look like golden water). Try to keep the water at a slow simmer.

Many folks feel boiling the honey water ruins the bouquet or smell of the mead, so if that is important to you, do not allow it to come to a full boil. The point of boiling is to keep it at a high temperature to kill off any wild yeast. Each type of yeast will give it a different flavor, and therefore wild yeast left living in the honey will spoil the taste of the mead. Otherwise, you must use Campden, a chemical to sterilize the mix, and this can alter the taste of the honey as well. As this recipe calls for using heat for sterilization, the use of Campden tablets will not be covered here. However, if you do not heat the honey water, you cannot remove the pollutants in the honey (flower pollen, dirt, and so forth), and these are the primary causes of mead hangovers, not to mention will also alter the taste of the mead. Once all the scum is skimmed from the top of the honey water, allow it to cool for a hour and place in the fridge overnight. If you wish, add the tannic acid or tea and allow to simmer a while longer. The purpose of tannic acid or tea is to keep the mead from having a super sweet taste, to give it a bit of bitter bite.

You can, of course, completely leave out this step, and have a super sweet mead. For a sack mead like this recipe, the alcohol content generally give bite enough. You now have what is called must. By the way, you can use a hydrometer at this point to test its potential alcohol content. Prior to fermentation, use the hydrometer to find out how much sugar is in the must. This may help later in determining if fermentation has stopped.

Once the must has cooled, pour it into the primary, add the yeast, and put on the vapour lock Allow the mead to ferment in the carboy one week, then rack the mead into the other carboy. This is done by siphoning the mead from one carboy to the other. Do not allow the sediment or dregs to go into the second carboy. Allow the mead to set for a month at least and then rack (siphon) again into the other carboy.

239

Continue alternating between carboys for about three months, or until fermentation seems to have stopped, and then rack into bottles and cork. You can usually tell if fermentation has stopped by the fact there will be few to no bubbles on the top of the liquid. Alternately, you can rack out a small amount of the mead, and test its alcohol content and compare this to the potential alcohol reading you made before fermentation began. Allow the bottles to age for at least 6 months. This recipe can also be used to produce a dry mead. To do this, merely lower the amount of honey used to about 3 lbs per gallon of water.

# Appendix V
## Making a Drinking Horn

One of the most significant elements of Modern Heathen equipment is the drinking horn. Regardless of whether folks dress like the ancient Heathens for ritual or not, the vast majority will own at least one drinking horn. Raw horn is not fit to us as a vessel for drink, however, and several steps must be done to make it so.

1) Obtaining a Horn:

With the closure of most Tandy's across the USA and elsewhere, it may be difficult to obtain horns. However, many locally owned leather stores still carry them as well as Ren Faires, pioneer events, and a few craft outlets. If you buy your horn from a Ren Faire vendor, chances are it has already been crafted for drinking, and you need not do anything. However, if buying a raw horn, you must check for certain attributes.

a. Has it been punched? - Horns do not come off the neat (cow, steer, or bull) punched or cored. They are filled with a substance similar to dentine in your teeth or marrow in your bones, and this needs to be taken out. For your own sake then, its best to get a horn that has already been punched or cored.
b. Does it have thick walls? - You want your horn to have relatively thick walls. If the walls are too thin, you can easily sand through, or if carving, punch a hole through the wall.
c. Does it have an appealing color? - This is a totally subjective observation, but since you are the one using the horn, you are the one that has to live with its color. Note however, that a raw, unhanded horn will look much duller than the finished product. The whites will appear whiter, the blacks blacker, and grays grayer when you are finished. The entire horn will have glossy finish when you are done. Raw horns have a dull tone that will disappear with sanding.
d. Is the horn surface scratched? - Deep scratches in a horn

can mean trouble. They are hard to sand out, and can make you take much more time in the sanding process. A lot of small scratches are just as troublesome, sometimes requiring a lot of sanding.

e. Is it of a size suited to you? - While it may be appealing to have one gallon drinking horn, remember you are the one that has to lift it, and horns are not easily set down and picked back up even with a stand. On the other hand, too small a horn may mean frequent refills.

2) Cleaning the horn:

Raw horns can be rather nasty with dirt and bugs inside, and the remains of the horn innards. Therefore a good washing may be needed before starting work. This will help get any dirt off the outside of the horn that may interfere with work as well. Usually hot water will do the trick. For really nasty horns, boiling water or bleach may be needed. If a horn is very nasty, you may want to fill it with water, stand it upright, and add up to a capful of bleach. Then let it set for 10 minutes, and rinse with very hot water.

Once the horn is clean, you may want to leave it standing overnight with water in it. Raw horns have a very bad odor and this will also affect the taste of anything put in a horn. Therefore, before the horn is cured for drinking, you will need to let water stand in it overnight, or repeatedly pour boiling water in and out of it. This will get rid of most of the odorant leave the horn smelling fresh.

3) Sanding: Sanding is actually a two stage process, sanding and polishing. For sanding you will want a fine grade sand paper, and maybe another finer grade. Start with the less fine sandpaper and sand the entire body of the horn. Do not sand the horn up and down, but try to keep circular motions not sanding too much in any one place. Make sure you round any rough edges around the mouth of the horn, and work to get out any rough spots. Once most of the rough spots are worked out, and the lip of the horn well rounded, you can then start with the finer grade sand paper. Again repeat the process, smoothing the lip and any rough spots. Once the lip

is smooth as well as any rough spots, you can begin polishing. You will want to start with the emery cloth, again using the same method as you did with the sandpaper. If you want a high gloss, you may want to switch to an even finer grade emery cloth, once through with the entire horn. Once you have sanded the entire horn with the emery cloth, you can then use the steel wool. Make sure you use a fine grade, rougher grades of emery can scratch the horn. Again you may wish to use finer grade once you have went over the horn at least once. Once you have achieved the finish you desire, you are ready to finish the horn.

4) Finishing: For finishing you will want to use linseed oil. Linseed oil will bring out the shine of the horn and not damage it in any way. If you do not wish to use linseed oil, wax will also give a nice finish to the horn. Do not do the inside of the horn however, the oil can affect the taste of any drink. Also do not use lacquers or enamels on the horn. Many of these dissolving alcohol and water and will leave your horn looking as if it had not been polished.

a. Waxing - Many folks like to wax the inside of their horns. Natural horns after first being cured sometimes add a bitter taste to the drink, and waxing prevents this. However, a waxed horn gradually attracts dirt on the inside of the horn, and cannot be washed in hot water. To wax the inside of your horn, you will need to melt bees wax, pour it in the horn swirling it until the entire inside of the horn is covered. Do not allow excess wax to solidify in the horn however. Make sure you pour it out.

b. Curing - Perhaps the best way I have found for making a horn suitable for drinking. Again repeat the cleaning process using hot water. Some folks have found that denture cleaners help clean the inside of the horn. I have not tried this, but it seems reasonable it would work. If all else fails adding bleach to the water in a horn does help. Once the horn is clean, fill it with mead, hard cider, wine, or beer, and allow it to stand overnight. I suggest using cider or wine as the acids left in the drink help clean the horn. Beer and ales seem to be the least effective. However, I have even use vodka and PGA to cure a horn and these seem quite effectives well (and they disinfect too!). If the inside of the horn still has a "horn" odor in the morning, repeat the process. Most horns are "cured" within one to two days. However, my ex-fiancée once had a horn that took two weeks before it was suitable to drink from. Patience in curing is a virtue.

d Enameling - There are enamels designed for use on such things as horn, and many of the Ren Faire horn crafters use them. If you want an enameled horn inside and out, I would suggest asking one of the Ren Faire craftsman what they use. From here there are several ways to make the horn suitable for drinking. The advantage to enameled horns is they can be washed without water like an unwaxed horn, and are easier to clean.

Once your horn is finished, you may wish to decorate it with Heathen motiffs. To do this you can use a Dremel, wood working tools, exacto knife, or wood burner to carve or burn decorations straight into the horn. Or you can fasten gold or silver leaf to the horn to form a lip or end cap. There are any number of ways a horn can be decorated. The main rules area horn like wood is hardest worked against the grain. With a horn the grain runs lengthwise. And second, be careful not to punch through the walls of the horn.

Appendix VI

# Making A Blowing Horn

A good blowing horn can greatly enhance the ritual experience at a gathering. Many a Heathen has learned to respond to the sounding of a horn when nothing else may get his or her attention. Making such a horn is actually relatively easy, and can be done in one afternoon's setting.

1) Obtaining a Horn:

With the closure of most Tandy's across the USA and elsewhere, it maybe difficult to obtain horns. However, many locally owned leather stores still carry them as well as Ren Fairies, pioneer events, and a few craft outlets. There are criteria for selecting a good blowing horn.

a. Has it been punched? - Horns do not come off the neat (cow, steer, or bull) punched or cored. They are filled with a substance similar to dentine in your teeth or marrow in your bones, and this needs to be taken out. For your own sake then, it is best to get a horn that has already been punched or cored.

b. Does it have thick walls? - You want your horn to have relatively thick walls. If the walls are too thin, you can easily sand through, or if carving, punch a hole through the wall. This is not as critical as with a drinking horn, but still an important consideration.

c. Does it have an appealing color? - This is a totally subjective observation, but since you are the one using the horn, you are the one that has to live with its color. Note however, that a raw, unsanded horn will look much duller than the finished product. The whites will appear whiter, the blacks blacker, and grays grayer when you are finished. The entire horn will have a glossy finish when you are done. Raw horns have a dull tone that will disappear with sanding.

d. Is the horn surface scratched? - Deep scratches in a horn can mean trouble. They are hard to sand out, and can make you take much more time in the sanding process. A lot of small scratches are just as troublesome, sometimes requiring a lot of sanding.

e. Is it of a medium size? - Overly large horns often take too much breath

to sound, while small horns sound more like whistles. The best blowing horns therefore seem to be of an average size. One that will hold from3/4 of a bottle of wine to one bottle should do.

2) Cleaning the horn:

Raw horns can be rather nasty with dirt and bugs inside, and the remains of the horn innards. Therefore a good washing may be needed before starting work. This will help get any dirt off the outside of the horn that may interfere with work as well. Usually hot water will do the trick. For really nasty horns, boiling water or bleach may be needed. If a horn is very nasty, you may want to fill it with water, stand it upright, and add up to a capful of bleach. Then let it set for 10 minutes, and rinse with very hot water.

A blowing horn need not be as clean as a drinking horn, you will not need to cure it, but it still needs a good cleaning nonetheless.

3) Carving the horn:

Once the horn is clean, you can carve the mouth piece. To do this, you will need a good strong but thin bladed knife, and a hand saw. You need to saw the tip of the horn off. This can be very tricky, as you want to do it at the very spot where the horn tip is no longer solid. There is no sure fire way of doing this. One way is to insert a wire into the mouth of the horn until you hit bottom to measure the depth of the horn's empty space. You can then use the wire to mark off where to saw on the outside of the horn. Some horns have too long a tip however, and thus if sawed at the end of the horns empty space would be too large to carve mouth piece. If this appears to be the case, pick a spot nearer the tip of the horn (where the horn tip is about the diameter of a trumpet mouthpiece) and saw it off. Then using a hand drill and a small drill bit, drill lengthwise through the solid tip into the empty space of the horn. Once you have sawed off the tip of the horn and have a hole in the tip end (either drilled by you, or part of the horn's cored empty space), you can begin carving. Your aim is to create a "V" shaped mouth piece leading into the horn. This is easiest done by inserting the blade into the horn at an angle blade tip pointing outward and slowly carving around the entire circumference of the horn tip. Once you have a slight "V" shape started, stop and sound the horn, after clearing away any splinters. Continue carving until the horn sounds as you wish.

4) Sanding: Once the mouthpiece is finished, you will wish to sand and polish the blowing horn. Prior to sanding, you may need to grind the rough straightedges of the mouthpiece in order to round them. You can do this using a Dremel with a grinder tip, or a table top grinder. You will want to do this

very lightly and in a circular motion with the edge 90 degrees to the grinder. Grind only as much as to leave the straight edge flat. Once it is flat, using a rough grain sand paper, you can round the mouthpiece off so as to give a smooth surface comfortable to the lips.

You can then sand and polish the horn. For sanding you will want a fine grade sand paper, and maybe another finer grade. Start with the less fine sandpaper and sand the entire body of the horn. Do not sand the horn up and down, but try to keep circular motions not sanding too much in anyone place. Make sure you round any rough edges around the mouth of the horn, and work to get out any rough spots. Once most of the rough spots are worked out, and the lip of the horn well rounded, you can then start with the finer grade sand paper. Again repeat the process, smoothing the lip and any rough spots.

Once the lip is smooth as well as any rough spots, you can begin polishing. You will want to start with the emery cloth, again using the same method as you did with the sandpaper. If you want a high gloss, you may want to switch to an even finer grade emery cloth, once through with the entire horn. Once you have sanded the entire horn with the emery cloth, you can then use the steel wool. Make sure you use a fine grade, rougher grades of emery can scratch the horn. Again you may wish to use finer grade once you have went over the horn at least once. Once you have achieved the finish you desire, you are ready to finish the horn.

4)Finishing:

For finishing you will want to use linseed oil. Linseed oil will bring out the shine of the horn and not damage it in any way. If you do not wish to use linseed oil, wax will also give a nice finish to the horn. Once your horn is finished, you may wish to decorate it with Heathen motiffs. To do this you can use a Dremel, wood working tools, exacto knife, or woodburner to carve or burn decorations straight into the horn. Or you can fasten gold or silver leaf to the horn to form a lip or end cap. There are any number of ways a horn can be decorated. The main rules are a hornlike wood is hardest worked against the grain. With a horn the grain runs

247

lengthwise. And second, be careful not to punch through the walls of the horn as this can affect the sound of the horn.

# Appendix VII

Making Recels

Recels is the term commonly used amongst practitioners of Ásatrú for herbs burned during a ritual or a spell working whether in the form of dried loose leaves and roots or in the form of incense. In ancient times it is assumed that the ancient Northern Europeans used only loose leaves, bark, and roots in their rites, if any at all. The concept of incense came from the south with the arrival of Christianity and largely was not seen in books until the late Dark Ages to early Middle Ages. It is known that the Northern Europeans felt fire and its smoke to have a warding quality. This can be seen behind the concept of need fire, fires lit with a fire drill or bow on particular holy days. The cattle were driven through the smokes of these fires to drive off pests and disease and some people were known to have leaped through them as they did the bonfires at May Day and Midsummer. In other sources we are told that nine kinds of wood played a role in the bonfires used in cremation. From these and other bits of folklore we therefore know that fire and its smoke was used magicly by the Northern Europeans. It is no far leap of the imagination then to assume that the magical properties of the plants burned in these fires affected the potency of the fire and its smoke in whatever rite they were a part of.

Drying Herbs

Whether one plans to burn loose bits of plant matter or burn incense in their rites or magical work, the herbs collected will first have to be dried. This can be done a variety of ways. The easiest and fastest way is to use a food dehydrator like those used to dry fruits and vegetables for camping trips. Anyone planning to use recels extensively in their rites would be wise to buy one of these units. Another, more natural way is to obtain a sheet of tin and place it in a sunny window of a dry room and lay the leaves and roots upon it. Depending on the plant, it can take up to three weeks for the leaves and roots to dry. Yet, a third way is to place the herbs in a tin can on a sunny hot day and place them outside on a slab of concrete. The can should be brought in at night to avoid the morning dew and the process repeated daily until the herbs are dried. Finally, one can lay the herbs out on a cookie sheet and place it in the oven. The temperature should be set at 350 degrees and the process usually takes half an hour to an hour. One must remember, regardless of what method they use, the faster herbs are dried, the greater the number of essential compounds of the herbs that are lost. It is therefore better perhaps to use slower methods when drying herbs for magical use.

Making Incense

Incense is thought to have been unknown to the ancient Northern Europeans, although the Romans were quite fond of using it even prior to the adoption of Christianity in the empire and its use did travel north with Christian missionaries. While perhaps not traditional for the Ásatrú, incense is convenient. It is easily stored and easily transported. Anyone can make incense cheaply with only the slightest bit of effort.

Incense is actually made up of three components: 1) The aromatic, which is the herb itself being burned for its magical effect. 2) The chemical agent, which is what actually makes incense burn so slowly. Usually this is salt peter (potassium nitrate), although charcoal can be used if it is ground up fine enough. In ritual it might be wise to use charcoal made from a wood sympathetic to one's spell working. 3) The bonding agent- This is the "glue" that holds the incense together. Gum arabic is the most commonly used bonding agent in incenses and tragacanth is also widely used. Nearly any gummy substance like the sap of a tree and even honey can be used as a bonding agent however. Some bonding agents do not burn as well as others, and others simply refuse to harden. It is often therefore difficult to find a good bonding agent that does not conflict with the magical properties of the herbs. It such cases, one is best to experiment and keep a record of what bonding agents seem to work best. When one cannot find a bonding agent sympathetic to their ritual needs, it is best to either burn loose leaves or use incense made using gum arabic (which I have found to be pretty magically neutral).

To make incense, one will need the following items: 1) a motar and pestal or something to crush the dried herb into powder, 2) Incense sticks (if one does not plan to mold the incense into cones) 3) A bread pan or cookie sheet on which to mix the three agents of the incense.

1) Crush the dried herb into a very fine powder using the motar and pestal. If one is using a wood or hard roots it will be necessary to sand it and use the dust from that. One will also wish to crush and grind the chemical agent into a fine powder as well.

2) If the bonding agent is in a solid form it will have to be made liquid. To do this one will need to boil the agent in water or allow it to set in water for several hours. Generally, one will need two parts water to the bonding agent.

3) Mix the three components together and knead them into a very fine paste. Make sure the paste is thoroughly mixed and has the aromatic, the chemical agent, and bonding agent thoroughly spread throughout it.

4) Mold the paste into cones or dip incense sticks into it and allow to dry.

Making incense is not a difficult process, and may take a few tries to perfect. However, once one gets the hang of it, they will find it is a quick and easy way to meet any needs for recels in ritual or spell use.

A Warding Incense

Ingredients: 3 ounces garlic powder 3 ounces dust from linden wood 3 ounces juniper leaves 4 ounces saltpeter Gum arabic as needed

Make sure all parts are ground to a fine powder and mixed well. This recipe is useful in warding and defensive rites of all kinds and can be burned in a house to drive off unwanted wights.

An Incense for Prosperity

Ingredients: 5 ounces clover leaves and/or blooms 9 ounces dust from birch bark 4 ounces vervain 3 ounces saltpeter Gum arabic as needed

Grind all parts together and mix well. Use this incense with rites to make material gain or to keep what wealth one already has.

An Incense for Love in Marriage

Ingredients: 3 ounces rose petals 9 ounces thyme leaves 3 ounces vervain 3 ounces flax seed 8 ounces saltpeter gum arabic as needed

Make sure all parts are ground into a fine powder. This incense can be burned during romantic interludes with one's spouse or simply to keep a household happy and bright

253

257

25733659R00150

Made in the USA
Middletown, DE
08 November 2015